PAUL ROBESON

Ron Ramdin

PAUL ROBESON
The Man and His Mission

PETER OWEN · LONDON

ISBN 0 7206 0684 5

PETER OWEN PUBLISHERS
73 Kenway Road London SW5 0RE

First published in Great Britain 1987
© Ron Ramdin 1987

Photoset and printed in Great Britain by
WBC Print Barton Manor St Philips Bristol

The artist must take sides.

PAUL ROBESON

Contents

Illustrations

Preface

No one who knows anything about Paul Robeson doubts his greatness. C.L.R. James, the Marxist historian, Pan-Africanist and thinker (who wrote the play *Toussaint*, which starred Robeson), in a recent interview said: 'Robeson is the most extraordinary man I have ever met.' He added emphatically: 'And I have met a few!' However, few people know enough about Robeson, and too much about him has been taken for granted.

Nevertheless superlatives came easily to those who had seen, heard or met this controversial interpretive artist. Yet many Americans have remained hostile or ambivalent towards, even ignorant of, his unrivalled achievements and, indeed, of the true significance and meaning of his life. The taboo of Robeson's communism led to a dichotomy in the American public mind: there were those who defended him as a black 'hero' and those who accepted, for various reasons, the prevailing orthodoxy of him as a 'traitor'. In spite of this, his great eminence, at home and abroad, proved too pervasive to destroy. Fortunately much has survived for posterity in the way of written material (manuscript and printed), films, photographs, recordings, and so forth. But even this legacy of his struggle remains lost to a new generation, although there is increasing interest among the socially aware and book-buying public.

Most of the biographical accounts on Robeson were written during his lifetime. Of the two exceptions, one was published in 1976 (only months after his death), the other, a small paperback work, was published in 1980. Now in the wake of the tenth anniversary of his death it is timely to take a fresh look at this American phenomenon; to pull together the main strands of his fascinating, multi-faceted life in a way that will help towards a clearer understanding of the uncompromising stand he took. Hitherto books on Robeson have

9

had one common drawback: they lack comprehensiveness, omissions that amount to providing less than a total picture of the man. In this biography – given the available material – I have tried not only to fill this gap, but more fundamentally I have attempted to trace Robeson's political development (a steady progression) in relation to his artistic career (a corresponding retrogression), especially in the United States of America. These themes are, of course, set against the background of the historic national and international issues and events of Robeson's time. Furthermore, previous accounts of Robeson's life, with the notable exception of Marie Seton's book published eighteen years before he died, have tended to neglect his crucial twelve-year residence in Britain. As well as examining the known documents I have been able to gain new insights of Robeson from his relatively neglected speeches, writings and interviews and from in-depth interviews with two eminent persons in the acting profession who worked closely with him in what was undoubtedly his greatest acting achievement, *Othello*: namely, Dame Peggy Ashcroft, Desdemona in the 1930 production at the Savoy Theatre in London; and Sam Wanamaker, the American actor-director who played Iago in the 1959 production at the Shakespeare Memorial Theatre, Stratford-upon-Avon. What emerges from Robeson's monumental struggles is the indomitable spirit of an uncommon man.

Robeson's impact has been incalculable. Indeed the controversy which surrounded Robeson in life, continued after his death. Black intellectuals and artists continue to assess his work and struggle; were (and are) divided as to the merits of the play *Paul Robeson*, starring James Earl Jones; and sought long overdue recognition of Robeson in the form of a star on Hollywood's Walk of Fame. Eventually this was granted. But as Sidney Poitier put it: 'There would need to be a ceremony like this every day for the rest of our lives for us to ever begin to be aware of the impact he had on the role of Blacks in the [film] industry.'

Reviewing Robeson's life in *Horizon*, two years after his death, Colin Campbell wrote: 'He is too lively . . . to allow careful biographers and intense political factions to keep the man all to themselves. He was a large man, and it will be a long time before most people fully comprehend him.' Today, he is still 'lively' and few people still 'fully comprehend him.' (It is perhaps useful for readers to note that throughout this work Blacks have also been referred to by

the term 'Negro' – Robeson's consistent usage, common in his day –
or 'coloured'.)

Writing this book has been a demanding but always an exciting
experience, particularly because many people have been encouraging
and helpful. My thanks to Paul Robeson Jr for answering questions
that needed some clarification; C.L.R. James for a long and revealing
interview; Dame Peggy Ashcroft for a clear, interesting and helpful
interview; Sam Wanamaker, for an exhaustively informative, first-
hand view of artists in the 1940s in the United States, his views of
Robeson then, when they acted together in London, and on various
aspects of Robeson's life and thought; Jonny Brown, for rare tape
recordings of the American production of *Othello* and of songs
(spirituals) sung by Robeson between 1925 and 1929.

Many others must also be thanked, especially Peter Owen for his
commitment to this project and Michael Levien for his major
editorial contribution; Rey Booven; Ghazala Faizi; Louise Floyd;
Irma, Ronnie and the De Freitas family; Elizabeth Grace; Nick
Jacobs; Jim McGeachie; Winston Major; Robert Mayall; Jen
Scallan; David Shoblaske; the staff at the British Library, par-
ticularly at the Reference Division, Bloomsbury, and at the
Newspaper Collection, Colindale; and Margaret Witham of the
Morning Star picture library. Finally, I am grateful to my parents,
brothers and sisters for their continuing encouragement.

Ron Ramdin

1 · Childhood, High-School and College Days (1898–1919)

Freedom was more than just a word; it was *the* goal, which had not only symbolic but absolute meaning for the enslaved. For most of his fifteen years William Drew Robeson had thought about escape from the driver's lash. In 1860, as he fled from the plantation and left his parents, the idea became a reality. He was born in Martin County, North Carolina, on 27 July 1845. His parents, Benjamin and Sabra, slaves on the Robeson plantation near the city of Raleigh, had several other children, of whom little is known. It was said that 'W.D.', as William was called by the older Blacks in Martin County, bore a strong resemblance to his 'royal Bantu' ancestors in Africa. The initials stuck until he escaped to the North.

About the time of William Drew's birth, many slaves were escaping from the South to the Northern states, as the anti-slavery movement became international in character. One of the leading black abolitionists was Frederick Douglass, an escaped slave. This remarkable man came to England in 1845 as 'a representative from the prison-house of bondage'. His first-hand accounts of the slaves' condition had a powerful impact on British abolitionists and working-class leaders. William Drew, desperately unhappy with life under his master's whip, followed the path of Douglass. This was a difficult and dangerous decision for him to make. To risk flight from his master was one thing, but parting from his beloved parents, brothers and sisters, was quite another. None the less, his mind was firmly made up.

As a free man in the North, William Drew adopted the name of his former master – Robeson. Years later, his son Paul Robeson recalled the story behind the misprinted name 'Mr Paul Roberson', which was perhaps the ancestral name of the slave-owning Robesons.

William Drew and the mass of human beings under the yoke of

bondage in the South adhered to a religion that had engendered an abiding faith in the ultimate deliverance from their evil masters. From the cradle to the grave, this supreme belief symbolized the importance of the 'Chu'ch' to the black community. Thus fortified, many black men rose to become preachers; positions through which their service and leadership afforded them respect, prestige and influence in their parishes. But although many were 'called', few were successful in winning the confidence, admiration, support and love of their flocks. For the leader and the led, then, Church life in the North was as important as it had been hitherto. It was at once a link with their lamentable past and a hopeful future.

By the turn of the twentieth century, Princeton, New Jersey, less than an hour's journey from New York City, had attracted many Blacks. Initially those who escaped and those who were free after emancipation, made their way in increasing numbers from the South in search of work and wages. This migration created black settlements in and around Princeton, where Southerners joined their relatives and friends. Apart from being 'free', Princeton none the less had assumed many of the characteristics of the black section of the South. But in this environment there were certain improvements. Their new homes were marginally better than the old log cabins; their children were schooled and, importantly, they had a real Church – a source of great pride and meaning. Some things, however, remained unchanged. Notable among these was the fact that Blacks continued to be employed as manual labourers and domestic servants – the only form of work they had been allowed to do.

Amidst the social problems confronting them in their new communities, the Church helped to bind the battered, disorientated black groups together. And these black people displayed many Christian virtues: they worked hard, saved and gave generously of their time and energy, and generally helped the less fortunate. Moreover, on Sundays they offered their pennies in praise of and thanks to the Lord.

Through religion, many found physical, mental and emotional release. Church contrasted sharply with the 'big house', where meekness and quietness were what was expected of them. In church on Sundays especially their pent-up feelings would be released, bursting forth uninhibitedly in songs of praise, as they swayed rhythmically to spirituals with exultant cries of 'Hallelujah', 'Praise the Lord' and 'My Jesus'. The sermons guided and disciplined them for the harsh realities surrounding them and they eagerly surrendered themselves to the 'will of God'. These poor, work-weary folk derived a soul-satisfying happiness and fulfilment from the so-called weekly spiritual 'Sit Down' which, in part, reads:

> I'm goin' up to heaven an' sit down,
> Goin' up to heaven an' sit down,
> Oh, sit down, sister, sit down, child,
> Sit down an' rest a while.

In the black communities in the North (as in the South) the black preacher fulfilled an important role within the community, in that he personified for these literal-minded people their religion. The preacher's oratorical powers and (sometimes) his educational background projected him in the eyes of his people as a spiritual and practical confidant; God's emissary on earth. In response, the preacher tried to live up to the expectations of his flock by co-ordinating a number of activities such as fund-raising, socials, picnics, concerts, dinners, fairs and entertainments, all of which helped to bind the community together. The initial goal, however, was to build a community church, and through persistence, sacrifice and labour many such churches were built. Indeed they have, through the years, become a source of pride among its members who became even more closely identified with its activities as they grew older, lonely and in need of comfort. It was also the place where the young were introduced to certain Christian and human values.

Against this background William Robeson set about building his new life in the North. A year after his escape, he was caught up in the conflict between the 'free' Northern states and the slave states of the South, when civil war broke out. Together with 200 Blacks, and mindful that his family was still enslaved, in 1861, at the age of sixteen, he enlisted with the Union Army to fight for black liberation. With President Lincoln's emancipation proclamation in 1863, an estimated 3 million slaves were set free well before the eventual defeat of the Confederate Army, two years later.

For the young William Robeson, this historical moment heralded a new dawn; the beginning of a fresh epoch in his people's struggle. Young and hopeful, he worked and studied diligently. After getting through an elementary education, he enrolled at Lincoln University, the well-known 'Negro' institution near Philadelphia, where he read for the ministry because he was 'called' to the Church. Throughout his youth he had witnessed the profound effect of the Church on the lives of his people. He was, however, aware of the significance of Princeton University which he could not attend because it excluded black students. This fundamental barrier in the crucial area of education was a clear indication of what he had suspected: that although black people were no longer slaves, they were a long way from being equal to Whites even in the North. He saw his calling as a minister as one way of advancing the cause of his people.

The central role of the Church in the concerns of the black community fulfilled his aspirations, providing the means through which the best interests of his race could be served. This devotion to service made him 'a man of God in the truest sense'; a rare man with rare gifts. As one member of the Robeson family later put it, he was tolerant and, in addition to his belief in God and the Bible, he possessed natural dignity, intelligence and integrity, together with a sense of humour and the qualities of sympathy, love and respect, which made him a spiritual leader.

By all accounts, William Robeson had an attractive and winning personality. While still at Lincoln he met Maria Louisa Bustill, who taught at a school in Philadelphia. Born on 8 November 1853 in Philadelphia, Maria was a member of the noted Bustill family whose ancestry can be traced back to 1608. Her great-great grandfather, Cyrus Bustill, was of mixed Negro, Indian and white Quaker stock. Over generations an outline history of the family was recorded and handed down. The Bustills were essentially a family of teachers who held liberal views. They spread their learning in Philadelphia and the neighbouring cities. Cyrus traced his ancestry back to a 'powerful Indian tribe'. He was born in Burlington, New Jersey on 17 March 1732, bought his freedom and moved to Philadelphia where he worked as a baker. Among the growing community of free Blacks he became one of the most active workers for the religious, moral and intellectual progress of black people. His leadership led to his becoming a founder of the Free African Society in April 1787, the 'first mutual aid organisation of American Negroes'.

At the outbreak of the War of Independence Cyrus Bustill fought with the colonists against the British. He not only baked bread for the rebels, but took it to George Washington's hungry soldiers at Valley Forge, about twenty miles from Philadelphia. This notable war effort was not forgotten. According to one account Cyrus Bustill is mentioned in the original draft of Benjamin Franklin's autobiography.

Physically Maria Louisa had a fine blending of Indian, English and Negro features. She and her sister Gertrude were educated in Philadelphia. It seemed natural, amidst widespread illiteracy, that she should become a schoolteacher and she was known to use the Quaker form of address, 'thee' and 'thou'. She was a striking woman. Her hair was straight and black, and her light brown complexion contrasted sharply with William Robeson's dark skin and 'Bantu features'. On 11 July 1878 their deepening friendship carried them to marriage, when she was twenty-four and he was thirty-two. William Drew was proud of his tall, slender bride who possessed many unusual qualities. She was described as having an alert mind and a remarkable memory, and was also blessed with a calm disposition. Together, this talented couple faced the future.

According to one writer, William and Maria had six children. Of the five who survived infancy, the last, a son, was born on 9 April 1898, when William Robeson was still a vigorous man of fifty-two. Maria, then forty-four, was partially blind. Their youngest child, born in the parsonage of the Witherspoon Church (where his father was pastor for twenty years), was named Paul Leroy Robeson. Very quickly this baby attracted unusual attention and became the 'pet' of both the family and the church congregation. The child, whose parents were by no means rich, lived a healthy and happy life. The other four children were: William Drew Jr, known as 'W.D.', who became a doctor in Washington, DC; Reeve, who became a businessman in Detroit; Benjamin, who followed his father's calling and became a minister in New Jersey; and Marion, who followed in her mother's footsteps by teaching in the public schools of Philadelphia.

Life for the Robeson family, as indeed for other black families, was dogged by immense difficulties. Yet as a child Paul was not deprived of warmth and love by his ambitious and hard-working parents, whose goal was self-betterment. He grew up in the comfortable parsonage where his mother wrote fine sermons for his father and helped to educate the children. Unlike her husband, Maria was not a Presbyterian, but a Quaker. She taught her children to be peace-loving and kind. Her understanding and devotion to the family ensured the security of home life amidst which Paul thrived. Her husband, though in a different way, was equally caring and concerned.

As a minister of the Church, the Revd Robeson had attained perhaps the highest position possible for a black person at that time in the United States. His work as pastor of the Witherspoon Street Presbyterian Church brought justified esteem from the black community. From this vantage-point, in a predominantly white community, he clearly saw the relationship between Blacks and Whites. Evidently those who had money were white people, while those who worked for them were black people. In essence, chattel slavery was replaced by wage slavery. In these circumstances the Revd Robeson played a central role. Paul wrote later that the pastor acted as a bridge between the rich and the poor, serving his community by finding jobs, raising money and seeking 'mercy from the law'.

Paul's childhood was interrupted by tragedy when his mother died in a fire accident at home. The fatal morning was 19 January 1904 when the Revd Robeson was in Trenton on a business trip. Many years later Paul, who was not six years old when she died, could not remember his mother, although his memory of other things went back before her tragic death. While he did recall her lying in her coffin, her funeral and the relatives who came, it seemed that the pain and shock of her death blotted out all other personal recollections. Others had told him of her intelligence, strength of character and spirit which contributed so much to his father's development and work. 'She was a companion to him in his studies,' Paul wrote. 'She was his right hand in all his community work.'

After his wife's death the Revd Robeson was again struck by misfortune. He lost his position as minister of the Church and was faced with the prospect of raising his family alone. He struggled to feed, clothe and educate his children. These hard times, and his father's stature, left an indelible impression on Paul. He wrote later that poverty was his beginning, the family slept four in a bed, a time when his father showed restraint and concern for his children, especially for him.

The Revd Robeson moved to Westfield with Paul. The other children were making their way in the world: W.D. was at medical school; Reeve, now married, had moved to Detroit; Ben was at Biddle University and Marion attended the Scotia Seminary. As the relationship between father and son developed, William Robeson's strong character and example had a profound effect on his son. At Westfield a new life had begun. Here the Revd Robeson worked in a grocery store owned by a Miss Fannie. Paul and Ben joined their father to share the attic accommodation above Miss Fannie's store. With few Blacks in the town, Paul attended integrated schools. Already he had begun to learn the necessity of combining work with study. Each morning he delivered groceries for Miss Fannie before going to school. He remembered that the cramped living conditions forced them to use the shack at the back of the store as their washroom. Yet his father's courage and ambition never flagged. Paul watched him wrestle with the many problems of building a small church and parsonage. The demands on his father's time, none the less, allowed them enough free time together. As Paul grew, they became inseparable. He loved walking at his father's side. Years later Paul underlined the true significance of their relationship, stating that his father was the glory of his boyhood years, a patriarch among those he served and a man who had the respect even of the most aristocratic Whites in Princeton.

In word and action young Paul grew to know more about the 'text' of his father's life: '. . . loyalty to one's convictions. Unbending. Despite anything'. From his youngest days Paul was imbued with this concept, which formed the bedrock upon which his own integrity and life were built. He reflected that his father did not so much preach as express himself each day through his life and work. A man of ordinary height, the Revd Robeson was broad-shouldered with a physique that was rock-like. He exuded strength of character and dignity. Notable too was his remarkable speaking voice, the greatest Paul had ever heard, a deep, melodic and refined bass. This was music to the boy's ears. He was very proud of his father. He received a great deal of attention because he was the youngest child and the only one permanently at home. Father and son communicated easily, and although his father was fifty-two years old when Paul was born (and near sixty when his wife died), the considerable difference in their ages seemed to bind them even more closely together. In every sense, they needed each other. The Revd Robeson's calm countenance masked deep feelings for his family. This undemonstrative man (in expressing either love or praise) had nevertheless commanded the full respect of his children, who learned to know what was expected of them. Paul knew when to come home from play, his duties in the household and his time for study. He almost totally accepted his father's discipline and never quite forgot his one regrettable act of disobedience to his father. He was ten years old, and still living in Westfield, when he refused to do something his father told him to do. Years later he wrote of the acute sense of shame and ingratitude he felt. Above all, Paul and his brothers and sister learned one fundamental lesson from their father, which they never questioned: '. . . that the Negro was in every way the equal of the white man'. Each of the Revd Robeson's children had resolved, in one way or another, to prove it.

Paul learned other lessons from his father, especially how he kept his dignity whatever the circumstances, as for instance when, after more than twenty years of dedicated Church leadership, his father was removed as pastor, following a factional dispute among Church members. This unchristian-like act was all the more painful in that some of his father's closest kin were among his opponents. The Revd Robeson was now unemployed; a preacher without a church or congregation. Soon, however, this resourceful man acquired a horse and wagon and began to earn his living hauling ashes. The ever-growing, dark-grey mound in the backyard fascinated his son, and the job brought its own rewards – Paul became fond of the horse, a mare called Bess. His father also worked as a coachman and in the 'hack business'.

Throughout this lean period Paul never heard his father complain of either his poverty or misfortune. He seemed to be without bitterness as he struggled to earn a livelihood and see to his children's education.

There were lesser, though important influences during Paul's childhood. Paul was attached to his brother Reeve, or Reed, as he was called. Paul admitted frankly that Reeve did not live up to the high expectations of the other Robeson children and that his father was very disappointed in his son and disapproved of his undisciplined ways. None the less Paul admired his rough elder brother, from whom he learned that the way to combat racial insults and abuse was by militant opposition. Indeed, Reeve's sensitivity to racial slurs, more often than not, brought confrontation. He was prone to dealing out rough-and-ready justice, particularly to Southern gentlemen-students, with his fists. To protect himself, he carried a bag of small jagged rocks which, as it turned out, were quite inadequate in fending off the law. These brushes with the law troubled the Revd Robeson, who warned Reeve that he would have to leave home, because he was setting a bad example to Paul.

Circumstances, however, cut short both the playful and serious moments Paul spent with his brothers and sister, who were absent from home for long periods. But there was always his father with whom he could engage in some playful activity. He enjoyed the winter evenings at home with 'Pop', who loved playing checkers. During these moments they were very happy together. Gradually Paul began to see a pattern emerge from his father's mysterious past. Although the Revd Robeson never talked about his early years as a slave or about his parents, Benjamin and Sabra, and it was not until many years later that Paul learned from others that, before his mother died, his father had made maybe two dangerous trips back to the plantation to see his mother. Paul could not imagine that a noble man like his father was the property of another man 'to be bought and sold, used and abused at will'. As the playful child grew, many disturbing thoughts entered his mind; thoughts that would become defined and sharpened with experience.

In Princeton he met few white people, except for some white playmates, among whom was a boy his own age. They did not go to school together, but during the long summer days they became inseparable companions at play. They came to blows once. After landing a blow on each other's noses, they both parted screaming as they ran for their homes. The next day they resumed their friendship.

The death of his mother left Paul entirely in the hands of his father; a dependence which bred a relationship that had, by its very nature, a measure of imbalance. Understandably there were moments when Paul felt the sorrows of being a motherless child, but it was a deficiency of which he seemed to be more aware in retrospect. During his childhood what he remembered most was 'an abiding sense of comfort and security'. Indeed he received ample mothering, not only from his father, brothers and sister, but from the whole close-knit community. His aunts, uncles, cousins and non-relatives 'adopted' him, especially when his father was away attending Church conferences.

This deep compassion and magnanimity of the hard-working poor and the uplifting community spirit struck him forcefully. It was to become more than another fleeting childhood impression. It became an integral part of his life. He wrote of the human goodness and spiritual strength of Blacks after centuries of oppression, and of homes (where there was a warmth of song) that served as theatre, concert hall and social centre.

These images of black solidarity became an essential part of young

Paul's life. During his early years in Princeton he became conscious of a special feeling the Negro community had for him. This made him self-conscious, since other children in the neighbourhood were to all intents and purposes no different from him. Yet people saw that, like his father, he had some exceptional quality of his own. Although this quality was not identified, many felt that Paul was destined for great things and they gave him their unreserved affection.

Like other children, however, Paul had no ambitious plans. Becoming a minister like his father or a teacher like his mother were possibilities. Whatever the vocation, it seemed clear to those around him that he would grow up to be a 'credit to the race'.

Paul was nine years old when the family moved from Princeton, first to Westfield, later to Somerville, places that were quite unlike Princeton. Over the years, when the Revd Robeson had lost his church, Paul remembered the encouragement his father received from friends to resume his calling as a preacher. The opportunity came to William Robeson when at the age of sixty-two he joined the African Methodist Episcopal Zion (AMEZ) Church. Here the black community was much smaller than in Princeton. And, at least to begin with, the Revd Robeson had no more than a dozen members in his congregation. None the less, with their help and his passion for his people, he dug the foundation of the Downing Street AME Zion Church. For the three years Paul lived in Westfield, he attended a mixed school.

In 1910 the Robesons moved from Westfield to Somerville, a larger town equidistant from Westfield and Princeton. Here the Revd Robeson served as pastor of St Thomas AME Zion Church until he died, eight years later. In both towns Paul came to know more white people; a departure from his Princeton experience. Although barriers between Blacks and Whites existed, they were not so rigid and there were more friendly relations between both groups. Paul's natural friendliness led to frequent visits to the homes of his white schoolmates, where he always received a warm welcome. For many years, he accepted this as the norm, the natural, Christian way to live. On reflection, he wrote that moving easily between the two racial communities came about essentially because he was the preacher's son, but also because of his success in sport and with his studies.

In the all-coloured school in Somerville Paul continued his studies. The Revd Robeson now spent most evenings at home with Paul. His interest in his son's school work was as keen as ever, and he was a patient and thorough teacher. He examined Paul's report cards monthly, but showed little interest in merely good reports. His son had to aim for perfect reports, and when these materialized he was full of praise. Paul was quick to learn and eager to please his father, and in time the rigorous tutorials he received from his father helped him achieve an unusually high standard of self-application. Already he was much more mature than any of his contemporaries, and soon his report cards were near perfect. Even so, more was expected of him.

Predictably, Paul pursued his studies with his father's suggestion as to how to improve his school grades uppermost in his mind. As he put it later, his father was never satisfied with ninety-five when a mark of a hundred was possible. Also, he was impressed by his father's argument that a successful life should not be measured in terms of money and personal advancement but by aiming, through personal integrity, for the 'richest and highest development of one's own potential'.

When the Robesons moved from Westfield, Paul attended the school in Somerville run by James L. Jamison, a graduate from Lincoln. This courageous man and his wife went to the Deep South after the period of reconstruction, to impart their knowledge to black children. During cotton-picking time they defied local convention by keeping their school open. The seriousness of this 'crime' was compounded by the fact that every black person over the age of seven was compelled to work in the fields as in the days of slavery. The bosses told Jamison to get out. When he refused to close his school, the Ku Klux Klansmen burned the school to the ground and beat him. Thereafter, the Jamisons came to Somerville determined to educate black children.

Under the watchful eye of Jamison, Paul grew. At the age of twelve, he was already the tallest boy in his school and was top of his class. In 1911, when Paul entered Somerville High School, he became colour conscious. There, even under severe provocation, he was not allowed to retaliate, which underlined the awful burden of being a black child in a white school.

He knew the Whites' comfortable background and lives were different from his. Indeed at the age of twelve he had to find employment to pay for his school fees. His schooling followed the 'classic pattern' which has been, as he later put it, 'largely displaced by an emphasis on technology'. In political terms, he did not know where his father stood in the great debate between the militant policy of W.E.B. DuBois and the conservative concerns of Booker T. Washington, as they clashed in the attempt to bring about 'Negro progress'. It was clear, however, that the Revd Robeson had rejected Booker T. Washington's accommodationist idea that Negro education should be limited to manual training. He believed that the freedom seeker must be allowed to attain the heights of knowledge. Therefore such treasures of learning as Latin, Greek, philosophy, history and literature must also be the Negro's heritage.

It was therefore not surprising that in high school Paul did four years of Latin (followed by another four years of Latin and Greek in college). His father took a keen interest in his studies of Virgil, Homer and other classics, and significantly, became Paul's first teacher in public speaking. The Revd Robeson's love for the eloquent and meaningful word, and his insistence on purity of diction, had a strong impact on his son's interest in oratory. There were many evenings of recitation in the Robeson home. The voice as an instrument of communication would become one of his main preoccupations.

In spite of the difficulties he encountered, as Paul later put it, high school in Somerville was not Jim Crow. There he formed close friendships with several white classmates and was welcomed as a member of the Glee Club, the Dramatic Club and integrated after much struggle into the school sports, and awkwardly in the social activities. He remembered his teachers who were friendly. Miss Vosseller, the music teacher, was especially interested in training his voice; Anna Miller, an English teacher (who first introduced him to Shakespeare's works), attended to his development as speaker and debater. Indeed, it was Miss Miller who coached him to play Othello in a high-school dramatic performance. The experience was unforgettable, and so trying that he thought he would never act again.

The Latin teacher, Miss Vandeveer, seemed to be without racial prejudice. Miss Bagg, who taught chemistry and physics, made every effort to make Paul feel welcome and at ease in the school's social life. Her sense of his discomfiture and her encouragement, however, could not change the way Paul felt. He kept away from most of the social affairs which he found embarrassing.

Even at that early age, Paul was aware that demonstrating he is really an equal (and strangely the proof must be superior performance!) the Negro must never appear to be challenging white superiority. This matter was particularly disturbing and instructive to him. Years later he wrote that one should not act 'uppity', but rather show gratefulness for one's success. Provoking fear would ultimately unleash the 'oppressing hand' to force the black aspirant down.

Thus the boy at high school, trying to 'act right', never allowed the rare opportunities to slip by. He made the most of his chances. In line with his father's teaching, he measured himself only against his own potential rather than trying to compete with anyone else. Yet although he had no thought of challenging the way things were, and was courteous and practised restraint, he was not immune to hostility. If there was racism in the school, he identified it in no lesser a person than the school's principal, Dr Ackerman. The hateful man did not disguise his bitter feelings. As far as he was concerned, the black boy had to be put in his place. Ackerman responded with contempt to Paul's hard-earned successes. The boy's popularity among fellow students and his outstanding skills on the football field irked him, and it was the last straw when the music teacher selected Paul as the Glee Club's soloist. Ackerman protested furiously. This headstrong black youth was clearly stepping out of line!

About this time talents hitherto inert began to emerge. Paul began to use his voice increasingly in song. His brother Benjamin, who was particularly close to him, recalled his kid brother's budding musical talent. One afternoon in July Ben, Bill and Paul (at Bill's suggestion) sang a few songs. Amidst the discordant sounds Paul's voice emerged. Bill ecstatically asked Paul to 'hit that note again'. Paul did so, at which Bill told him he could sing. But Paul thought he was kidding.

After this revelation, the brothers broke for a game of baseball in the nearby lots. On their return home, Bill was insistent that Paul should sing again. Paul obliged. Bill listened as he warbled and concluded: 'Paul, you can *sing*.' Of course Paul and Benjamin thought it all a joke, since singing was the last talent of the Robeson family, and even after singing in the church choir and the high school's Glee Club Paul still remained sceptical about his ability to sing. Concert work was the furthest thing from his mind. Ben, however, always maintained that Paul's life as a singer started that July afternoon.

Religious songs became one of Paul's main interests as he began to take part in church affairs and assist in his father's work. According to one relative, after his lessons and discussions with his father, he would inquire about the parishioners, the growth of the church fund and would talk over plans for the Sunday school, in which he always took an active part. His responsibilities grew with age. He became superintendent of the Sunday school, often helped his father with the services, and led the singing in church with his natural, uncontrolled, vibrant bass voice. Significantly it was here in his father's church that his life reached an important juncture: he became an essential part of that church, and, in turn, the church, the music and people became an essential part of his personal development. It was therefore natural that he was able to sing the music of his people, evoking all its glorious simplicity and sincerity, so that, years later, audiences felt the songs he sang were really a part of him. Already, the singer and his songs were inseparable. As his brother Benjamin has pointed out, it was Bill who first saw this unity in their young brother.

In later life Paul acknowledged the debt of gratitude he owed to his brothers and sister during his years of striving at school and college. Bill, the eldest of the Robeson children, was accorded first place as far as brains were concerned, and in his tutorial role he was invaluable to Paul as a young student. For his part, brother Ben was the one who most inspired Paul's interest in sports. He was an outstanding athlete by any standards and, according to Paul, he would have been chosen All-American had he attended one of the prominent colleges. Ben was closer in age to Paul than to his other brothers, and Paul did not hide the fact that Ben was his favourite in the family. It was Ben who took him out in the world beyond the life of their neighbourhood. When Paul was fifteen and still at high school, Ben was working during the summer vacation as a waiter at Narragansett Pier, Rhode Island, where many black students found vacation-time employment at the resorts of the wealthy. Ben took Paul along. There, Paul worked as a kitchen-boy. This kind of employment, essentially reserved for Blacks, was specially instructive of the outside world to the school-bound Paul. It was the hardest work he had ever done, beginning at 4 a.m., at the end of his working day he would emerge from a mountain of pots and pans, scrubbed to a gleaming finish. He was the last to leave the kitchen. Highly conscious of this unusual experience, Paul, grateful for the reassuring presence of his brother Ben, monitored his brother's bewilderment. Paul came to realize this was something they all had to endure. He never lost sight of the value of the job (for all its unpleasantness) as he tried to meet the cost of his education. Later, in college days, he would go back to Narragansett, where, among the waiters, bus boys and kitchen help, he made lasting friendships. Many leading black professionals came from among these student workers.

Sister Marion was at this time perhaps less close to Paul, essentially because she was not at home as much as Ben. She was a self-assertive girl who was not prepared to do housework and just generally hang around. She was full of warm good humour, which her brothers loved. On her visits home, during her school vacations, Marion gladly did the cooking. But she firmly believed that a woman's place was not in anybody's kitchen, at least not for long. If cooking for her brothers was fun, she always left the big stack of dishes for Paul to wash. In spite of her happy disposition, Marion was resolute in maintaining her independence. She was keenly aware of the double burden a black woman bears in striving for dignity and fulfilment.

Paul observed that Marion and Ben were like his father in temperament. Reserved of speech, strong in character, living up to their principles – and always selflessly devoted to Paul. The love they gave to Paul was overwhelming. Paul always felt enriched and happy when his brothers and Marion visited home. They gave him a sense of balance and perspective in his own development. While at Somerville High School, Paul's scholastic achievements were matched by his athletic prowess. Unusual physical attributes and agility of mind were invaluable assets which Paul evidently possessed. He became the mainstay of the football team, centre of the basketball team, catcher for the baseball team, and was active at track meets.

He was now in the final semester at high school and still had no vocation in mind. He could not see himself as a singer, because singing was merely for fun. And dramatics? Well, he thought, this was not to be his role either. For some time, however, he had thought of studying for the ministry, something his father avoided pressing upon him, since his life was already intimately involved with the church and the ordinary folk who worshipped and sang there. Paul thought a career decision should perhaps be deferred until he became a college student. The choice of college had already been settled. It was to be Lincoln University, where his father and brother Bill were both alumni.

As it was, during his senior year at Somerville High, Paul entered a competitive examination open to all students in New Jersey. The prize was a four-year scholarship at Rutgers College. Established in 1766, it was one of the oldest institutions of learning in America. Picturesque Rutgers stood proudly on the banks of the old Raritan River in New Brunswick, New Jersey. The town was an important manufacturing city situated between New York and Philadelphia.

Although Rutgers was close to Princeton University, views about them differed. At the time, it was said by some that it was more difficult to graduate from Rutgers than from Princeton, although the latter was more fashionable and better known. Many Rutgers graduates had distinguished careers, becoming Rhodes Scholars, governors of New Jersey, railroad presidents, economists, experts on agriculture and world affairs. It was important too for the fact that the first major football game ever played at that level in America was between Rutgers and Princeton in 1869; a match that Rutgers won. Thereafter, Rutgers became famous for its football team. Not surprisingly, Paul had heard about the college. He knew it had a reputation for being rather exclusive. In fact, only one or two Blacks had been there, and none had attended it for many years.

Against this background, and the family's preference for Lincoln (there was never any doubt about his going to college), Paul's father approved his taking the competitive examination, which was duly held in the Somerville Courthouse. Finance was a major consideration, and winning a scholarship would ease considerably the financial strain on the Revd Robeson's modest income.

Soon after the scholarship examination in 1915 he graduated from Somerville High School as an honours student, whose achievements could not be ignored. In the spring of that year he participated in a state-wide oratorical contest for high-school students, held at Rutgers. His earlier diligence and self-application emphasized his evident potential and served him well. He was not only a prize debater at Somerville High School but an ardent student of vocal artistry, some of which he learned from his father. Paul possessed both skills and the rare gift of winning the confidence of others. His family and classmates pinned their hopes on his winning first place. This did not happen. The first prize went to a black student, the second to a white girl. Paul was third. This disappointment, however, was counterbalanced by the news that he had won the scholarship to Rutgers.

At once this result became the decisive point in his life. Although he knew he would have been happier at Lincoln, he was not unduly concerned about going to Rutgers. For him, the vitally important thing was that deep in his heart, from that day on, was the conviction that none of the Ackermans of America would ever be able to shake. 'Equality might be denied,' he wrote, 'but I *knew* I was not inferior.'

Already, at the age of seventeen, he was beginning to form certain views and to adopt a 'revolutionary' stance, as is reflected in the subject he chose for the oratorical contest, which was Wendell Phillips's oration on Toussaint L'Ouverture. This was an attack on the concept of white supremacy delivered to an audience that was predominantly white.

Phillips's eulogy of the Haitian revolutionary was made before emancipation, both in New York and Boston during the first year of the Civil War. Many years later he quoted Phillips, who had challenged his audiences of 'blue eyed Saxons, proud of your race' to show him 'the man of Saxon lineage for whom his most sanguine admirers will wreathe with a laurel such as embittered foes have placed on the brow of this Negro!' Again he quoted Toussaint speaking to the Blacks after the victorious rebellion and Napoleon's dispatch of General Leclerc with some 30,000 troops: 'My children, France comes to make us slaves. God gave us liberty; France has no right to take it away. Burn the cities, destroy the harvests, tear up the roads with cannon, poison the wells, show the white man the hell he comes to make!'

The questions of chattel slavery, its abolition and the struggle for labour's emancipation were not unknown to Paul the teenager. But in the fall of 1915 he entered college for further study in Latin, Greek, physics, maths, history and to play football. As he left college to make his way in the world he was struck by the challenge facing him: that he was a 'Negro' in the United States.

By the time he was about to leave Somerville High School, he had of course already become the 'town possession'. Everybody seemed to know Paul. People liked and admired him. Although he enjoyed this popularity, it never made him conceited. Because he liked everyone, with few exceptions, he thought they in turn responded simply by doing likewise. As the summer of 1915 drew to a close, Paul's versatility was already evident.

In the fall of 1915 Paul became the third Black to enter Rutgers. The scholarship winner arrived there when Rutgers was already famous for its football team. He settled down quickly to the routine of college life and began to turn out for the various athletic teams. At that time football had assumed enormous importance in many large universities in the United States. To become a member of the varsity was a great honour. At Rutgers the football team was special, a group apart, almost sacred. The team's social distinction in college was clear: they always sat at a special table, known as the training table in the campus dining-room; they ate special foods; they enjoyed special privileges in classes, being excused for practice; and they were eagerly sought after by the various fraternities. Altogether, then, the desire to make the team was the secret longing of almost every boy entering the college.

Faced with this challenge, Paul tried out for the team in 1915. Tall and broad-shouldered, he looked more mature than his seventeen years. He played for the 'scrubs', as the second team was named. The varsity team, comprising giant six-foot and six-foot-three-inch players, had already been in training for several weeks before the opening of the new college term. All the players in the varsity team had at least one year's football experience; a considerable advantage over the newcomers. The daily practice matches between the varsity and scrub teams were gruelling tests of strength, stamina and skill. For Paul, other qualities were vital for survival, if he was to make the team. The most talented scrub player was the threat to those in the team who wanted to keep their place. In this sense, many members of the team saw Paul as a real threat. No black man had ever been in the Rutgers team, something the team members seemed proud of, when Paul arrived to make his challenge. Paul's growing confidence and improvement, as a football player, aroused deep hostility from the white team members. Thus, the lines of battle were clearly drawn.

A natural athlete, Paul became the most formidable of the scrub players, leading them in hard-fought games against the varsity team. He had to be stopped. In the scrimmages he sustained a broken nose, a dislocated shoulder, and was always badly battered. Yet he retained a fighting spirit, which impressed the coach Forster Sandford, 'an intelligent and fair-minded' man who was determined that Paul should have a fair chance of getting into the college team. Sandford gave him a week's rest, for which Paul was grateful. When he returned to play, he did so with renewed strength and determination. The varsity team had plans for him; he was singled out for special treatment. They battered him even more than they had done before; they were bent on breaking his spirit. At this stage Paul was convinced that they would do everything to keep him out of the team; that they would try everything possible. Several years later he related his experiences, particularly the violence of those who did not want him in their team, resulting in a broken nose (which troubled him as a singer) and a dislocated shoulder as well as cuts and bruises. Aged only seventeen he was unsure whether he could take any more. Certainly life was tough for him, but his father had impressed upon him that when he was out on a football field, or in a classroom, or anywhere else for that matter, he was not there just on his own: he was the representative of a lot of Negro boys who wanted to play football and go to college, and, as their representative, he had to show he could take whatever was handed out. His brother Ben had been through a similar experience at Pennsylvania and gave Paul whatever support he could.

Strangely, Paul's forceful retaliation against racist violence brought about the team's admiration and appreciation of his grit and skill. Near the end of his college days the team was built around Paul, who had achieved unprecedented heights. His intra-campus and Somerville popularity were now extended as he hit the headlines. In the 1917 football season several New York newspapers hailed him as a football genius.

His versatility in the sports field was increasingly evident at Rutgers: he was catcher in the varsity baseball team; centre in the basketball team, and threw the discus for the track team. Excellence in these sports demanded devoted and constant training. Paul made extraordinary efforts, not sparing himself. A black man can do it, he thought, except that he had to be twice as good as the white man. His brilliance at all games won him the nickname 'Robey' as Rutgers students cheered him on. Gradually Robeson of Rutgers made national news. Both the student body and faculty were proud of Paul's remarkable college record. In 1917 Walter Camp, the leading authority on football, listed Paul first on the roster of college stars. (No All-American team was picked that year because of the war.)

Through these outstanding displays which brought him growing popularity, Paul went home at least once a week. Predictably, his father examined his grades, which were on average about 95 per cent. Delighted, the old man was also proud of his son's accomplishments in sport. He attended many games in his preacher's coat, yelling with the crowd when Paul played well.

If versatility was earlier in evidence, it became characteristic in Paul's life at college. But he never lost sight of his studies. Hard work and concentration brought averages, at the end of his junior year, that were high enough for him to be elected to the national honour fraternity of Phi Beta Kappa – America's highest scholastic honour. After entering Rutgers he became a member of the debating team, of which he became captain. He represented Rutgers in intercollegiate debates and won many prizes for oratory. His father, a fine orator himself, helped Paul to work out his speeches.

Paul's phenomenal success, during the early part of his college life, was punctuated by his first great sorrow. His father died on 17 May 1918 at the age of seventy-two. Paul was heartbroken. Now, alone more than ever, Paul became more quiet and thoughtful. His father's words of wisdom and example, as a man of the people, guided him.

On 29 May 1919 he submitted his senior thesis, 'The Fourteenth Amendment, the Sleeping Giant of the American Constitution'. This theme was to be of major relevance throughout his life. He argued that the Fourteenth Amendment was the greatest force in strengthening the Union, protecting civil rights and guiding American institutions towards true nationhood. He went on to cite the inherent weakness of the original system of dual government in America. He saw the cure for this weakness in the Fourteenth Amendment.

Shortly afterwards he won the Ann Van Nest Bussing Prize in Extempore Speaking, and on 10 June he delivered his graduating class oration, 'The New Idealism'. When he graduated in June 1919, among the other honours he had won was his Phi Beta Kappa key and selection by Walter Camp for his annual All-American football team.

In July 1919 Paul left the small towns he had known and moved to Harlem, New York City, where his reputation as a football star preceded him. With distinction, he was now known fondly as 'Robey'. At twenty-one years of age, and with a matchless record behind him, Robeson was poised for a new beginning. He knew he was not an inferior black man. He had transcended seemingly insurmountable hurdles, with honour. In retrospect, he stated that the ideas relating to his fundamental concern, the struggle of his people for freedom, had their roots in these early years.

2 · Leaving America (1920–1929)

When Robeson arrived in Harlem, that 'city within a city', he was received as a hero, admired for his sporting achievements as well as for his intellect. If this attention was unexpected, as a stranger to New York he openly welcomed it, and he was accepted by nearly every class of the black population in Harlem. A casual stroll between the blocks from 153rd Street to 132nd Street took much longer than usual because of the many admirers who stopped him along the way. In a real sense, Harlem had become his constituency. He was frequently reminded of the stark realities of life in this black ghetto and the harassment meted out to Blacks only a few months before in various parts of America during the 'Red Summer' of 1919. Segregation had become the watchword, reflected in the popularity of the film *The Birth of a Nation*, based on the novel *The Clansman* by Thomas Dixon.

Towards the end of this period of racist violence in the United States the young law student was invited by the New Brunswick Young Men's Association to speak on social problems. In his speech on 'The Future of the Negro in America and What Shall His Place Be in American Life', he compared Whites with Blacks over the previous half-century, spoke of an unjust system and affirmed that closer co-operation between both groups would be the solution to the problem.

Paradoxically, in 1919 Harlem was entering its heyday; a period which became known as the 'Harlem Renaissance' when Whites with plenty of money and a liberal demeanour came to observe black life and listen to the exciting sounds of jazz as they imbibed illegal whisky. The Cotton Club and Small's Paradise were among the favourite haunts. Actually, many of the popular restaurants, bars and clubs were owned by Whites. But amidst this seemingly liberal atmosphere segregation persisted to the extent that even W.C.

33

Handy, the celebrated black composer of 'The St Louis Blues', was refused admittance to one of these clubs.

If Harlem was forbidden fruit, a tourist attraction offering pleasure to Whites who slipped in and out, for Blacks it was home. Here the creative efforts of the 'Renaissance' brought into being various forms of protest from black intellectuals against economic and social injustices. Uninterested in revolutionary politics, through novels, poetry, drama and music, many of them criticized the white establishment, especially during the 1930s. This coterie of black intellectuals included James Weldon Johnson, Claude McKay, Jean Toomer, Langston Hughes and Countee Cullen. Another Harlem resident, W.E.B. DuBois, the distinguished black scholar, had preceded them by a generation. This was the intellectual Harlem that Robeson called his homeland. Few Harlemites had the opportunity that now presented itself to Robeson. When this very sociable young man entered Columbia University Law School in February 1920, he made an immediate impression. William O. Douglas, who later became a Supreme Court judge, remembered Robeson as the most memorable of the few Blacks in his class and that Robeson was deep into his music. And he had had other interests too. He played basketball for the school and with other teams. His ability to make friends easily and his boundless energy quickly established him on the campus to the extent that when the graduating class held its annual dinner at the Hotel Astor in 1920 he was guest of honour at the speaker's table. The president of the class said that Robeson was one of Columbia's most brilliant men.

Thus far, his life was marked by a rare ability to communicate with a wide cross-section of people. Maintaining his general attitude which saw him through Rutgers, now at Columbia University it seemed he was as comfortable with his white classmates as he was with his black friends in Harlem. Participation in a number of activities in both institutions left little time for him to socialize. Yet Robeson refused to neglect the people he knew. Short of money, he took a number of jobs between his study periods to pay his school fees and maintain himself. For a while he worked as assistant football coach at Lincoln University, where he became a member of Alpha Phi Alpha fraternity, the oldest of the Negro college fraternities in America.

Perhaps for the first time during this period of financial difficulty at Columbia, Robeson sang to earn money. He sang with 'The Four

Harmony Kings' and with Florence Mills at the Cotton Club. Further attempts to raise money led to his playing professional football with the Akron Indians, and later with the Milwaukee Badgers.

Through all these time-consuming activities, he still maintained an essential interest in the theatre, occasionally attending plays at the Lafayette Theater in Harlem where the performances of Charles Gilpin and Abbie Mitchell impressed him. A succession of odd jobs later, Robeson was drawn into acting. This was not such an unusual step. Earlier at Rutgers he had, through his interest in drama, developed a warm friendship with an English professor. It was the influence of this teacher that led Robeson to see his first Shakespearian play. About this time black people were underplayed, misrepresented, in short stereotyped, in American drama.

The year 1917 was an historic one for Blacks in the American theatre. The play *Simon the Cyrenian* was first produced, breaking completely with all the theatre stereotypes of the 'Negro' character. Three years later the Harlem Young Women's Christian Association was about to stage a revival of *Simon the Cyrenian*. Not only did the original production give Negro actors the first major opportunity, it gave Robeson a chance to act the part of Simon, who was intended to be played by persons entirely or partly of Negro blood. In this play, which is set on the day of the Crucifixion, Simon, who has carried the cross to Golgotha, leaves the stage to bear the cross for Jesus. This role, given his religious upbringing, was to have enormous significance for Robeson, especially in relation to the manner in which he lived.

When he made his début in the 1920 revival of the play, many founder members of the Provincetown Playhouse were present, including Kenneth MacGowan, Robert Edmond Jones and Ridgely Torrence, author of the play. Although they congratulated Robeson on his performance, evidently he was unimpressed. 'I went home,' he said, 'forgot about the theatre and went back next morning to law school as if nothing had happened.' This attitude towards success, especially at a time when he needed a breakthrough, was an unusual Robeson trait, observed by those close to him. It was as though the private Robeson was separate from the public Robeson. This, of course, does not mean he had a split personality. More essentially, it was perhaps the behaviour of a man either unable or unwilling to accept his destiny. Perhaps his pressing studies led him to view the role of Simon as a one-off that just happened, reflected in his intuitive, rather than studied performance. At times like these his father's guidance mattered a great deal.

Whatever Robeson might have thought of his ability as an actor, members of the Provincetown Playhouse, impressed by his natural talent and outstanding performance, invited him to join their group and offered him the leading role in Eugene O'Neill's *The Emperor Jones*. Robeson turned it down because it was repellent to him. Although he had shown an interest in the theatre at this time, it was clear that he had no burning ambition to become an actor. What preoccupied him was how to become a successful lawyer. In pursuit of this goal, he alternated between odd jobs and studies.

He met Eslanda Cardozo Goode in 1921 when she was a graduate student in chemistry at Columbia University. Although they differed in background, the link between the two was clear. Eslanda (known as Essie) came from an educated, upper-middle-class family. She was a descendant on her mother's side from the Spanish-Jewish family of Cardozo. The Cardozos, who had settled in South Carolina, freed the black branch of the family from slavery. Paul and Essie were irresistibly attracted to each other, their differences drawing them together. He towered over her small frame. She was none the less a formidable opponent, aggressively intellectual. After months of courtship and a brief engagement they were married in August 1921.

Marriage did not prevent either Paul or Essie from pursuing their separate careers. While she worked in the Surgical Pathology Department at the Presbyterian Hospital of the Columbia Medical Center, Paul's studies were punctuated by less than attractive jobs. Not surprisingly, this enterprising and capable woman, better informed than most Blacks and with a number of important contacts, weighed up the possibilities for her husband's extra-curricular talents amidst the rising tide of creative energy and activity generated by the Harlem Renaissance.

Also present at the YWCA's production of *Simon the Cyrenian* was Augustan Duncan (brother of Isadora Duncan), who was preparing to direct the New York production of Mary Hoyt Wyborg's *Taboo*. In 1922 Miss Wyborg had asked Robeson to act in this play about the American South and Africa, in which he was cast opposite the English actress Margaret Wycherly. The offer surprised Robeson who admitted during rehearsals that he knew little of what he was doing at the Sam Harris Theater in New York. As it turned out, this loosely constructed and bad play not only gave Robeson the opportunity to earn some money, but more importantly the chance to sing several songs.

What of Robeson's performance? Margaret Wycherly's 'monstrously stagy' performance was counteracted by Robeson's generally good reviews, with one important exception. His sharpest and most brutal critic was Alexander Woollcott. Years later, Woollcott recalled thinking of Robeson as 'someone touched by destiny', a man with a quiet confidence moving along on an as yet unspecified mission.

For the first time in his life he was about to leave the shores of the United States. That summer he toured the English provinces with the same play, which was retitled *Voodoo*. Instead of Miss Wycherly, Mrs Patrick Campbell starred opposite Robeson, with the original black cast from New York in support. Robeson had met Mrs Campbell for the first time while she was rehearsing *Hedda Gabler*. Within a few minutes of their meeting, it was clear to him that this would be an exciting visit. He found her fiery, humorous and unpredictable, but very solicitous that all went well with him, 'a stranger in her land'.

When *Voodoo* opened in Liverpool Mrs Campbell, impressed by the young actor, urged him to prepare for the role of Othello. He was very pleased but baffled by her extravagant encouragement, since he thought he knew nothing of either acting or singing. In effect, out of a summer pastime, another career loomed large. The play was a success and Robeson received critical acclaim. An Edinburgh critic was struck by the part played by the big Negro whose simplicity was sound art.

During this first visit by Robeson to England his political thoughts were aroused. Arriving at Southampton, he sensed none of the prejudice he had left behind. His first impressions of the English people were formed by his close contact with the labouring folk. He shared their way of living, their food, their warmth and friendliness. Conscious of his ambassadorial talents and status as an actor, he believed that his success would help to raise the downtrodden black people of the world. Yet there were contradictions within him. The theatre and concerts, as a career, were the furthest things from his mind. Although he viewed the trip as 'just a lark', it was much better than waiting on tables in hotels to earn money. He was amused by the fact that he was paid £20 a week and expenses to walk on the stage, say a few lines and sing a song or two.

While in England Robeson met the black American Lawrence Brown, a man with whom he would form a close and long professional and personal relationship. A piano accompanist, Brown was keenly interested in arranging and scoring Negro spirituals, and he was impressed by Robeson's natural voice. But whatever his hopes, it seemed unlikely that they would meet again in the near future.

During the time he spent in England Robeson had forged a close relationship with English workers and saw a similarity between the labouring poor and black Americans. He was conscious of the way he was treated in England, and drew parallels with his American experience. The absence of Jim Crow laws emphasized the contrast. Altogether his tour of England was instructive. Now at twenty-four years of age, his acting and singing had given him a passport to unforeseen opportunities. In fact, his tour of England had given him a chance to see his American homeland in a new perspective. In the wake of his success, and preoccupied with his studies, he returned to America hopeful of qualifying as a lawyer.

In February 1923 Robeson graduated from Columbia University Law School. It was difficult for him to know what to do and how to begin to practise. He toyed with the idea that perhaps a political job would tide him over until he could build up a practice, but decided against it because of the political corruption of the Tammany Hall machine. After this principled decision, he found a legal job, well below his capabilities, writing briefs for a white law office. Even this job became unbearable; another matter of principle. When a white secretary refused to take dictation from him, he walked out of the law firm, and in so doing irrevocably turned his back on the one career to which he had devoted years of schooling. In later life, however, his knowledge and legal training would serve him well.

After this brief, abortive attempt at practising the law (it seemed as though he had expected it), Robeson felt that his maximum fulfilment could best be realized in the theatre, and not as a lawyer in America. At this stage in his life he knew well the barriers that would be placed before him. It was no coincidence that this educated black man was faced with the hard fact that there were no available jobs to suit his qualifications. In the trying months that followed he found he had come to know himself better. His attitude was, wait a little in the hope that something would turn up. Although something did turn up, Essie was concerned with his 'almost pathological laziness'. At times like these his ability to sing helped.

After appearing with Florence Mills at the Cotton Club early in 1924 Robeson was invited by Kenneth MacGowan and James Light of the Provincetown Playhouse to star in Eugene O'Neill's *All God's Chillun Got Wings* and in a revival of *The Emperor Jones*, the play he had earlier turned down.

The Provincetown Players was one of the most intelligent and non-commercial artistic groups in America. The Provincetowners wrote and produced plays essentially for intellectual and artistic self-expression and experiment. Robeson was attracted to this small group within which he achieved a remarkably quick assimilation. When rehearsals for *All God's Chillun Got Wings* began in the spring of 1924, his friends were James Light, Eugene O'Neill, Eleanor Fitzgerald and Harold McGhee. His entry, through O'Neill's plays, into the American theatre was historic in helping to change the prevailing perception of the Negro. O'Neill's *Emperor Jones*, which made its first appearance on 3 November 1920 with Charles Gilpin in the leading role, broke with tradition. Hitherto no black actor had been cast in a starring role in an American tragedy. Gilpin and the play had received favourable reviews.

On 24 February *The New York Times* published a biographical sketch of the twenty-six-year-old actor. Apart from choosing Robeson to play Brutus Jones in *The Emperor Jones*, O'Neill had also selected him to play Jim Harris in *All God's Chillun Got Wings*. After it was made public that Robeson would appear as Jim Harris and the white actress, Mary Blair, as Ella (Jim's wife), the play was published in *The American Mercury*. This pre-production exposure aroused strong critical reaction; a portent of the black/white controversy to come.

For those directly involved, the production was a positive commitment. James Light, who directed both plays, and O'Neill, were primarily concerned with getting the best from Robeson as an actor. At first, Robeson was self-conscious about his height in relation to the small stage at the Provincetown Playhouse. Light helped to instil Robeson with confidence in his acting by working on his ability to concentrate and by emphasizing the emotion in the character of Jim. He hoped that the emotional experience would reduce and eventually eliminate Robeson's fear of the stage, which caused the physical tension.

O'Neill's *All God's Chillun* was one of the first modern plays with the theme of intermarriage between a Black and White. In a crucial line in the play, Jim says to Ella: 'You with your fool talk of the black race and the white race! Where does the human race get a chance to come in?' Predictably, the play's last dramatic gesture (Ella kissing Jim's hand gratefully) sparked off public disapproval. The play, however, rose above the colour question.

According to O'Neill, the Negro question was not an issue in the play and was not the only one which could arouse prejudice. 'We are divided by prejudices,' he said. 'Prejudices racial, social, religious. Tracing it, it all goes back to economic causes.' In time, some of these lines by O'Neill would have an impact on Robeson's own developing interest in race relations. At this time, however, his growing interest was not in politics but essentially in art. Indeed there was no dividing line between his art and his politics. They were inseparable.

In summing up his new play O'Neill described it in terms that would later appear as part of Robeson's political and artistic philosophy: 'The real tragedy', he said, 'is that the woman could not see their "togetherness" . . . the Oneness of Mankind.' This 'Oneness of Mankind' (preached by his father) would later become an integral part of Robeson's philosophical development.

Art in the form of *All God's Chillun Got Wings* had stirred a hornets' nest. From the moment the leading players were announced, the main objections to the production came from the Hearst newspapers. O'Neill was the focus of their indignation. Among those who came to his defence in the face of criticism and abuse was the black scholar W.E.B. DuBois. Evidently the dramatic value of the play was overlooked immediately it became known that a black actor would appear with a white actress. One Brooklyn newspaper commented that because the play portrayed the love of a black man for a white woman and called for 'the kissing of the darky hero's hand by the blond heroine', interference by the Ku Klux Klan could not be ruled out.

On balance, it was clear that the attacks on the play were largely based on ignorance and racial prejudice, but many saw nothing objectionable in them. Assembling the cast presented no problems. O'Neill denied presentation of a theme that would incite racial feeling and supported the casting of Paul Robeson and Mary Blair. Before the play opened, Mary Blair, the young actress at the centre of the storm, considered it a great honour to have been selected for the part of Ella. She said she saw nothing in the part that should give offence to any woman desiring to portray life decently.

In New York, officials not only brought pressure to bear on the Provincetown Players to call off the production, they tried to intimidate the public. During the days of mounting tension the director James Light hid many things from Robeson, censoring Robeson's and Blair's mail because the letters written by the Ku Klux Klan were so filthy. O'Neill had received a letter from the head of the Klan in Georgia, threatening his son's life (if the play opened), and the Long Island Chapter of the Klan said the Provincetown Players would be responsible for the injury or death of hundreds of people if the play opened in New York.

Light and his Players, determined to press on with the production, told the Hearst press that their attacks were responsible for these threats. Although the attacks stopped, Mayor Hylan, allegedly connected with the Hearst press, became troublesome. At the last moment he rerouted traffic to cause the maximum disturbance.

In spite of the storm that raged about the play, rehearsals continued with a break in March when Robeson replaced Charles Gilpin in a revival of *Rosanne* in Philadelphia. Robeson's performance in the play was a preview of his major performances to come. The quality of Robeson's voice was now a matter of public notice.

On 6 May about a week before the scheduled opening of *All God's Chillun Got Wings* the Provincetowners hastily revived *The Emperor Jones* with Robeson in the title role. Although this put additional strain on Robeson, it was a clever, strategic move in that it was expected to earn revenue until *Chillun* was ready. Besides, attention would be focused on Robeson as an actor, rather than on his being at the centre of controversy.

Many of the first-nighters came to see *The Emperor Jones*, as the Provincetowners had predicted, because of the stir that was being raised over Robeson's role in the forthcoming *All God's Chillun Got Wings*. Remembering Charles Gilpin's brilliant performance as Jones, the audience was cool to Robeson at first. But by the time the curtain fell, the audience was won over by his outstanding, natural attributes, as opposed to the sensitivity and strength of Gilpin's more polished performance. With few outstanding black actors around, the comparison with Gilpin was inevitable and most found Robeson's evocation of the character strong in its own right. Again, his stature, physique and voice touched his audience. On this occasion,

Alexander Woollcott thought Robeson was brilliant. Even the black community, which had some reservations about the play, saw in Robeson a new talent on the American stage, not a 'Negro' actor, but actor pure and simple.

Reservations were, however, voiced some twenty years later by Dr Nick Aaron Ford, who contended that although the role of Brutus Jones and the play had created a major role for a black actor, the character of Jones was a stereotype, a 'superstitious dupe' and 'egotistical braggart'. It was argued that when such plays present the 'Negro' as morally or culturally inferior, yet 'another roadblock is thrown in the path of complete integration'. At this stage of his acting career, it seemed the idea of the Negro stereotype had not affected Robeson unduly.

Amidst this atmosphere of controversy, born out of prejudice, *All God's Chillun Got Wings* opened on 15 May 1924. And remarkably, having worked under great artistic and personal pressure, the Provincetown Players remained undaunted. James Light said: 'In spite of their threats, we knew that the Klan was made up of cowards.' The Provincetowners used husky steelworkers to protect the theatre and the cast and to guard the dressing-rooms and theatre lobby. This protection, it seemed, ensured that the performance went on.

Even so, there were forces at work to thwart performance of the play at that late stage. As curtain time approached, the chief clerk of the mayor's office refused to grant the theatre licences to permit eight children to appear in the opening scene. No reasons were given for this denial. None the less, Light's sheer determination shone through. He appeared on the stage, explained what had happened and read the opening scene. Without further interruption, the first performance of *All God's Chillun Got Wings* was successfully staged. There was neither a riot, nor even a good healthy protest. As O'Neill had intended, Mary Blair, the white heroine, knelt and kissed Robeson's hand and nobody said a word, nothing was thrown and no one hissed, booed or even 'smacked their lips derisively'.

Overall, the build-up to this performance was memorable. The play had received more pre-production publicity until then than 'any other play in the history of the theatre'. At once, through the agency of acting, Robeson had become a controversial name, and although the critics seemed to have been disappointed in the play, most of them regarded Robeson's performance with favour.

The performances by Robeson in *The Emperor Jones* and *All God's*

Chillun Got Wings dispelled any doubts he had had about his ability as an actor. In 1924, between July and December, in expansive mood, he talked about his possibilities and hopes and reflected on O'Neill's plays. And following his success in these dramas, he became more interested in the theatre and less so in law as a career. He loved the life and spirit of the group in Macdougal Street where he and Essie spent a good deal of time in the village restaurants and parks in the company of actors, writers and painters, some of whom were involved in radical political activity. The life-style greatly appealed to Robeson. He was happy with the work of acting which had become serious, worthwhile and important, yet it was fun. Moreover, everyone whose opinion he valued said he could act. Through his work in the theatre he formed many interesting and enduring friendships. Among his close friends were Carl van Vechten, Heywood Broun, Glenway Westcott, Emma Goldman and Antonio Salemme.

Robeson was proud of his Negro heritage. He showed his friends as much of Harlem as he knew, and introduced them to recordings of his favourite singers, Bessie Smith and Ethel Waters. In the presence of his white friends, he expressed frank opinions concerning the problems and progress of his race, and talked about his own hopes and ambitions in redressing the wrongs committed against black people and passionately argued the case for human brotherhood. Evidently his sense of responsibility was gaining strength.

Music had always been an important part of Robeson's upbringing and he enjoyed singing to his new-found group of friends. He felt the Negro had a definite contribution to make to art, particularly in the theatre and music. Through the peculiarly racial qualities of voice, temperament, vivid imagination and virility of spirit, he hoped for the development of a Negro culture: 'It would be splendid if Negroes would write books and plays and music about themselves.'

If his performance at the Provincetown Playhouse confirmed his ability as an actor, it was his role in *The Emperor Jones* that brought him closer to a career as a singer. In one scene he sang a Negro spiritual that the director James Light had introduced because he was impressed by the power of Robeson's singing voice, which he had heard at an informal gathering.

In spite of his growing popularity, Robeson did not have a regular income and so he happily accepted an offer from the film-maker Oscar Michaux to play the leading role in *Body and Soul*, a silent movie intended essentially for black audiences. However, his acting engagements were few and far between at this time, as a result of which he became discouraged. He had experienced much, and after he had made a second visit to England in 1925 the scope of his political thinking had broadened. Apart from the rights of the American Negro, he was concerned with human rights for all.

Essie continued to work as a pathologist at the Presbyterian Hospital of the Columbia Medical Center as Paul passed the long months of enforced idleness. Meanwhile, in London, Lawrence Brown was working on his arrangements of Negro spirituals. Brown recognized the quality of Robeson's voice and recalled that he immediately knew of Robeson's potential as a great singer. Both men loved and cared for the music of their people, and remembering this, Brown sent a copy of his musical arrangements to Robeson.

According to Essie, Paul's step from the theatre to the concert stage was a natural one. Throughout his childhood and youth the musical sounds in his father's church had become an integral part of his emotional life. When he heard his people singing, he was enriched by their soulful harmonies. He related these songs to the 'Negro's' speech which contained, as he put it, 'much of the phrasing and rhythms of folk song'.

His first reported public appearance on the stage as a singer was in a Somerville High School minstrel show, though while he was at law school he received payment for occasional performances outside. However, it was during his time with the Provincetown Players that he was effectively launched on a singing career. In *The Emperor Jones* he sang 'a little snatch of Negro music', as he had much earlier in the play *Voodoo*.

When Lawrence Brown heard his father was critically ill, he returned to the United States and, after his father's death, he went to New York where quite by chance he met Robeson. The conversation that followed had far-reaching consequences for both men. Brown accepted Robeson's invitation to join him at James Light's home. That evening in Greenwich Village Robeson told Light that he wanted to sing two of Brown's arrangements of spirituals to point up the contrast of spirit in Negro music. He sang 'Swing Low, Sweet Chariot' and 'Every Time I Feel the Spirit'. Brown joined in the latter as the second voice. 'It was completely spontaneous,' said Brown. His joining in excited Light who said, 'Why don't you fellows give a concert?' That, as Brown recalled, was how it all started.

Light's suggestion was revolutionary in American musical history in that there had never been a concert concerned only with Negro spirituals and work songs. Hitherto, spirituals performed in public were interpreted only in choral form. Light was gratified to have Robeson's support and the approval of his influential friends. The Provincetowners agreed to hold a concert in the larger theatre, the Greenwich Village Theater, and the entire concert was arranged on Provincetown credit.

According to Brown, he and Robeson had only three weeks to arrange a programme and rehearse before the first concert on 19 April 1925. For this special occasion they chose what they felt were the most beautiful of the spirituals. In the publicity campaign many of Robeson's friends offered their services. Carl van Vechten sought the help of his most influential friends, while Heywood Broun in his *New York World* column recommended the concert to his readers, and Walter White, the black writer, added his untiring support.

By the evening of 19 April all tickets for the concert were sold out. The programme, representing a selection of songs reflecting the inner life and aspirations of an oppressed people, was subdivided into four groups. Nervously Robeson and Brown strode on to the stage to make their concert début. Accompanied by Brown, Robeson sang beautifully, and at the end of the programme the entire audience remained seated, clamouring for more. This memorable evening brought rave reviews from the music critics. Robeson's voice was described as one in which 'deep bells ring'; a voice that evoked the 'sorrow and hopes of a people'. At a second concert given on 3 May 1925 *The Evening Post* critic compared Robeson to Chaliapin singing Mussorgsky; a portent of things to come for the young artist.

The audience at the Greenwich Village concert had witnessed an historic event. Given the prestigious patronage and publicity, this concert marked the beginning of a change in musical and public acceptance of the richness of Negro music. Robeson had become one of the best interpreters of this folk music. These successes brought him closer to the concert stage.

Robeson was now committed to singing the songs of his people. Indeed he would make famous the songs and music of his race, which he felt was the 'happiest medium of expression' for his dramatic and vocal skill. He considered that the meaning and message of his songs could be achieved only by doing them dramatically. At the outset, he felt his singing to be not merely a means of artistic satisfaction. He was conscious of its social aspect. He said: 'I want to sing to show people the beauty of Negro folk songs and work songs.' Through this medium, Robeson accentuated and transmitted a sense of the real plight of Blacks. He firmly believed that Negro music had its own distinctive message and philosophy and was unquestionably a body of folk music as genuine as English, Russian, German or French folk-songs. This music, peculiar to America, had indeed evolved out of a condition of slavery. He felt that the spirituals were spontaneous outbursts of religious fervour, most of which were never composed, but came to life 'ready-made out of the white heat of religious emotion during meetings in Negro camp or church, as the utterances of simple minds'. He placed the origin of these songs before the Civil War. He did not find the music gloomy. On the contrary, it was full of hope, courage and exaltation, portraying the hopes of those who faced the hardships of slavery. 'They fled to God through their songs,' he said. 'They sang to forget their chains and misery.'

Against this historical experience of Blacks in America, Robeson was ready to take the message across the land. In 1925 he and Brown were signed up by the Pond Bureau for an extensive concert tour the following year. To assist her husband in this undertaking, Essie quit her job to act as road manager. Robeson also signed a recording contract with the Victor Talking Machine Company.

At the beginning of the 1926 concert tour Robeson was described as 'one of the best interpreters of Negro music' and as possessing a voice that brought to it a 'velvety softness that is racial'. His performances moved audiences from tears to laughter and won many fans. By the end of the tour he had begun a process of at least establishing the Negro spiritual firmly in the American consciousness. Amidst a rising chorus of popular and critical acclaim, Brown observed that Robeson had remained unaffected, unmoved; he sought, it seemed, as yet unknown horizons.

A few weeks before their scheduled concert tour in early 1926 Paul, accompanied by Essie, arrived in London to play in *The Emperor Jones*. By then, both Robeson's fame and O'Neill's play had not yet affected the London theatre world. The idea of a black dramatic actor was something new to British audiences, although the black American Ira Aldridge, one of the great Shakespearian actors of the mid-nineteenth century, had played Othello with Edmund Kean as Iago and Madge Kendall as Desdemona. If this was little known, contemporary audiences were quite familiar with black actors as comedians. In 1903 Bert Williams had played a command performance for Edward VII and, later, Florence Mills was an outstanding success in the American revue *Black Birds*. In 1925, however, Robeson's name was unknown to the general public when it was announced that he would star in *The Emperor Jones* in September at the Ambassador's.

James Light and Harold McGhee, an old friend of Robeson's and stage manager of the Provincetown Playhouse, came to London to assist in the production. The rest of the cast, apart from Robeson, were English and African or West Indian. Robeson's colour, and appearance as a star on the London stage, were revealing. Light told Marie Seton (a friend and biographer of Robeson) that he had rehearsed the Africans, most of whom were dockers, for the pantomime scenes and the last scene before Robeson arrived from New York. He recalled that because some of the Africans were illiterate, the Ambassador's stage manager said to him, 'You must have had a hard time teaching Robeson all his speeches.' The manager looked surprised when Light told him that Robeson was not only a barrister, but had achieved the highest American academic honour.

Robeson, in buoyant mood, was glad to be in London to play the part of Brutus Jones which he rated highly. Meanwhile Brown travelled through the South in the States in search of new material for the first scheduled full-scale concert tour.

When the play opened at the Ambassador's on 10 September 1925 Londoners were eager to see the play and particularly Robeson. During the opening performance many of those in the audience seemed restless. McGhee observed that sections of the audience reacted more strongly to the incessant beating of tom-toms than the New York audience. If British nerves were frayed by the drumming, this was precisely the playwright's intention. The reviewer in *Punch* had never heard the tom-toms 'so terrifyingly employed before'.

None the less, Robeson's commanding presence made an immediate impact. During the interval of the opening performance people talked about Robeson rather than the play, and when the curtain fell he received an ovation. It was clear that London had not seen anything quite like *The Emperor Jones* or Paul Robeson. The *Westminster*

Gazette critic said that 'The play . . . sure is a weird play. I do not think anything comparable with it has been seen in England before', and the *Daily Mail* wrote of a 'Giant Negro' actor who held his audience 'spellbound'.

Predictably, many English people with strong views on black people were not interested either in Robeson or the play. Others marvelled at the black actor's physique, intelligence and voice. James Agate felt his voice was 'one of the finest' he had ever heard, 'warmer in tone than Forbes-Robertson's, and apt, one thinks, for the role of great verse'.

Showered with unprecedented accolades, Robeson, the untrained actor (aware that there was much to learn of his art), was amused by all the fuss, not to mention the reviews that praised his acting technique. He could not understand what they were talking about. He said he was ignorant of acting technique and of the actor's art.

When the play closed, after an unexpectedly short run, Robeson was disappointed. He was conscious that although his performance was well received, the play was not. It seemed that the cultural gap was too great for the British audience. As one London critic wrote: 'Negro plays do not evoke the emotions in London that they are understood to do in, say, Kentucky, and the sight of a half-naked wretch gradually becoming more demented leaves an English audience cold.'

After the London production of *The Emperor Jones* and his earlier success in *All God's Chillun Got Wings*, Robeson's fame as an actor spread steadily and many people speculated about his future roles. Lawrence Stallings, wondering if Robeson would play Othello, commented that 'Shakespeare must have thought of Robeson'. Robeson pointed out that good acting performances by Negro actors invariably led to talk of Othello. For him, Othello was a 'sort of culmination'. In his modest way, he underlined the significance of being a performer. As he saw it, becoming a top-class actor would be more effective than argument and propaganda in helping people to understand the 'Negro problem'.

Whatever the experts considered ought to be the future aspirations of Robeson, there were powerful forces in the press that worked against him as a black person. For instance, while most American reviewers and critics in the 1920s wrote 'negro' without a capital N, it was in the British press that one found racist language. The *Daily Sketch* described Brutus Jones as a 'full-blooded nigger', and *Cleo* as a 'huge buck nigger'. But the problems of the black artist were not entirely lost on English writers. Writing in *The Sphere*, Alan Bott pointed out that in order to achieve distinction, a black man has to overcome no less than twice the difficulties which an ambitious white man faces. And even when he transcends the disadvantages and gains respect through his intellect, instead of being accepted as an equal, he is seen as a freak. Although Robeson had proven that he was an extraordinary artist and an educated and cultured man, Bott added that he was told by a man whom he had hitherto regarded as being of sound judgement that praising Robeson as an artist was misplaced, because it would arouse conceit from Negroes all over the world.

With his undoubted success, Robeson became increasingly conscious of the difficulties he faced as a black artist. He believed it was difficult for a black actor to make a name on the stage. 'Folks won't believe he can act,' he argued, 'and prefer to see Al Jolson or Frank Tinney blacken his face and imitate us.'

The stint in London was rewarding in other ways. Robeson loved England. He felt more at home in the capital than he had in the United States, his wife said. Among the things that attracted him were the great stretches of parks and the quiet squares in the heart of the city. He was fond of strolling along the Embankment and became a cricket enthusiast, spending sunny days at Lord's and the Oval.

Robeson's stardom afforded him certain social exemptions. There were few inconveniences for him as a black man in London. He did not have to live in a segregated district. He leased a flat in Chelsea, near his friends, and dined often in the pleasant surroundings of the Ivy, directly across from the Ambassador's. And he ate at many other restaurants in London without fear of the discrimination that all Blacks encountered in America, and was a welcome guest in hotels at the seaside, where he spent many weekends. This was important for his general well-being. By comparison, while playing at the Provincetown Theater in New York he could not get a meal (in most good restaurants or hotels) unless he dined with friends or in the Village itself. At none of the first-class eating-places could he be served as a black guest. This was a great practical inconvenience. And as a traveller, he could not secure good seats in a pullman train. At hotels outside New York it was almost impossible for him to get accommodation, and in places where he knew no one, this was intolerable. So in England where everyone was kind, cordial and reasonable, Robeson was happy.

In England he had experienced an extraordinary sense of freedom of movement. By nature, he loved travelling and meeting people. He and Essie remained in London for about a month until the bad weather set in. Then they headed South to Villefranche-sur-Mer. Among the friends they met were Glenway Westcott, the writer, and Claude McKay, the black poet. McKay invited Robeson to meet his friend Max Eastman. Both McKay and Eastman had been to Russia together.

While in the South of France Robeson also met Frank Harris, who told him he had on his staff of *The Saturday Review* three of the most promising young writers in England – George Bernard Shaw, Arnold Bennett and H.G. Wells. Other notables whom the Robesons met were the singer Mary Garden, Rebecca West and G.B. Stern. Gertrude Stein, whom Robeson had met, did not like hearing him sing Negro spirituals. 'They do not belong to you any more than anything else, so why claim them?' she said. Wisely, Robeson remained silent.

Whatever were Gertrude Stein's views of Negro spirituals, Robeson returned to New York a few days before Christmas to begin his first extended concert tour. Billed as the 'Music Sensation of the Season', Robeson fulfilled the expectations of his audience at the opening concert in New York on 5 January 1926. Along the East Coast and through the Midwest the 'almost perfect blend' of Robeson and Brown brought more critical acclaim.

This successful tour informed Robeson of the degree of racial discrimination in America. He tended to see art as transcending racial prejudice. A firm believer in equal rights, he encountered a series of incidents of racial discrimination in hotels, theatres, trains and, of course, restaurants. Perhaps the worst experience was in Boston, where Robeson, his wife and Brown had arrived to give a concert. After travelling on a draughty train, Robeson had caught a cold. They needed a warm place to rest before the concert. They were refused accommodation at several hotels and drove around aimlessly in a taxi trying to decide what to do next, as Robeson's cold got worse. The light-skinned Essie eventually passed for white and booked in at the Copley Plaza. But by the time Robeson reached the concert hall his condition had deteriorated dramatically. He never sang so badly in his life as he did that evening. Essie had been a strong influence on her husband's career, and when they returned to New York after their ordeal, concerned with the state of his voice she sought voice help. But how would the famous natural voice respond to being trained? Robeson accepted his wife's initiative and worked diligently to improve his vocal range and technique. He had come to accept that it was his responsibility to preserve and protect this God-given asset.

The artist, however, faced cold and insistent racism, which forced him willy-nilly to reappraise his views. His next role was not only racial but realistic. After he returned to New York from his concert tour, the producer Horace Liveright announced plans for him to star in *Black Boy*. The play, essentially a drama, portraying the rise and fall of a black prize-fighter, again afforded Robeson an opportunity to sing. Both his singing and acting were highly rated; a performance seen as the one bright spot in the play. The drama aroused dissent from the black newspaper, the *Pittsburgh Courier*, which found *Black Boy* a play of propaganda both for and against the Negro, much of it against; and that the Negro was characterized as 'a lowly, ignorant perverse child . . . more pathetic than noble', arousing pity rather than admiration. This criticism seemed justified. Robeson, recognizing the shortcomings of the play, said more could have been done about the way the Negro really lived and felt. In this context he lamented that white people were intolerant of truth and intellectual honesty.

It seemed the Negro as actor and subject for drama had suffered a setback since the critical and artistic success of O'Neill's plays. None the less, Robeson had begun to emerge as a symbol of what a black person might achieve. After *Black Boy* closed, although Robeson the singer packed the Comedy Theater with Sunday night concerts, he continued his search for a suitable acting role. While he sought an appropriate vehicle through which he could bring to life his social-theatrical philosophy, he was simultaneously interested in commercial projects. Increasingly, he was moving closer to the social, economic and political realities confronting him and his race. Since his schooldays he had dreamed of a great play about Haiti, about Blacks, written by a Black and acted by Blacks. He dreamed of a moving drama that would have none of the themes which offer targets for advocates of racial supremacy. He feared the stereotyped format of plays and the commercialization of the Negro's characteristics and talents, but seemed to accept its coming as inevitable in the American theatre. He believed actors should decide whether plays offered to them would tend to uplift, degrade or create wrong impressions of their people. He was particularly concerned about the advance of the

Negro as the leading man in good plays and the reaction of the audience to such plays. In his estimation, *The Emperor Jones* and *All God's Chillun* were a far cry from *Uncle Tom's Cabin*-type productions. As Whites discovered the Negro's talents, he said, intellectual bondage was being diminished.

If Robeson was absorbed by his work and its implications, marriage had brought its own moments of joy. In the spring of 1927 Essie was pregnant. Assured that she would be all right with her mother, Robeson left for London in the fall to appear again with Mrs Patrick Campbell in a London revival of *Taboo*. In his absence his eldest brother Bill died. The heightened sense of becoming a father was now affected by a grievous personal loss. The sadness that tinged his voice brought out the beauty of the spirituals for which he was becoming famous beyond the shores of Britain and America.

Robeson and Brown, who had joined him, went to Paris where they sang for the first time at the Maison Gaveau. The French press was enthusiastic and Robeson commented that 'people, no matter what their race or nationality, find something of high order in [black] music'.

Essie gave birth to a son, Paul Jr, a 'replica' of his father. The likeness was so amazing, Essie said, that it became a joke among their friends. Apparently no one ever asked his name, but just called him Paul. Essie was at the centre of Robeson's professional career. And gradually as she regained her health, after a difficult childbirth, she returned to manage her husband's expanding affairs, while her mother looked after the baby and the household.

Although Robeson continued to give concerts, he hoped for a play that would satisfy his interest. The play that turned up was *Porgy*, which opened in New York on 10 October 1927, featuring an impressive black cast: Frank Wilson as Porgy, Rose MacClendon as Serena and Jack Carter as Crown. When Carter left the cast after a short stint, Robeson was perfectly cast as his replacement. The musical numbers originally left out of the play, were now written in for Robeson. But, after only a few weeks, Robeson left the show because of the strain on his voice. Commenting on Robeson's brief appearance in *Porgy*, Woollcott put it in perspective: he saw Robeson's occasional theatre performances (in between his main activity on the concert platform) in plays such as *Porgy* as being essential to earning him a place in the Negro theatre.

An offer that had been at various times under consideration since 1926 became increasingly viable. Jerome Kern went to see Robeson in Harlem with the song 'Ol' Man River' which was perfect for the bass baritone. At the time, Robeson liked it and agreed to appear in *Show Boat*, but other commitments intervened. Now, two years later, Robeson accepted the role of Joe in the London production of the play. But he was not entirely free of commitments. Before he had agreed to appear in *Show Boat*, Robeson had signed a contract with Mrs Caroline Reagan to appear in a revue due to open in October 1928. Robeson accepted an advance and heard nothing more about the production. Since then he had appeared as Crown in *Porgy*. Engagement in the revue, however, may have slipped his mind as he constantly sought more appropriate roles for his burgeoning talents. In April 1928, five months after the birth of his son, he arrived home and told Essie to pack her things, as they were going to London where he was to sing 'Ol' Man River' in the production there of *Show Boat*. Robeson might well have been happy, for he could have lost the part. The producer of the play did not want to engage him to play Joe, arguing that it was an unimportant part, that the song was not the hit song of the play, and that Robeson was too big a man for such a small part.

The rehearsals which began in April inaugurated what was to become one of the biggest productions at the Drury Lane Theatre. The play, costing about £30,000, included a cast of over 160 people who wore over a thousand costumes. Now that Robeson was committed to the show, Mrs Reagan sent him a cable asking that he be available for her revue. Robeson refused to honour his contract and stayed in England. According to one account, Essie went to New York to negotiate with Mrs Reagan and Equity, which had taken up Mrs Reagan's case. Essie explained that singing the blues in a revue would be a strain on her husband's voice. But Equity threatened him with suspension if he did not honour his contractual obligations. Although Robeson returned the advance, Mrs Reagan brought a suit against him, while Equity suspended him. The suspension, however, had force only in the United States and affected his acting alone. At that time Robeson considered himself to be more of a singer than an actor and signed for a concert tour with a London agent.

To resolve the matter Equity exerted strong pressure on Robeson, introducing a racial note by stating that it would be a great pity if this outstanding member of his race should take such a narrow view of the obligations he had incurred when he signed the contract. The racial overtones had an effect on the black community, members of which showed concern that Robeson should be careful of the harm he might do to his career and representative role as the 'Idol of his race'.

In England the columnist Hannen Swaffer commented: 'It seems to me a pity to drag Mr Robeson's colour into this question.' The issue was no longer simply a legal and artistic matter but had become tinged with race. Although Robeson made attempts to settle the matter legally, an injunction was sought by Mrs Reagan to restrain him from playing in *Show Boat*. In response to the seriousness of the matter Sir Alfred Butt, manager of the Drury Lane Theatre, argued that if Robeson were to leave, it was possible that the show would lose its popularity, which could lead to its withdrawal.

In spite of the Reagan setback, plans for the show went ahead. In the cast of *Show Boat* during rehearsals were Edith May as Magnolia, Cedric Hardwicke as Captain Andy, Marie Burke as Julie, Howett Worster as Ravenal, Colin Clive as Steve and, as already noted, Paul Robeson as Joe. As the opening night approached, although the show was laced with musical numbers, Robeson and the song 'Ol' Man River' were expected to be one of the big hits. In anticipation, public interest had grown and a queue had built up in front of the box office twenty-four hours in advance.

The opening night was a truly rare event for many seasoned theatregoers. Robeson's rendition of 'Ol' Man River', a fusion of art and experience, moved his audience as if by magic. In addition to the show's favourable notices, Robeson and 'Ol' Man River' were singled out for special praise. His powerful projection established an essential link with the audience seated in the gallery to whom he would later exclusively direct himself.

The success of *Show Boat* had resulted in a phenomenal demand to see and hear Robeson. This demand was in part satisfied through Sir Alfred Butt, who experimented with Sunday afternoon recitals. These recitals were probably the only times an actor had appeared in a musical comedy while being a solo artist in the same theatre where he played nightly. The experiment was a success. According to the *Daily Mirror*, Robeson sang spirituals at the Drury Lane Theatre for one and a half hours to an enthusiastically attentive audience. Lawrence Brown, who had come over from Paris to accompany Robeson, attributed this success to English taste and appreciation of naturalness and straightforwardness and their sense of fair play made the English wholeheartedly recognize Robeson's great talent.

As the crowds flocked to see *Show Boat* the pervasive impact of Robeson was like a chain reaction. They came from Mayfair, Bloomsbury and Chelsea; from the country, and young people from Clapham and Tooting were heard discussing Robeson on buses and in the Underground. According to one first-nighter, the expression on Robeson's face was not that of an actor. He spoke in song. In his moment of triumph, as they clapped wildly, Marie Seton observed that even as Robeson acknowledged the applause, although he was apparently touched, he seemed remote from it all.

Robeson communicated friendliness and warmth, to which his audiences responded. He possessed an essential quality important to any performing artist. As one critic put it: '. . . with or without a name however, his singing was a delight, and his stage personality has that aspect of bigness which makes him a friend, despite the intervening footlights'. The praise was punctuated by one major dissenting voice. The *Pittsburgh Courier* objected to the use of the word 'nigger' and saw the show as white America's attempt to export to Europe its anti-Negro propaganda, by yet again giving a Negro a role of little value.

Robeson, already concerned, was sensitive to the manner in which he projected the problems affecting the Negro in America. Indeed it was at this time that he began to publicize his intention to establish a repertory theatre in London where he could produce plays of his own liking. He had realized that until he could exercise some control over the plays produced, his ability as an actor would never be enough.

It is important to bear in mind that, even prior to *Show Boat* in London, Robeson's fame in England had no effect on American social attitudes. While he was lauded by the British, the US Embassy in London chose to ignore him. Although he was perhaps the most popular and respected American in England (he was lionized by English society), the American ambassador did not invite him to the Fourth of July party in 1928 or thereafter.

This snub had no bearing on Robeson's increasing popularity. He had become the man of the moment who moved in high social circles. His experience was quite unlike those of the few Blacks he had come to know in Britain. He was intrigued that Lord Beaverbrook (a staunch imperialist) should invite him to sing at a private reception.

Was Beaverbrook anxious to know what he thought? Robeson wondered. At least H.G. Wells was, since he put several questions to Robeson on one occasion when they were both Beaverbrook's guests. Unwilling at this time to entertain preconceived ideas about British society, Robeson absorbed the new and sharply contrasting impressions. He could not quite understand the primness of William Rothenstein of the Tate Gallery, his wife and family, 'and yet', he said 'they were kind and pleasant and I enjoyed myself'. What he perceived as the quaintness of English society brought him closer to his own sense of reality. England was the theatre within which his art developed.

Robeson saw much of the English countryside and waxed lyrical about English music, especially the gay and gentle lilt of the songs. He said that soon after playing the 'Emperor', and the London critics had hailed him as one of the great actors, he was persuaded to sing in public; something he did after much discussion. Almost immediately, he was proclaimed one of the great singers! He was baffled (as he had been by the acclaim for his acting) by the profound effect his voice had on others. He was always guided by instinct, while singing. He said he would only rarely act in plays because he felt he could achieve more by singing than by his best acting in a good play.

In the minds of the pundits, Robeson had achieved a unique position by 1928. The *New Yorker* published a 'Profile of Robeson' in which he was called 'King of Harlem' and 'the promise of his race'.

It says much for Paul Robeson and the rest of the cast that a London production of *Show Boat* ran through the autumn and winter of 1928. Towards the end of the year, the Robesons had decided to settle in England permanently. Prospects in America were less encouraging for a black artist. As Robeson put it, this decision was based partly on 'the same reasons as those which had over the years brought Blacks out of the American South'.

Essie found a house in Hampstead overlooking the Heath and brought her mother and son from America to live with her. By all accounts, this was a comfortable habitat for the Robesons. The poet Hart Crane, who visited the Robesons, wrote of a 'sumptuous home rented from an ex-Ambassador to Turkey', where seated at a large desk near french windows overlooking the park, Essie transacted all her husband's business.

In the following six months Robeson's fame had elevated him into a new crucial sphere of meetings and discussions of ideas that would put his artistic development into an historical, as well as a social and political, context. Few actors, indeed few black men, have been appreciated in this way. Among those with whom he was in contact were the leading experts on the British Empire, on such subjects as economics and politics. Essentially, these experts were members of the British Labour Party.

Robeson's inquisitive mind was most receptive to discussion of the British Empire. As probably the first actor to be so honoured, he was invited by a group of MPs to lunch at the House of Commons on 17 November 1928. On that occasion he sat next to Ramsay MacDonald, the former Prime Minister. Both men spoke about the future of the British colonies and socialism. At this time, agitation by colonial nationalists was gaining momentum, and Robeson epitomized the black man's cause. He was very popular in Britain, and given the potential capital that could be gained from him, this was, perhaps, the reason why he had been invited to the lunch. It was evident that the political views of these politicians interested him. He had found something in common with these MPs who later escorted him with all the formality accorded guests into the Distinguished Strangers' Gallery. The guided tour was an education for the artist who had hitherto remained outside the realm of politics, and had never before seen anything as unique as the House of Commons, with all its pomp and rhetoric, echoing the politics of the 'white man's burden'. Surveying what he took to be an edifice of British imperial power, his eyes fell on a most un-English face in the House. The man he saw was dark brown. During the tea interval he learned from James Maxton that the dark MP was the Indian Shapurji Saklatvala who had been elected in the Battersea North constituency in 1922. Robeson was told that the outspoken Saklatvala would in all likelihood have been in gaol had he been in India. Some ten years later Saklatvala, the uncompromising communist, became Robeson's friend.

Robeson may not have systematically thought through his position or the merits of socialism *vis-à-vis* his personal involvement in politics, but his claim not to have known anything about socialism is at variance with discussions he had had earlier in his life. The idea of socialism had been bandied about in New York circles for some time and many of Robeson's friends were of a radical bent. William Patterson recalled that he, Robeson and Heywood Broun talked often about the subject. Essie, too, in her account of her husband's chance meeting with Claude McKay and Max Eastman in 1928, wrote that

'Paul listened eagerly to the talk about Russia and Socialism'. Possibly what Robeson meant was that his knowledge was superficial. Certainly at this point, he had not developed his ideas on socialism.

During this period, as Robeson was being entertained, on the one hand by staunch imperialists, and on the other by traditional opponents of British imperialism, he was closely monitored. According to the historian A.J.P. Taylor, 'Paul Robeson received a more appreciative welcome [by Beaverbrook] and came four times in succession, at a fee of eighty-four pounds, 10 shillings for each recital – a large sum for those days.' When the Robesons and the actress Pola Negri lunched at Lord Beaverbrook's in June 1929, a guest recorded in his diary that Robeson 'is a pleasant enough Negro whose ambition it is to play Othello in straight drama'. Interestingly, he added, 'Robeson danced with all the white women.' Apart from his wife, who was the only black woman present, it seemed Robeson had little choice.

Overall, Robeson was happy enough with the contacts he had made in Britain. He felt he was treated as a 'gentleman and a scholar' and was impressed with the sense of justice among the British.

The spring of 1929 saw the beginning of Robeson's European tour, accompanied by Lawrence Brown and Essie. After several days in Vienna, Robeson and Brown gave their first concert to a hall crowded to the roof in the Musikvereinsaal on 10 April. If the audience had expected a cheap sensation from this giant black performer, they would have been surprised to find themselves present at an important artistic event. Robeson's selection of spirituals (including 'Water Boy' and 'I Don't Feel No Ways Tired') took them gently through a variation of moods.

This incident-packed concert tour had a powerful influence on Robeson's developing social concerns. Through his Negro spirituals he found he could communicate at a common level with people from other cultures. He was deeply stirred when those whose language he could not speak grasped his hands. This act, expressive of the 'oneness of mankind', engendered in him a desire to understand other languages. More significantly, however, it was in Vienna that Robeson's growing political consciousness was heightened by a memorable experience. Whatever his preconceptions of Europe, he was now faced with something quite unexpected.

He knew nothing about the conditions in or the politics of Europe at that time. The poverty of the Viennese people was surprising; something he could not forget. After the concert he was approached by a young man, knowledgeable in music. The youth said he had no money and could not have attended the concert if someone had not given him a ticket. He asked Robeson to visit him at home. Robeson accepted the invitation and never forgot the poverty in which the young man lived with his mother, a cultured woman. 'I knew they were Jewish,' Robeson said, 'but at the time I didn't understand the position of the Jewish people in Europe.'

This contact with Jewish people in poverty would lead Robeson towards a fuller understanding of their 'problem', and to see the problem of his own people in a broader context a few years later.

When the Robesons and Brown arrived in Prague for the next concert they were surprised and pleased to find a formal and deeply cordial note of welcome from Mr Einstein, the US minister to Czechoslovakia. Einstein and his staff attended the concert held in the Smetana Hall, entertained the Robesons at supper and invited the distinguished people of Prague to meet their fellow Americans. Conscious of the snub from the US Embassy in London, the Robesons were impressed by this official act of appreciation.

Robeson's concert in Budapest brought critical acclaim. His performance reminded the newspaper *Pesti Kurir* of 'the great Italian masters'. His presence in Hungary was not only a new experience but a revealing one, for it was there that he discovered that Negro music had an affinity with Hungarian, Czech and Slovak folk-songs. Robeson did not then understand why there should be any similarity between the expression of the Negro people and the people of Central Europe.

After this enlightening tour he returned to London to appear in his first concert at the Royal Albert Hall on 28 April 1929, the anniversary of his opening in *Show Boat*. Since that grand opening in 1928, Robeson had become the most discussed singer in London and, predictably, the Hall was full.

Robeson's voice, which to many was reminiscent of Chaliapin, moved his audience. The *Evening Standard* critic, however, wondered if Robeson would include in his repertoire 'a more sophisticated type' of song. It seemed Robeson was more concerned about the type of audience he was reaching; he wanted to include in his audience the low-income British working class. He said that although it was not usual for a singer on tour to give summer concerts at the spas and seaside resorts, he was willing to sing on a percentage basis in order to do so.

Robeson's success, both in the theatre (he had, at last, agreed to appear with Maurice Browne in *Othello*) and the concert stage, seemed limitless as his ability to move audiences with simple folk-songs gained him more and more popularity. On 8 September 1929 he signed a long-term contract with the American impresario F.C. Coppicus, who had managed the tours of Caruso and Chaliapin, among others, in the United States. Coppicus had neither met Robeson before, nor heard him sing. But having seen him in *The Emperor Jones*, he said he had never met a man of any race with so many talents.

Just before Robeson left London for concert engagements in the United States he was involved in a disturbing incident which shocked the British public, and more than likely brought Robeson closer to the British working class and to politics. The Robesons were invited to attend a party in their honour in the Grill Room at the Savoy Hotel, but on arrival they were refused admittance. In the United States Robeson had come to expect, though he never accepted, this kind of discrimination, but not in London. Outraged Africans and West Indians in Britain called a meeting in support of Robeson. They invited the press and read details of what had actually happened. In the glare of publicity the Savoy's management felt shamed but said that the affair could not be traced. This was unacceptable to many people. A few days later, the 'colour bar' re-emerged as a political issue. James Marley, MP, had intended to raise the issue in the House of Commons and Ramsay MacDonald, guarded because of his political prospects, and in characteristically British diplomatic style, said: 'It is not in accordance with our British hotel practice, but I cannot think of any way in which the Government can intervene.' Although Robeson was assured that the general attitude among English people was anti-discrimination, the experience rankled deeply with him.

He would never forget this incident. The colour bar was alive and growing uglier in Britain following the shipping depression and increased presence of West Africans and West Indians. Even Robeson's celebrity status did not protect him altogether. The complaints of black seamen and students were in fact well founded.

His experience in London had brought Robeson up against the unacceptable face of racial England. On this sour note, he left for his singing tour of the United States. The Savoy incident marked a turning-point in Robeson's feelings towards racism in England and made him more politically aware.

In the United States Robeson's mesmeric qualities thrilled his audiences across the country as the work song 'Water Boy' became a hit. By the end of the 1920s Robeson had emerged as a brilliant interpretive artist poised to interpret Negro spirituals as an integral part of a repertoire that would extend far beyond his homeland.

3 · Finding a Voice: From Interpretive Artist to Political Artist (1930–1940)

By 1930 Robeson had achieved undisputed international acclaim. He appeared in the British *Who's Who* (though not in *Who's Who* in the States); his head was sculpted by Jacob Epstein, but permission to display his nude statue by Tony Salemme in Rittenhouse Square was refused by the Philadelphia Art Alliance. Furthermore, his first biography, *Paul Robeson, Negro*, written by Essie, was published. While Robeson was being lionized, however, his marriage had been undergoing difficulties. According to one report, during that year he was temporarily separated from Essie, notwithstanding the public image of the Robesons as one of togetherness.

Robeson's commanding presence and voice had brought him superstar status, and naturally among his vast and growing audience there were many inquisitive female admirers. But although women were always around, as a close friend put it, women were not Robeson's primary interest. The first public statement of marital discord came with the publication of Essie's book. In frank admissions Essie remarked to a friend that, after eight years of marriage, she and her husband had never agreed on anything. Although they were good friends and she loved him more than ever, she described him as a blessed, confounded but admirable nuisance.

Robeson, according to Essie, was displeased by her remarks. He was 'mad' that she treated him as though he were a child. He in turn considered her unreasonable and absurd. Did Essie have doubts about her husband's faithfulness? When asked, at the time, if he was faithful to his wife, Robeson refused to be drawn. However, Essie recalled his saying that admission of unfaithfulness on his part would simply be met by her disbelief.

During these early years of marriage Robeson was clearly dependent on his wife both emotionally and in his career. She not only dealt with his business affairs and his growing correspondence, but overall she wanted, as she put it, 'to make a good job of Paul and Pauli, but it was a whole time job'. In spite of her loneliness while her husband was away on tour, she completed her biography of him which was described as 'offensive' in its simplistic explanations of racial phenomena. The book revealed much of the state of their marriage as well as Robeson's shortcomings which, she maintained, derived from his laziness. Essie was unhappy about the female attention Robeson received. She dismissed the loud protests about the harm the book might do to her husband as coming from jealous white women, whom she laughed at in her book. According to one account, Robeson was upset by the book. One writer observed that Essie 'discussed him as if he was her possession and somehow mentally inferior'. Robeson, on the other hand, who had a great capacity for friendship, was not a male chauvinist. Rather, he genuinely liked and respected women as equal human beings.

Now that Essie had made their private lives public, Robeson had to cope as best he could with any personal and professional repercussions that might be directed at him. If he was really upset by his wife's statements, was this a reflection of the state of their marriage? Time would confirm or deny the truth of Essie's deep feelings and concern for Robeson and their marriage.

By 1930 the United States was plunged into depression, as poverty and unemployment spread across the country. The Great Depression, precipitated by the Wall Street Crash of 1929, had world-wide repercussions. In Britain, unemployment dramatically rose from 1 million to over 3 million. Against this background of world events Robeson prepared for his historic appearance in *Othello*.

Behind the scenes there was an air of excitement. The idea and repeated suggestions that Robeson should play Othello was not only announced but had now begun to take shape. Robeson approached the play with the respect it deserved. He felt the play was a modern one, 'for the problem is the problem of my own people'; that it was a tragedy of racial conflict, a tragedy of honour rather than of jealousy, and that Shakespeare presented a noble figure, a man of singleness of purpose and simplicity with an uncluttered mind. Further, he emphasized that Othello was important to the State, but the fact that he was a Moor incited the envy of 'little-minded' people. Desdemona's love for Othello and their marriage sowed the seed of suspicion. 'The fact that he is alien among white people makes his mind work more quickly,' said Robeson. 'He feels dishonour more deeply. His colour heightens the tragedy . . . I am approaching the part as Shakespeare wrote it and I am playing Othello as a man whose tragedy lay in the fact that he was sooty black.' Aware of the historical moment, like Othello, Robeson the sooty black was made to feel 'alien among the white people'.

On his return to London, after his American concert tour, Robeson again appeared at the Albert Hall. At the end of March he was invited to Berlin by Max Reinhardt to perform in *The Emperor Jones*. This was Robeson's first trip to Germany. The production, performed in English with an all-white cast at the Kunstler Deutsches Theater, was directed by James Light, who also played the role of Harry Smithers. The German critics praised Robeson, 'the first great American actor seen in Germany'.

Robeson returned to London for rehearsals in *Othello* and continued his intensive study of the English language during Shakespeare's time. He read works on phonetics, listened to records to improve his enunciation and studied English pronunciation with the help of the Furness Variorum of *Othello*, in which the text was printed in Old English. He learned, for example, from the spelling of *chaunce* and *demaunde* how to pronounce the words chance and demand with an English accent.

Robeson was particularly careful about his interpretation of the role. He studied the play, his part in it and the language, reading everything he could, and absorbed all the relevant knowledge. In the process he came to know Frank Benson, the Shakespearian actor, whom he visited regularly. Although he had learned much about Shakespeare and Shakespearian actors from Benson, he could not apply this tradition to himself and was unable to grasp the concept of 'thinking one's role'. Indeed Robeson, having embarked upon a major acting challenge, would come to accept and explain later that he was essentially an *intuitive* actor. He told a *New York Times* reporter that having read a good deal of Shakespeare, and given his understanding of England and the English people, he was confident he could play Othello.

Overall, Robeson's preparation was thorough. He understood Othello in a way that would be quite unlike any interpretation of the character by a white actor.

The rehearsals for *Othello*, an extraordinary experience for Robeson, increased his love of the theatre. Maurice Browne, the American actor/producer, who played Iago, recalled that Robeson's 'movement was not always good, but his emotional power was terrifying. In the "jealousy" scenes he – literally – foamed at the mouth; I used to wonder whether one day he might not seize Iago and pluck out his arm'.

In line with Browne's policy of developing young talent, Peggy Ashcroft, the English actress, who had not yet made a name for herself, was selected to play Desdemona, after Robeson had seen her in *Jew Süss*. She was then twenty-two years old, and recalls that she knew nothing of Robeson's politics. (At the time Robeson was a supporter of the Labour Party. She had known of him through his records, and says he was a 'hero' in Wales. Theirs was a significant meeting, none the less. In fact she became aware of racism for the first time when Robeson was refused entry at the Savoy Hotel.) Other members of the cast included Sybil Thorndike as Emilia, Max Montesole as Cassio, and Ralph Richardson (then little known) played Roderigo.

Since the production had been announced, public reaction was aroused. Robeson's starring role opposite a white woman yet again shored up feelings of racism. Although the opposition was not like the New York experience (centred on *All God's Chillun Got Wings*), there were newspaper articles and letters, many of which came from women. One woman wrote that while Robeson was a fine actor, she did not think he was right to play the Moor; another, addressing herself to a columnist, asked him to use his influence to stop 'such an exhibition'; while yet another wrote: '. . . we are not against Negroes, but we do not like them near us'.

This reaction to the casting was indeed a surprise. By contrast, the black American Ira Aldridge's Othello, opposite Dame Madge Kendall's Desdemona, over half a century earlier, seemed to have caused little excitement. Robeson may have thought optimistically of his Savoy experience as an aberration, but now once again he was confronted with the reality of race and colour. Although it seemed to him that the fuss in London was 'all nonsense', nevertheless he was affected. For the first weeks, during his performance in the scenes with Desdemona, he backed away from Peggy Ashcroft. He felt as clumsy as 'a plantation hand in the parlour'. This difficulty was overcome only after he had received favourable notices.

For her part, Peggy Ashcroft said that racial prejudices were 'foolish at the best of times, but I think it is positively absurd that they should even come into consideration where acting is concerned. . . . I see no difference in being kissed by Paul Robeson and being kissed by any other man. It is just necessary to the play'. She considered it an honour to be acting with Robeson, and any discussion about her kissing or being kissed by him seemed 'merely silly'.

Another issue thrown up by this production of *Othello* was whether Shakespeare imagined Othello as a Negro or a Moor. Among the diverse views expressed (that Othello was Arab or Negro, light brown or black) one writer felt that the part of Shakespeare's Moor was not written for a coloured actor. Robeson expressed his opinion later: he argued that Shakespeare had intended Othello to be a black Moor, a noble African, and that later on English critics saw a black Othello in a colonial context, regarding him as less than noble. Here, the connections of Europe, Africa, slavery and colonialism were part of Robeson's history, an ever-present past, as it were. Moreover, Robeson saw the problem in the play as allied to the problem of black people. He related Othello's colour, race and marriage to a white woman in the Venice of that time to the experience of the black man in contemporary America. As a Negro Robeson underlined the fact that for once at least he had started with an advantage. 'An English actor who plays Othello has to spend three-fourths of his time convincing the audience that he is really black,' he said. 'At least I haven't that to do!' He also pointed out that although Othello was a member of an alien race, facing a highly developed white civilization, knowing exactly where he stood, and a great general, he was placed in a precarious position because of his race. Feeling his way through the part Robeson argued that colour was a secondary issue in that it emphasized the cultural difference – Othello's love and honour were embodied in his culture.

By the time Robeson trod the boards at the Savoy, his appearance was transformed. He had added a moustache and a beard. It was, however, not only colour that interested Robeson. He was absorbed in trying to determine exactly what Shakespeare meant. He felt Othello to be a character demanding the inner feelings of an actor and that his jealousy was honourable. Furthermore, Robeson's singing talents were brought into play. He was in tune with the verse in the play which 'holds a rich music all its own'. He explained that the verse offered him as a singer the opportunity of enhancing the

Shakespearian rhythm that now lay within his grasp.

Robeson found the rehearsals enjoyable and developed a love for the theatre. Although he had played a number of roles in the United States, and had always preferred singing, he now wanted to act. As the opening drew nearer, the cuts in the play revealed the obvious deficiencies to Robeson, which in turn affected his interpretation of the role.

After all the preparation, gossip and speculation, the production opened on the evening of 19 May 1930. The modern settings were a departure from those generally seen in a London production of Shakespeare. Robeson had spoken of Shakespeare's lines as coming from the heart, yet some critics considered his performance to be 'too reasoned'.

In spite of the criticism and flaws in the Savoy Theatre production, at the end of the first performance there were twenty curtain calls before the applause subsided amidst cries of 'Robeson! Robeson! Robeson! Speech! Speech!' If he had previously been unmoved by applause and accolades, now he was almost speechless. 'I am very happy,' he said. At that moment he had fulfilled the expectations of many who had seen him act, including Mrs Patrick Campbell, one of the first to recognize his talent and encourage him to prepare for *Othello* way back in 1922.

Othello, which set box-office records for the opening night, ran for six weeks. There is no doubt that Robeson had added a new and interesting dimension to Shakespeare's Moor. At the close of the production and acting performance, J. Dover Wilson, the Shakespearian scholar, wrote of Robeson and the production: 'I was lucky enough to see his Moor at the Savoy in May 1930. It was an unforgettable experience which taught me to understand the play as I had never done before; to understand it in the way I am convinced Shakespeare meant us to.'

With his Othello Robeson had truly established himself as an actor. Generally, he pleased the reviewers and the public. Not only had they found an Othello as Shakespeare must have planned him, but the talented Peggy Ashcroft as well. Robeson's triumph in London aroused great interest in the United States. On 9 June 1930, for the first time, he did a broadcast to the States through the BBC. He explained how the daughter of Ira Aldridge had helped him in his preparation for the role. For black Americans, the significance and nuances of the play had stirred provocative responses. Whatever hopes there might have been of a New York production of *Othello* in 1930, racial prejudice there remained a contentious and divisive issue, acting as a barrier to progress. The climate of opinion, it seemed, was not right for it. Although the possibility was always there to titillate liberal and progressive Americans, Robeson had previously expressed doubts about the reception this play would receive in his native land. He said the kissing and rough handling of a white actress on the stage would not be tolerated in certain parts of the United States. He feared audiences might become dangerously hostile. His concerns were not totally unjustified. An editorial appearing in a Georgia newspaper in May 1930 responded to Robeson's remarks by stating that although Robeson had queer ideas about art and the stage, he had the good sense to know that the people would not welcome that kind of entertainment 'now or ever'.

By now, Robeson had scaled new heights as a performer; he fascinated many people. Although he was not 'political', he had been the centre of considerable controversy, which pointed up many sensitive social questions. Nevertheless, his stature as an artist and his commitment to his race were particularly attractive to some. Marie Seton, then a budding dramatic critic, was puzzled and went to see Sybil Thorndike (Emilia) in the hope that she would illuminate the dark, brooding phenomenon that was Paul Robeson. Miss Thorndike told her that Robeson was a wonderful person – the nicest man with whom she had worked in the theatre, a feeling that was shared by the entire cast of *Othello*. But even this view did not satisfy Marie Seton's curiosity about Robeson's ability to command respect.

Following *Othello*, the British public saw Robeson as a 'great artist'. Of necessity his fame presented him with many subtle problems, for he was a man who needed to keep his inner self intact and one to whom material success and acclaim were inessential. The banal and superficial disturbed him and he could take nothing for granted. He felt that he understood the British people and had become part of the English scene. As Lawrence Brown observed: 'I would say that the audiences in England and abroad were always more friendly and enthusiastic than in America.' And as England became more and more a part of him, he felt a new kind of individualism asserting itself within him, one that seemed to have no race or nationality; a consciousness neither black nor white but of the world. 'Paul always had a bigness,' said Brown. 'There was nothing petty about him, and he cut through the mass of details and arrived at a larger understanding.'

Othello marked an important juncture in Robeson's artistic development. When the play closed in July, Robeson returned to the concert
stage. About that time O'Neill had been working on *The Hairy Ape*
for Robeson. Apart from his eager interest in the play, Robeson had
hoped for a revival of *The Emperor Jones* and a production of *All God's
Chillun* in London. Looking to the future, he wanted to reach a wider
audience. To achieve this goal, he had to overcome real difficulties.
He was particularly concerned with the high prices of admission
which were prohibitive to the low-income working people. He
identified strongly with the lower-income patrons of the theatre and
concert halls, who understood him best. He demanded their accommodation in theatres at prices they could afford.

By late August 1930 Robeson was back at the Savoy to perform
the first parts of *The Emperor Jones* and to sing Negro spirituals.
Songs by Schumann and Mozart were to follow. Robeson and Brown
toured England, Wales and Scotland, appearing in Manchester,
Liverpool, Bradford, Cardiff, Glasgow and Edinburgh. The audiences
were in tune with Robeson. Brown had no doubt as to Robeson's
special appeal. It was as a singer, he said, that Robeson captivated the
provincial audiences. He was gradually learning to understand the
significance of this medium of communication.

However, his acclaim as an artist had not dulled his social and
political awareness and development which had not yet asserted itself
in a positive way. Marie Seton noted that at this time, and several years
later, Robeson's thoughts and experiences were not clear-cut. He
tended to hide his innermost feelings from his close friends in
England. He spoke little or not at all about racism in the United States
because it was precisely this historical and contemporary experience
which invested power in the folk-songs he sang. It was clear to Brown
that the concert tours on both sides of the Atlantic between 1929 and
1932 revealed Robeson's mastery of his art and his increasing acclaim
as an individual artist. But how did this individuality relate to the
wider scheme of things in world affairs? And why should it?

Under the exigencies of fame he discovered that many Blacks had
betrayed their heritage. Of his own volition he pushed aside those
personal contacts which were in any way inimical to his pride of race.
The success of Robeson, a member of an oppressed race, pointed up

the real and deplorable disadvantages of his people. He became increasingly troubled by social questions. Almost twenty years later he recalled a lesson he had learned in London. While he was being fussed over by people in fashionable Mayfair, he overheard an aristocrat speaking to his chauffeur as though he were a dog. This reminded Robeson of the way white Southerners in the United States spoke to Blacks. Thus he saw the fight of all oppressed people as one struggle. The class differences in England seemed clear-cut, and while black servants in the United States resented their status and sought escape, in contrast servants in England accepted their status.

Robeson was still searching for direction, yet he was conscious of the strides he had made, and felt a growing sense of responsibility to fellow Blacks. In London, his contact with Africans and Afro-West Indians generated a search for the roots of 'Negro music'. If he was concerned with the biblical and African melodic basis of the spirituals, he seemed wary of the value of jazz which, he said, had 'no spiritual significance' and therefore would not seriously affect 'real music'.

If Robeson had no clear purpose at this time, as one writer put it, 'there was no more indescribable suffering for Paul than his emotional state during this period of his great public acclaim and his private humiliation'. Even as the great artist, he was not spared from being subjected to undisguised racial prejudice and discrimination. This became a constant preoccupation, as each day brought him closer to a clearer understanding of his place in the world.

Before the end of *Othello* the film *Borderline* was shown at film societies in several European countries. Robeson's curiosity in film resulted in his teaming up in *Borderline* with the experimental film-maker Kenneth McPherson. Essie also acted in this film essentially for the avant-garde cinema. With its weak story-line, there was no enthusiasm for it in England and it was not shown in the States. To its credit, however, was the fact that it showed Blacks as human beings and not as racial stereotypes.

Increasingly, Robeson came to see films, plays and music as the media through which he could (and should) express his concerns. After all he was assured of a captive audience to whom he could deliver his message. By the end of 1930 Robeson was also preoccupied with other more personal matters. The malaise in his marriage had reached breaking-point and, according to one report, he and Essie were 'quietly separated'. About this time Robeson employed Robert Rockmore who, from 1931, would attend to his professional affairs.

According to Dorothy Butler Gilliam, during Robeson's concert tour of the United States early in 1931, his comment that he would be rejoining his wife and son at the end of the tour, was 'only a cover'. Robeson's home was a rented flat in the Strand. In fact his wife was not there with him. Accompanied by her mother, she had taken her son to Vienna, where she worked on a novel and a play. For his part, the ever-industrious Robeson moved closer to learning the Russian language. Already he spoke German well and studied French, which helped him to expand his repertoire of songs.

In April 1931 Robeson returned to London to start rehearsals for *The Hairy Ape* under the direction of James Light. The play encountered difficulties with the censor who, it was reported, had cut thirteen expletives from the play. Robeson had worked himself convincingly into this 'tough guy part' by the time the play opened in May 1931 at the Ambassador's in London. This was, however, a first night with a difference: the audience paid 24 shillings for the stalls, twice the usual first-night price. And symbolic of Robeson's stature in the entertainment world, the famous Epstein bust of him was on display in the theatre lobby.

Robeson played Yank Smith, an alienated by-product of the technological age. Yet again Robeson was involved in a play in which 'race' had become an issue. Referring to Robeson's 'racial characteristics', one critic wrote that when Robeson's 'eyes roll and glitter and his strong white teeth flash in angry grimaces, we admire a spectacle of animal energy, but without experiencing the thrill of fear. The explanation probably lies deeper than the actor's art, and in the characteristics of his race which, capable of wild excitement, is remarkable also for its sweet nature of docility'. Another felt that because Robeson 'is a Negro. . . . He plays the leading part in one explosion and he himself the personification of another potential explosion . . . that of bitterness in the hearts of the coloured races against the overlordship of the whites'.

Physically Robeson was perfect as Yank the stoker in the hold of a ship, of which he saw himself as an integral part. When the curtain fell on this play, Robeson received loud applause. In the next day's newspapers, reviewers used superlatives describing Robeson's dominating performance. With this play Robeson moved nearer to being in a class of his own as a performer.

During the play, however, one of Robeson's fears was realized: he lost his voice and, after less than half a dozen performances, he left the show suffering from laryngitis. To the disappointment of theatregoers, the theatre refunded the advance receipts and Robeson was strongly advised to rest his voice. Many factors contributed to this illness, he said. Although his voice had regained its former strength and power, he did not recover fully from the physical fatigue, the accumulation of wear and tear of four years of continuous work – physical and mental – without adequate rest. Nevertheless, this illness brought out one of Robeson's many remarkable qualities. Apart from his own disappointment, he was particularly concerned about the English actors who were made redundant as a result of his illness. He knew well the difficulties of making ends meet as an actor. Alarmed by this first major setback in health, he made the important decision to forgo the stage and acting for about three years so that he could concentrate on his concert performances.

Robeson went back to New York the following year to appear in the 1932 revival of *Show Boat*. During that year he received an honorary Master's degree from Rutgers University. This was a proud moment for him, but it could not hide the fact that his private life was in the doldrums. His wife, according to one source, had planned to sue for divorce.

According to Alexander Woollcott, Jerome Kern had earlier telephoned him to say he had just finished a new song, 'Ol' Man River', which he wanted Robeson to sing in his new musical, *Show Boat*. Although Robeson had sung the song in the 1928 London production, it was Jules Bledsoe who played Joe when the show had its première in New York, because Robeson had a previous engagement to honour – a concert tour. When the 1932 revival was planned, however, Robeson agreed to appear. Edna Ferber, author of the book, thought a revival was premature. After reconsideration she attended an extraordinary opening night, which was characterized by a mad rush for seats.

The show was considered even better than its first production. Robeson's part attracted particular notice. Superlatives seemed appropriate. As one reviewer put it, the 'brilliance of the original cast is heightened by the presence of Paul Robeson, whose singing of "Ol' Man River" in the first scene is one of those perfect things to put away in the corner of your memory and never forget'. Most outstanding of all was Robeson's 'celestial' voice; a triumph, playing the role of Joe. But it was not only his voice that mattered. 'It is his understanding that gives "Ol' Man River" an epic value,' the critic Brooks Atkinson explained. 'When he sings it out of the cavernous [sic] depths of his chest his face is a mask of the humble patience of the Negro race, and you realize that Jerome Kern's spiritual has reached its fullest expression.'

At about this time of unusual critical acclaim, however, Robeson's troubled marriage was again spotlighted and divorce for the Robesons was again reported. Much intrigue surrounded Robeson. He was linked with a famous titled English woman – namely Edwina Mountbatten, the wife of Lord Louis Mountbatten.

Robeson's sensational first night at the Savoy Theatre as Othello was a society event that Edwina Mountbatten had attended. His voice, physique and mind fascinated her. She had never met a black man with all these qualities and with such charm. In 1932 the gossip columns took note of her attraction for 'dark-skinned gentlemen', one of whom was the well-known singer and pianist 'Hutch' – Leslie Hutchinson. The names of these men were never mentioned by the columnists as companions of Lady Mountbatten. But in May *The People*, 'that vulgar socialist Sunday paper', as Lord Mountbatten described it, touched on an extremely embarrassing story headlined SOCIETY SHAKEN BY TERRIBLE SCANDAL. According to the biographer Richard Hough, Edwina Mountbatten's reputation was so well known that 'even the lowest echelons of society' had no doubt as to the identity of her 'associate'. *The People* stated that as one of the 'leading hostesses' in Britain 'Associations with a coloured man became so marked that they were the talk of the West End. Then one day the couple were caught in compromising circumstances. The sequel is that the society woman was given the hint to clear out of England for a couple of years to let the affair blow over, and the hint comes from a quarter which cannot be ignored.'

The potential damage this publicity could inflict on the Mountbattens was a matter of the highest concern. On the advice of the King and Queen, the Mountbattens (whose marriage was shaky) were required, as Hough argues, to deny Lady Mountbatten's association with a 'coloured' man. Accordingly Lord and Lady Mountbatten initiated proceedings for libel against the owners of *The People*. During the hearing in camera of this 'most monstrous and most atrocious libel', as Norman Birkett, acting for the Mountbattens, put it, Lady Mountbatten denied that she had ever met the man referred to. Moreover, in her diary she denied ever having met the man in question.

Hough suggests that she did know Robeson, who had been a guest at her Brook House parties. 'Even if one accepts that she lied in her private diary and that she was prepared to perjure herself,' writes Philip Ziegler in *Mountbatten*, 'it seems inconceivable that none of the many fellow guests who must have witnessed Robeson's presence was ready to testify to that effect in court.' The case ended with a 'grovelling apology' from *The People*, and Lady Mountbatten refused damages. In fact the case had long-term damaging effects of a different nature. Hough argues it was not Edwina Mountbatten but Paul Robeson who suffered most, and that Robeson never deviated from the belief that his colour was the decisive factor in the whole affair.

Other rumours linked Robeson with the Englishwoman Nancy Cunard who was in Harlem researching a book on Negro life. The press hinted that they were lovers merely because they happened to be staying at the same hotel. Intimates of Robeson's thought another black man was involved, a composer who had been living in Paris. But even this was doubtful. Robeson was angry about the publicity.

By now Robeson had become a more sophisticated artist; he had changed somewhat, as though his visit to the United States had reinforced and clarified certain things in his mind. He had learned much, having moved easily and freely among London's upper classes, and was now able to put into perspective the fact that English aristocrats' treatment of white servants was on a par with the disregard Blacks received from Whites in America. This simple observation affected Robeson deeply. More clearly now he saw economic class and the poor in relation to society as a whole. And somehow his earlier experiences (of poverty in Europe and the plight of the Jews) began to make proper sense. Yet in spite of his growing awareness, he was still reluctant to relate race and politics to himself, a reluctance that was soon to be threatened from all sides.

In 1931 the Depression had struck deep in the United States and Britain, bringing widespread poverty and unemployment. A chain of events followed: Britain went off the Gold Standard and the repercussions in India, Africa and the British West Indian colonies were especially profound. In London, the Pan-African organizations – the West African Students' Union and the League of Coloured Peoples – campaigned for an end to colonialism; the former more militantly than the latter.

Although Robeson wanted to live in Germany for a time in order to make an extensive study of the language and music, that ambition now seemed impossible to fulfil. Early in 1933 Adolf Hitler came to power, and under his dictatorship the Jews became 'impure' people. Thousands fled. In Britain John Strachey, a leading spokesman for the Left, Victor Gollancz, the publisher, and James Maxton, leader of the Independent Labour Party who had earlier taken Robeson around the House of Commons, aroused British socialists and pro-labour supporters to act against fascism, which had resulted in the presence of Jewish refugees from Germany in London.

Amidst these depressing world events Robeson continued his work as an actor. The sensitive producer André van Gyseghem was interested in producing *All God's Chillun Got Wings* at the Embassy Theatre, London, but knew that it depended on Robeson's availability for the part of Jim. He was concerned with Robeson's fee in view of the fact that the Embassy (a laboratory theatre, similar to the Provincetown Playhouse in New York) could not pay the sort of salary Robeson commanded. Although Ronald Adam, director of the Embassy, could not see Robeson playing at the theatre for £10 a week, van Gyseghem persisted. His perseverance paid off. But, in the event, both the producer and the director of the theatre had misjudged Robeson's capacity for helping others in distress, especially (as he had now come to accept) if his art could be used towards this end. This approach towards Robeson was, however, understandable, since at that time he was not known to be political. In fact, before he agreed to do a benefit performance of *All God's Chillun* to aid destitute Jewish refugees in London, he said, 'I'm an artist. I don't understand politics.'

In the autumn of 1932 Robeson had agreed to do the play with Flora Robson, the English actress, as Ella. The meeting of these two performers, which held great promise, was a revelation. Three weeks before rehearsals for the production of *All God's Chillun Got Wings* began, van Gyseghem, who was especially concerned with plays representing some social or political problem, went on a short trip to

Moscow to obtain the rights of the anti-Nazi play, *Professor Mamlock*, and to see Alexander Tairov's production of *All God's Chillun* at the Kamernay Theatre. Apart from its artistic objective, this hurried visit also had its social and political significance.

By the time *All God's Chillun* opened on 12 March 1933 public interest in the controversy it had generated and in Robeson had mounted steadily. Theatregoers jostled to get seats, and to accommodate increased demand, the usual run of a fortnight was extended to three weeks and all performances were sold out. Reaction to the production was focused on the play and the acting. The critic Ivor Brown commented: 'To this part [Jim Harris] Mr Robeson brings a kind of Promethean pathos. He is the impotent giant whom the gadfly can destroy, the gadfly of race prejudice . . . Robeson towers above the squalid scene with . . . dignity.'

Robeson now began to search for a medium and a theatre through which he could combine his artistic talents with his ideas. To achieve this purpose, he hoped to rent a theatre, assemble a company and put on plays. Theatre for him then was not merely about entertainment, and he was interested in roles that were not specifically for Blacks. In search of a proper place and play, he came to the Arts Theatre Club, a private theatre group of 3,000 members, and to a play entitled *Basalik*.

In May 1933 Robeson returned to New York to star in the movie of *The Emperor Jones*, which had a mixed reception. With the experience he had gained, Robeson became enthusiastic about the technical aspects of the cinema. But he was faced with the central problem of finding scripts he liked. He believed that the film industry should rethink its stereotype image and begin to show the 'Negro' as a human being. Hitherto, Hollywood's only interest was in visualizing the plantation type of Negro. These were clear statements, a declaration of intent by Robeson to the film industry. His hope was that after British film companies had seen *The Emperor Jones* they would not only recognize but also act upon the potential of films relating the Negro in the United States and elsewhere to Africa. He saw the African setting as particularly attractive and cited the historical importance of such characters as Emperor Menelik, Chaka and the Zulu king Umbopa from Rider Haggard's *King Solomon's Mines*.

In August 1933 Robeson returned to England and concentrated on his singing and the study of languages. It was an intense period during which he became acquainted with African students in London, among whom was Jomo Kenyatta. Naturally, Paul and Essie Robeson gravitated towards these Africans, who made them honorary members of the West African Students' Union. The Robesons had devoted much thought and study to Africa. If Robeson had found a voice to express certain issues concerning his people, he now earnestly sought his African roots. How much Marcus Garvey's 'Back to Africa' movement influenced Robeson is left to speculation. But it must be remembered that Garvey's Universal Negro Improvement Association was enjoying huge popularity while Robeson was a student and at the time he was in Harlem; and that Garvey was also in London during the 1930s. In fact at one time Garvey's house was made available as a WASU meeting-place.

Robeson now became an ardent student not only of black folk-music and spirituals but of the folk-music of Mexico, Russia, Finland, Ireland and South America. Moreover, through his study of African languages, he began to acquire a knowledge of Yoruba, Efik, Benin and Ashanti, as well as a smattering of Chinese and Arabic. His ability to speak Russian engendered a special affinity with the Russians. Of central importance was the fact that the background knowledge he had gained from his studies encouraged him to increase his understanding of Africa. He had become well acquainted with African students who regularly attended his concerts. West Indians and Indians also respected Robeson, who symbolized the emergence of black people. He was their hero, albeit a non-political one, at the time. Taken together, many of these militant students were passionately engaged in the struggle for freedom from colonial rule, for national independence. This dedication was communicated to Robeson, who came to know and appreciate their political aspirations.

Robeson had also become a celebrated black figure for white radicals among the intellectuals at English universities who supported socialism and racial equality. The Socialist Club at Cambridge University invited him to speak 'even though he had not yet made public a political point of view'. This mattered little to the student socialists; Robeson's presence alone, it seemed, was enough because he embodied 'a new man bringing forth a new society'.

At the beginning of 1934 Robeson turned to the study of Hebrew and Hebrew music. It had been a matter of some concern to close friends that Robeson should extend his repertoire of songs. On his return from the United States in 1933, he reached an important decision in his career as a singer. He confided in Lawrence Brown that he could not feel the sentiments of classical songs. It was then Brown realized that Robeson was essentially an uncompromising folk-singer who sang only those songs that moved him. And so Brown looked through the songs of other peoples and made a collection of all the traditional and folk-songs of the English, Irish, Welsh and Scottish people.

Along these lines, then, Robeson and Brown put together a programme and went on an extensive tour of celebrity concerts early in 1934. By now Robeson's critics in the States, Britain and in Europe were agreed that he was a unique artist who moved audiences by the force of his sincerity, artistry and personal dignity. Underlining his special attraction, as his repertoire of songs expanded, was the warmth with which his audiences greeted and embraced him. During his 1934 tour of Midland and Scottish towns Robeson emerged far closer to the people's minds and feelings than other national and international artists appearing in the same celebrity concert series. In January 1934 he attracted one of the largest audiences in Leicester during the season's concerts. The Liverpool *Evening Express* reported: 'It would seem as if his own idea of singing to the "man in the street" by means of folk song is certainly popular in Liverpool.' Robeson had touched the heart of working-class Britain. A Manchester cotton-spinner wrote to Robeson explaining why he liked to hear him sing and what his singing meant. This gesture moved Robeson. 'I've always remembered that letter,' he said to Marie Seton. 'This man said he understood my singing, for while my father was working as a slave, his own father was working as a wage-slave in the mills of Manchester.'

While on tour in Dublin, Brown said something had happened that made him see Robeson in a new light. He realized Robeson had power beyond that of an ordinary singer. After one concert Brown said five Negro medical students came to see Robeson. Their attentions verged on worship. Brown thought they saw Robeson as Moses, a man to be trusted, a leader of the Negro race. Certainly with his mass following and stature Robeson looked the part. When Brown posed the question of his becoming such a leader, Robeson replied that he had never considered it and had no such desire.

But Brown felt sure that this incident did have an effect upon Robeson.

This power beyond that of an ordinary singer and the leadership qualities necessary for the Negro race that Brown recognized in Robeson had begun to emerge and attract other individuals and groups. Robeson, the symbolic leader for some time, now found himself being irrevocably swept forward. His leadership qualities were evident not only to Blacks but to Whites too. At a summer concert in Cambridge in 1934, among the undergraduates was an Australian, Geoffrey Innes, who later became a film director. According to Innes, Robeson was 'an inspiration to members of the Socialist Club because even though he had as yet never expressed any political views, he seemed to symbolise the kind of man who would emerge in a new society'. Here again we see Robeson being projected as a model for a 'new society'.

The adulation Robeson received from Africans in Britain encouraged him to delve into African culture and languages, and their relation to other cultures and languages. Their mutual search for their identity brought Paul and Essie closer to their African roots. The Negro problem, as they saw it, was not and should not be confined to the 13 million Negroes in the United States of America, but also to the millions of Negroes in Africa, the West Indies and elsewhere in the world. This essential view of black Americans invoking the value of Africa was, needless to say, far ahead of the later surge of Black Power in America.

African culture, which Blacks around the world shared, was related to Arabic, Chinese and Jewish culture, Robeson wrote in an article published in March 1934. He felt that his task at this time was to 'introduce a fresh spiritual and humanistic principle' to the world. That same month, Essie, on her husband's behalf, declined an invitation from the Jamaican Dr Harold Moody, founder and President of the League of Coloured Peoples in London, because in her words she and Robeson thought that Negroes who decided to remain in England were of no importance whatever compared with the major problem of Africa's 150 million.

This was a crucial period for Robeson. His views were in a state of flux. Several years abroad had increasingly brought his American concerns into clearer perspective. America was an ever-present past and would remain so while he was abroad. He was now absorbed in European life and current thought. As in the United States, in Europe he could not pretend that he was not a black man in a white-dominated world, uninterested in progressive social change. He was, at least physically, indistinguishable from the Africans in London with whom he felt a deepening sense of brotherhood and solidarity. His understanding of this scenario could either have led him up a cul-de-sac of silence or to give expression to strong feelings in song and speech. His seeming aloofness and silence, which many had observed, was part of that deeper preoccupation to free his people and himself from the tyranny of racial inequality and oppression. This had become the larger purpose that concerned Robeson during these years in London. Those who knew him well recognized that money and comfort did not mislead him. In a personal sense, material possessions rarely if ever entered his conversation, though of course his star status had relieved him of the pressing daily needs for survival, a preoccupation of Blacks and the poor. Yet he did not at the time own a car, and he lived modestly.

People in the theatre world, and particularly the film industry, were perplexed by Robeson's detachment. He was not pushy and did not seek the roles he played. If anything, he had to be induced to act, a trait that Essie had labelled 'laziness' in her book. Producers found Robeson elusive. They could get in touch with him only with difficulty. This was not so much because he had put himself above their reach as that he had found his dealings with them to be discouraging. The inferior material offered to him was, more often than not, extremely offensive. The white Hollywood world was asking Robeson to play the Negro as they saw him – the racial stereotype which was anathema to him. At a time when few Blacks offered resistance, Robeson objected strongly. Although he was cautious about the parts he was offered, even those he had accepted were not entirely free of ambiguous interpretation.

Robeson had met some of the leading British spokesmen on the question of colonialism, among whom were Sir Stafford Cripps, Harold Laski and Archibald Sinclair. He began to see the links between the position of Blacks in the United States and the oppression of Negroes in the British Empire. During these days in London the colonial question was an important issue, particularly among colonials themselves. Not only was Robeson friendly with the Ugandan prince, Nyaboiga, a Cambridge student, but he showed concern with the problems in India. He met Krishna Menon, Secretary of the India League, and Pandit Nehru.

As early as 1928, while Robeson was appearing in *Show Boat*, the idea of the film *Sanders of the River* was put to him. He was selected to play the role of Bosambo, the native chief, by Alexander Korda, producer of *The Scarlet Pimpernel* and *The Private Life of Henry VIII*, although Charles Laughton had originally been mentioned for the part. There was no reason to doubt Korda's competence. What, however, was Korda's true interest in this film? For his part, Robeson hoped the film would promote African culture. Korda, Hungarian born, admired British colonial rule. It is not clear whether Robeson knew anything of Korda's political views. The *Sunday Dispatch* quoted Korda as saying: '. . . the British characteristic which most completely compels the admiration of the world is the genius of Britons for governing native people. Some day I will make a film about it'. His opportunity came with *Sanders of the River*.

The film crew travelled thousands of miles, shooting 60,000 feet of film. Korda had to hand an array of pictures of native dances. Although much of this was used as background material, Robeson, who had not been to Africa, found the war, ceremonial and fertility dances instructive. The preparation, aimed at conveying authenticity, was elaborate. Studio shots were taken near Shepperton, where an African village was built. Among the 200 Blacks employed, both as actors and workers in constructing the African village, was 'Johnstone' – Jomo Kenyatta. The central characters of *Sanders of the River* were Sanders, a British administrator in Africa, played by Leslie Banks, and Bosambo, an escaped convict, who was dependent on the goodwill of Sanders. In the final version of the film, Robeson's part as Bosambo was cleverly worked in to support the benevolence and patronizing attitude of Sanders's control over the African jungle dwellers.

The film première at the Leicester Square Theatre in London attracted wide publicity, as crowds of onlookers greeted the stars and celebrities. Hollywood's contribution at this première was the showing of the first Mickey Mouse film in colour. On the whole, the film reviewers and critics found the film and Robeson acceptable. Korda had achieved his objectives of showing the 'white man's burden' and, as one critic put it, it was certainly propaganda for the British Empire.

But why did Robeson do the film? In the light of his interest in

Africa and African culture, it is understandable that Robeson would have been enthusiastic about it. He felt this was an opportunity to convey African culture to Americans and Europeans. Moreover, the dignified image of the African would help to eliminate Negro stereotypes.

While making the film, Robeson mixed with many Africans and was curious of the languages they spoke, the link to his roots. Listening to an African speak his native tongue one day he was amazed how much he could understand. He identified the African as an Ibo, the tribal background of his father. At once his historical inquiry made practical sense.

During the filming of *Sanders of the River* Robeson and Kenyatta had several conversations. The likeness of the Asiatic peoples and the people of East Africa that Kenyatta spoke about, struck deep responses in Robeson. Contact with Africans clarified his understanding and sharpened his perception of being black in England. He sympathized with the League of Coloured Peoples and was patron of the West African Students' Union.

Although Robeson had found peace and freedom in England, it disturbed him that his African friends were the victims of racial prejudice. He declared that he was leaving England. He wanted to live among Africans in Africa, because he felt it would relieve him of the loneliness he always felt among white men. This was a clear statement, and a strong position, reflecting the cumulative resentment of a sensitive black artist who had witnessed and experienced years of hostility from white America.

While Robeson was still engaged in making *Sanders of the River* Sergei Eisenstein, the Soviet film director, had been considering him for the leading role in a film based on the life of Toussaint L'Ouverture, the Haitian revolutionary, after reading the book *Black Majesty*. He felt Robeson was perfect for the part and through Marie Seton he contacted Robeson in the hope that he would visit Moscow so that they could discuss ideas for a film.

On the eventful trip to Russia that followed, the Robesons were accompanied by Marie Seton. They left London for Moscow in December 1934. Their long train journey was broken by a day spent in Berlin, where they had to wait for another train. Since Robeson's last visit to Germany in 1930, during which he played *The Emperor Jones* at Max Reinhardt's theatre in Berlin, things had certainly changed. Reinhardt had become a refugee in the United States and

Adolf Hitler had come into power in Germany. The ubiquitous storm-troopers and others in Nazi uniforms instilled fear in many people. The presence of a black man at the station in Berlin was conspicuous amidst the cold-looking, blond Nordic men in uniform, who stared at him with apparent contempt and hatred. Robeson recalled what a Jewish man had told him about the horrors of the concentration camps, and so he and his wife and Marie Seton stayed in a cinema until it was dark. On their way back to the station, Essie went to collect their luggage, while Paul and Marie Seton made their way to the platform. This black and white couple seemed to have drawn unwelcome attention from the storm-troopers, who had lined up in such a way as to separate Paul and Marie Seton from the other passengers on the platform. This provocative action was underlined by insolent Nazi stares. As the uniformed men muttered obscenities Robeson, struggling to contain his rising anger and disgust, said to Marie Seton, 'There's time for you for get out.' Expressionless, he was now on the spot and had to consider the safety of his travelling companions. His blackness made him more and more uneasy. 'This is like Mississippi,' he said to Marie Seton. 'It's how a lynching begins. If either of us moves, or shows fear, they'll go further. We must keep our heads.' It seemed a hopeless situation. Robeson's anger grew and there were echoes here of the inner turmoil he felt preceding the violence directed against him by white Rutgers football players. None of the storm-troopers reached much above Robeson's shoulder. Fortunately for all concerned the baiters did not attack Robeson, whose very physique may have forestalled a challenge.

Anger did not come quickly to Robeson; he was not a violent person. Yet the danger of violent confrontation increased with each moment before their train connection arrived.

The three passengers arrived at the custom-house at Negoroel on a very cold day; snow had fallen heavily. Rested and more his normal self, Robeson smiled at the words 'Workers of the World Unite!' on the wall inside the custom-house. Apparently the Robesons' passports did not meet the requirements of the customs officers. As communication was being made to Intourist in Moscow, Robeson, who had been travelling with his gramophone and some of his records, played one of his songs. The sound of his voice quickly won the attention and approval of the customs officers and soon a crowd had gathered to listen. The Russians applauded, 'Robesona! Pavel Robesona! Krasivo! Beautiful!' But many of those who had assembled, did not immediately realize it was the voice of the man among them until Robeson sang in person. If at that stage there were any doubts in the custom officers' minds, Robeson's ability to speak Russian finally laid them to rest.

With this unexpected response from the Russian people, a sharp contrast to the Berlin incident, Robeson journeyed on to Moscow in a better frame of mind, although he was still unsure of what to expect. He was surprised to find how popular he was in the Soviet Union. As his train pulled in he was greeted by a waiting crowd on the platform, among whom were Sergei Eisenstein, Weyland Rudd, a black actor from Philadelphia, and Herbert Marshall, who was studying with Eisenstein. Robeson and Eisenstein established an immediate rapport. Although physically different – Eisenstein was short and white, while Robeson was tall and black – both men, who had achieved international fame when they were twenty-seven years old, were united by common concerns, namely a dedicated search for knowledge and a love of art. By all accounts they were impressed by each other's achievements and liked each other. Within twenty-four hours of their meeting Eisenstein, a sceptic and critical of 'great men', attributed human genius to Robeson because he was 'without falseness'. Robeson in turn regarded his meeting with Eisenstein as one of the greatest experiences of his life.

Robeson learned much during the two weeks he spent in Moscow. He was particularly interested in Eisenstein's impressive film *General Line*, which portrayed the evolution of Russian village life. He felt this aspect of Russian life had parallels with Africa and saw the cinema as the freest form of expression. During his stay in the Soviet Union, language, art and music dominated his conversation. With meticulous care, he expounded on his view of music to Eisenstein. In Moscow he met many non-Russians, such as the Indian student, D.G. Tendulkar, who was studying the art of film directing. Rudd's presence in Moscow was of particular interest to Robeson, because the black American's view of the Soviet Union was in agreement with other Blacks, who felt that the country was free of racial discrimination. Of significance, too, was the fact that the children he had met in Moscow gravitated towards him like pins to a magnet. This strong attraction was due in part to his massive size, but perhaps more essentially to his caring attitude and natural warmth, which led them to embrace him.

In Moscow Robeson was not always surrounded by people. Often, he went out alone to take in this part of the country, if only briefly. It was during his stay in the city that Alexander Tairov, founder of the Kamernay Theatre, in a grand gesture, produced O'Neill's *All God's Chillun Got Wings* to celebrate the theatre's twentieth anniversary.

When on another occasion Robeson attended a performance of *All God's Chillun Got Wings* the entire audience was composed of factory workers. Inevitably Robeson was invited to sing. Appropriately he sang 'Go Down Moses' and from Mussorgsky's opera *Boris Godunov*. Later Robeson visited William L. Patterson, the black American communist who as head of the International Labour Defence courageously defended the Scottsboro boys. This internationally famous case received the support of the communists. Robeson welcomed this support, a clear indication of his political mood.

On the day Robeson was invited by Eisenstein to meet members of the film industry he said in Russian, 'I will try to sing something you know.' Marie Seton explained what happened: the end of the song aroused a spontaneous rush of people towards Robeson and a need to hug and kiss as they laughed, wept and called him *Pavelushka!*

Before he left the Soviet Union Robeson sang Negro spirituals at Moscow's Kaganovich Ballbearing Factory. This appearance again before workers (and his growing interest in taking his art to them) would serve him in good stead later in Britain, the United States and around the 'civilized' world.

If this trip was designed as a public relations exercise to impress Robeson, there could not have been a more welcoming programme. According to one report, however, Essie was less enthusiastic about Russia. If in fact this was true, Robeson might have seriously considered his wife's concern, but all he had heard about the Soviet Union seemed fully justified. As if summing up his thoughts on the country he said that he had hesitated to come, listened to what everybody had to say, but he did not think Russia would be any more different for him than any other place. However, the few days he had spent in the Soviet Union, he said, had profoundly affected him. Here for the first time in his life he felt like a human being. 'You cannot imagine what that means to me as a Negro,' he added.

For better or for worse, this statement underlined a firm belief that would carry him forward for the rest of his life. When Robeson and

Essie left Moscow on 6 January 1935 for London, the die was cast. Comparison with England and the United States of America was inevitable.

On their return journey the Robesons visited Leningrad, Helsinki, Stockholm, Copenhagen, Oslo and Bergen. In Bergen Robeson heard disturbing reports of political developments in Germany. There were fears that fascism would spread throughout Europe, a concern also expressed in Copenhagen and Moscow.

Before Robeson left Moscow he told Eisenstein he was unavailable for work on the proposed film *Black Majesty* until the autumn, because of his commitment to act in the play *Stevedore* which had earlier interested him. In the euphoria of this Russian visit Robeson returned to London. There was still some unfinished work to be done on *Sanders of the River*. Retakes for the film, and various editorial manoeuvres, resulted in what he described as one of the most unpleasant discoveries of his life. Increasingly he hoped for the day when Africans would be free people, controlling their own destinies. But through this film he considered he was being used to support British colonial rule. This, of course, was the last thing he wanted to do. As Marie Seton has pointed out, Robeson was not consulted on a number of new scenes which were written into the scenario of the film, glorifying British imperialism.

In answer to those who criticized his role in *Sanders of the River*, Robeson was at first defensive. He argued that, given the circumstances in which Negro artists were placed, it was unrealistic automatically to expect them to reject roles that were ideologically disagreeable to them. In retrospect, he stated that the attacks against him for the role were correct. 'I committed a *faux pas*,' he told an interviewer years later, 'which . . . convinced me that I had failed to weigh the problems of 150,000,000 native Africans . . . I did it all in the name of art . . . I hate the picture.'

The distorted presentation of the nature of colonial rule in *Sanders of the River* led Robeson to reappraise his views of art and life. He studied the works of Karl Marx and investigated the theory and practice of racial equality in the Soviet Union. Among those to whom he spoke on the questions of imperialism, colonialism and Marxist theory were Kingsley Martin, Maurice Hindus, Andrew Rothenstein and George Padmore, the Trinidad-born ex-Comintern agent and Pan-Africanist. Padmore became known as the father of African emancipation. Robeson's discussions with these intellectuals lasted for several months. At the end of this period, as he began to express his opinions, he was drawing closer to active socialists. It was, however, through the theatre that he reflected his political ideology and race pride most vividly. The socially conscious artist was now more conscious than ever of his art and entertainment as a dynamic social force that would mould the attitudes of the public. Witness how the character of Bosambo was used to distort the realities behind colonial rule.

In the spring of 1935 Robeson played the title role in *Basalik*, a play about an African chief who suspects a British colonial governor of planning to give concessions on the natives' land. Although Robeson's portrayal was credible, the role lacked substance. None the less, he felt that unlike the humiliation of Bosambo, *Basalik* was about an African of dignity and honour.

A month later, and several months after he had first expressed an interest in the play, Robeson finally appeared in a production of the American drama, *Stevedore*. It was Robeson's ambition to establish a theatre for Negro drama, and it was with this interest in mind that he accepted the play that struck at the real problems facing black workers in the United States. Bringing together the cast in London, which involved a large number of 'Negro' characters in the play, was a problem. But van Gyseghem managed it. Although there were a few American singers and dancers in London at the time, they could not appear because their work permits prevented them from doing so. Marie Seton suggested to van Gyseghem that Africans and West Indians might be willing to participate. She was active in the search for potential black actors, visiting Aggrey House, the club where African and West Indian students met. The black community rallied round. Among those involved was Mrs Marcus Garvey, who suggested the names of would-be actors. George Padmore was also consulted, and his friend Robert Adams, a student from British Guiana who earned money as a wrestler while he studied, played the part of Blacksnake Johnson, which was a success. Employing non-professionals did not bother Ronald Adam of the Embassy Theatre. What mattered to him especially was that there should be unity of atmosphere in the performance which he felt only a cast of 'Negroes' could provide.

Robeson's instinct about the unity of his brothers was evident by the time rehearsals for *Stevedore* began. The play came alive, as the cast around Robeson gave convincing performances. This experience with Blacks in England brought a qualitative change in Robeson's mood and social approach. Perhaps as he grew in confidence he acquired greater understanding. More to the point, however, was the essential fact that he was relating to Negroes from Africa and the diaspora through his art in a socially sensitive play, and in a trusting way. Blacks in America were not the only oppressed ones; the oppression was linked with others. Although he seemed naturally inquisitive and curious about the world about him, this change was noticeable. According to Marie Seton, since the party following the first night of *All God's Chillun Got Wings* in March 1933 Robeson had become less reserved. He was more accommodating towards people, mixing freely and taking a leading part in discussions. This change was also noticed by Adam, who recalled that it was 'infuriating to argue' with Robeson. 'We called him the autocrat of autocrats,' he said, 'yet everyone who worked with him loved him.'

Stevedore was important for Robeson, who played the role of Lonnie Thompson, a 'bad nigger' who not only tried to organize black workers but to make them a part of one union with white workers. Hostility came from both the white employer (whose divide-and-rule strategy was vital to effective labour exploitation) and some black workers, who were sceptical. One of these characters asked: 'Who ever heard of black and white getting together in a union anyway?' Lonnie would not be discouraged. He countered: 'Lawd, when de black man gwine stand up? When he gwine stand up proud like a man?'

As the story unfolds, Lonnie, the militant trade-union trouble-maker, is framed, arrested and charged with the rape of a white woman. He escapes and is helped by friends, among them the white trade-union leader. As a white mob in lynching mood approaches to round up all the 'wharf niggers', Lonnie exhorts the black community to defend themselves. During the conflict, as Blacks defend their homes, Lonnie is killed. In the ensuing struggle Blacksnake Johnson assumes the leadership of black and white workers who fought together against the white mob.

The play undoubtedly reflected Robeson's political outlook. The idea of black-white unity and labour solidarity appealed to Robeson, who was well aware that there were West Indians and Africans in the cast who had come from the colonies where nationalists were organizing the masses. At last, it seemed, Robeson had found a role worthy of his developing ideas grounded in the life of ordinary black Americans.

When the play opened in May 1935 to a packed house, *The Star* and the *New Statesman and Nation* considered the play as 'propaganda' and of 'little merit', respectively. But for others, Robeson's acting and developing ideas fused effectively. Van Gyseghem was delighted by Robeson's performance and with the rest of the cast. (Later van Gyseghem went to South Africa and produced the Empire Pageant, in Johannesburg. He was impressed by the Africans' reaction to the Robeson recordings he played, and observed that their songs were remarkably similar to the spirituals.) Robeson's voice had been unanimously applauded by the critics.

Whatever else *Stevedore* might have represented, it was an important play which showed for the first time in the theatre Blacks, fighting for their rights, being assisted by white workers in their resistance against racism and oppression. Robeson recognized the essential message in the play and saw the practical possibilities of the theatre as a medium through which certain ideas could be presented to the public. In spite of some reviewers' reservations, public demand for the play was such that the run was extended for another week.

The year 1935 was also significant to Robeson in that Africa made headline news. The Italians, under the dictatorship of Mussolini, attacked Abyssinia. The appeals of the Ethiopian Emperor, Haile Selassie, for help from the League of Nations fell on deaf ears. Blacks in Britain, including Robeson, and in the United States were embittered. This act of aggression had a radicalizing effect on black people in many parts of the world. To Robeson's chagrin, fascism was, once again, on the move – this time the victims were Africans in Africa!

Robeson had hoped to return to Moscow in the autumn of 1935 to work with Eisenstein on the film *Black Majesty*. This chance was lost because Eisenstein had begun another project. Robeson was, however, in demand. On 25 September 1935 he left for a concert tour of the United States, his first in three years; and to appear as Joe in the film of *Show Boat*. Mrs Goode was looking after Pauli (now eight years old) in New York. The boy was sent to the United States to get 'to know his native land'. For Robeson, this trip was a chance of seeing his son, with whom he had spent so little time. Father and son were close, even though Pauli was not always as physically close to his father as Robeson was to his own father. To minimize the long absences between father and son, Robeson found it expedient to bring Pauli to live in England, under Mrs Goode's charge, when he returned.

The Robesons' sojourn in the film capital left little to be desired. Universal Pictures made them feel at home. What then was the catch? There had to be one, Robeson thought. This was soon revealed: Robeson would have no control over the finished film. The bitter experience of *Sanders* was still fresh in his mind, although the film company conceded that work outside California had to meet Robeson's approval.

On arrival in the United States Robeson performed concerts in Milwaukee and Seattle before the shooting of *Show Boat* began about mid-November. The filming was done quickly to facilitate Robeson's return to England to start a series of concerts in January. The total cost of the production was an estimated \$2 million. To make good any deficiences, new musical material was penned by Jerome Kern and Oscar Hammerstein, and sound equipment was introduced to communicate the full resonant quality of Robeson's voice.

When the film opened in New York, it was hailed as a spectacular musical. Robeson received special praise from most of the reviewers and critics. The song 'Ol' Man River' was particularly memorable, and Robeson's stirring performance, it was felt, was alone worth the price of admission. A month later, the film had its première in London at the Leicester Square and Piccadilly Theatres. At the Leicester Square Theatre a large crowd had gathered for what was described as a society event. A packed house burst into spontaneous applause after Robeson had sung 'Ol' Man River'.

Even Robeson's powerful and melodious voice, however, was not enough. The black press found the film to be only just about average. Another reviewer felt that Uncle Tom had a true exponent in Paul Robeson, and found that he had done more to project the black man as shiftless than he did in the role of Bosambo. The London *Jewish Chronicle*, which had previously criticized his role in *Sanders of the River*, again put him under scrutiny, commenting that the 'utter emptiness of the part' was the more lamentable because he was unquestionably one of the great personalities of his time.

When Universal Pictures bought the rights of Edna Ferber's book

Show Boat in 1929 they had intended making a silent movie, with Steppin' Fetchit as Joe. Before 1934 *Show Boat* was successfully staged. In 1934 Universal had already been interested in casting Robeson as Joe. Writers began work quickly and Oscar Hammerstein informed Robeson of his work on a film of *Show Boat*. At the time, Hollywood seemed out of the reckoning for Robeson, while he was enjoying huge success in England and elsewhere in Europe. But in the end the Robesons went.

Around the mid-1930s Robeson was involved in several films, one of which was a documentary, originally entitled *Africa Looks Up*, about the relationship between the achievements of the white man in South Africa and his attitudes towards the natives. The film was eventually retitled *My Song Goes Forth* and opened at the Piccadilly Theatre in March 1937. The theme song, 'My Song Goes Forth', about hope and progress, gives us a clue as to why Robeson sang it. Perhaps the outstanding merit of the film, however, was Robeson's introduction and commentary. What was the message Robeson was trying to convey through his art this time? A London newspaper observed that the film lacked militancy and should have penetrated deep into the vitals of the system. For the interpretive artist this was an important comment, a view that Robeson would come to accept.

In 1936 the Stage Society in London, which produced 'plays of high artistic merit' (though not of commercial viability) for short runs, scheduled three new plays to be produced that year. Flora Robson, a member of the Society, announced that one of the plays was C.L.R. James's *Toussaint L'Ouverture*.

At the time Robeson was offered the part of Toussaint, the Haitian revolutionary, he had just returned to England after filming *Show Boat* in Hollywood. In the play, Toussaint emerges as a man whose sense of honour is superior to that of the white men who contrived his downfall. Robeson held the play together. The *Times* noted that 'the action is generally vitalized by Mr Robeson', while another reviewer remarked, 'the play must have been a great pleasure for Paul Robeson to act, for Toussaint's opinion on the necessity of black people being educated has always been a plank in his platform'.

After *Sanders of the River* Robeson was wary of roles that stereotyped Africans as witch-doctors and chiefs dressed in leopard skins. He had come to realize that the motion-picture industry was more concerned with box-office demands than with human values, and that as an actor he was a cog in the wheel of the film-makers' scheme of production. The fact that they sought his opinion on certain films, especially those that depicted, or rather misinterpreted, colonial life and labour, compounded the dilemma he faced of self-exploitation. He would have liked to boycott American and British film producers. But among the documentary film-makers he had known, almost all were strongly anti-racist and relied upon him to suggest improvements in the characterization of Blacks.

Yet Robeson was not indifferent to the roles he accepted. Harry Watt, the film director, pointed out in 1936 that Robeson had turned down many offers because he felt they did not show the Negro in a sympathetic light. It is interesting to speculate that had Robeson not persisted in his efforts to improve the quality of films dealing with Blacks, it is more than likely he would not have made *Proud Valley*, perhaps his favourite film. Before doing so he had made three pictures: *King Solomon's Mines*, *Jericho* and *Song of Freedom*. Later, as he picked his way over the stony ground during these years of pioneering effort, a new generation of black actors would claim him as the forerunner in the struggle against presenting Negro stereotypes. At this time Africa was the key which opened up new vistas of thought, expression and action to black liberation movements.

In January 1936 Robeson had predicted that an Africa free of foreign domination would become reality 'some day'. Although he did not specify a time, he was certain it was going to happen. He had become skilful at speaking on matters concerning Africa and relating them to the rest of the world, and he laughed at the suggestion that the rise of black nationalism might create a menace to white civilization. He explained that it was not a race problem. He cited two examples: first, that during the Italian invasion of Ethiopia Blacks were fighting against Blacks, and in Manchuria yellow Japanese were fighting yellow Chinese. Race was therefore not the vital factor. He said of his own work that the film he hoped to do next would present an interesting tie-up between the Negro tradition in America and Africa and predicted that within five years the theatre and literature of the Western world would be taking as much interest in Africa as it was then taking in the culture of black Americans.

In February 1936 a film unit went to West Africa to shoot background material for the film *Song of Freedom*, including the famous 'Devil Dancers' of Sierra Leone. Robeson sang songs which were specially written for him. But, like a recurring nightmare, his unfortunate *Sanders of the River* experience made him cautious. He had a clause written into his contract providing him with the right to approval of the final version of the film. In essence, *Song of Freedom* reflects two main developments in Robeson's thinking. First, in social terms, there was the idea of a coming together of Western and Eastern cultures; and second, in artistic terms, as a way of bringing the relationship of the Negro and the film industry closer to reality, Robeson saw this film as an improvement. He liked the story of *Song of Freedom*. Under the direction of J. Elder Wills he played John Zinga, a London-born descendant of an African queen, while Elizabeth Welch starred as his wife. Like Zinga, Robeson had not only developed a deep interest in his African heritage but yearned to visit Africa.

Robeson's estimation of the finished version of *Song of Freedom* was in general echoed not only by critics but by those involved in struggle in Africa, fourteen years after the film had its première. In September 1950 the Convention People's Party, the leading political party in the Gold Coast, screened *Song of Freedom* during its second anniversary celebrations. Through the medium of this film, Robeson (who was dedicated to bringing about an end to colonization) and the writer Claude Wallace pointed audiences in the direction of a new society in West Africa. Indeed, in the light of the difficulties Blacks had been experiencing in the United States at the time, the holding of free elections was an historic occasion, for all Africa. Victory for the CPP, the prime ministership of Kwame Nkrumah and the eventual transition from colony to Ghana, the independent African state, in 1957, gave Robeson deserved satisfaction. This achievement heralded the beginning of Black Power in Africa, which would have repercussions throughout the African diaspora.

Song of Freedom was to be followed by a planned sequel, *Thunder Island*. Instead of that project, Robeson began work on *King Solomon's Mines*. The role of Umbopa in this film required Robeson to speak in an African language. This suited him, since he had learned Efik. Although the demands of this role kept him busy, he signed a new contract for the film *Jericho*.

King Solomon's Mines became acceptable to Robeson only after he had suggested changes in the script, particularly the parts representing the savage, violent stereotype. But if Robeson was satisfied, there was no unanimity of opinion either among critics or audiences. And although British reviewers found the film banal, it was successful in the United States.

Robeson's next film, *Big Fella* (originally entitled *Banjo*), based on a novel by Claude McKay, was a further improvement – perhaps his best role to date – but far short of his hopes. It was a delight to him not to be playing a half-naked native. At last it seemed the stereotype was giving way to better roles. He then began work on the film *Jericho* (originally entitled *Salt*). As Jericho Jackson, Robeson played the role of a court-martialled black soldier during the First World War. He escapes and, with a white American soldier on the run, they arrive in Africa where, as the chief of an Arab tribe, Jackson leads a trek across the Sahara Desert.

Making this film would take Robeson at last to the Continent of Africa, the land of his forbears. At the age of thirty-nine, he went to Egypt, the location of many scenes for the film.

If the New York press were not unanimously ecstatic and the English reviewers were tepid in their response to the film, the Washington *Afro-American* considered that Robeson had redeemed himself in it. This was perhaps even better than the previous role he had played in films, some argued. In it there was the element of the spiritual regeneration of a Negro who returns to his African homeland. The message in this film was important to Robeson.

The years 1936–7 were among the busiest in Robeson's career, particularly in films. And altogether it seemed that he had achieved part of what he hoped to communicate to his audiences. But this was not enough. Now in 1937 he said he intended to retire from commercial entertainment, and *Jericho* was to be a climax of his growing disenchantment with the film business.

During December 1936 and January 1937 Robeson returned to the Soviet Union on a concert tour. He sang in the Moscow Conservatoire, in factories and came into contact with the common folk, the village people. In the Caucasus and in Soviet Asia he saw people who were as backward as those in Africa. He was much impressed. In spite of his general optimism, he found it almost unbelievable that only a generation before these people had been destitute, hopeless and without a language. The strides they had made in the theatre, drama and education astounded Robeson. Clearly there was hope also for Africans. He was convinced that the simple solution for minority and racial problems was complete equality for all peoples, and that colour was not the cause of so-called backwardness, the real cause of which was oppression. There can be no doubt that at this point in his life Robeson believed 'complete' equality for all men was possible. The Russians had proved it! So convinced was Robeson of the Soviet system that he decided to place his son, then nine years old, in a Moscow school. He announced this decision in Moscow in December 1936. The protective father told American reporters that consequently his son would not have to face racial discrimination at a time when he was most vulnerable.

On his return to England from Egypt Robeson was preoccupied with the positive developments in Soviet Asia. Self-examination seemed inevitable as he pondered the possibilities both for himself and his people. He really wanted to be a 'teacher' (in a true sense he was that already) and seemed dissatisfied with what he was. He told some friends, 'I've never cared for fame.'

The East-West dichotomy nagged at him. Freedom and equality beckoned; he was prepared to follow this cause wherever it might lead him. At the end of his concert tour of the English provinces Robeson took another practical step which brought him closer to his beliefs: he abandoned his commitment to celebrity concerts, which were generally aimed at middle-class audiences. He wanted his music to reach the common folk.

In the autumn of 1937 Robeson's venues were music-halls and cinema palaces such as the Kilburn Empire, Gaumont State, Kilburn, Trocadero, Elephant and Castle, and the Gaumont, Hammersmith. In these centres of working-class entertainment he was able to reach vast new audiences who understood the emotional depth of his folk-songs and Negro spirituals. Here Robeson touched the pulse of the British people, and the demand was such that he did three performances daily.

Robeson could not separate the plight of ordinary working people from the larger issues of world politics. He regarded the Spanish Civil War not simply as the concern of Spaniards but as being of the greatest importance to the Negro peoples of the world. In short, it was a struggle against the tyranny and ravages of the fascist hordes.

In 1937 he made news in several newspaper articles. He spoke of his third visit to the Soviet Union for a concert tour under the auspices of the Moscow State Philharmonic. He took the opportunity to see more of the country, which confirmed his earlier impressions. When he sang the spirituals and work songs of his people to Soviet citizens he felt a bond of sympathy and mutual understanding between himself and his audiences. Thus Russian folk-songs and those of the Negro people were closer than he had thought. These songs were born out of the misery and suffering, exploitation and oppression of the people.

Robeson had arrived in the Soviet Union just as the Eighth (Special) All-Union Congress of Soviets had completed its historic work and had adopted the new Socialist Constitution. His study of and concern with the United States Constitution had encouraged new interest in the Soviet system. He said that after one had read this unforgettable Socialist Constitution, it was easy to appreciate the new humanism in the Soviet Union.

During 1937 Robeson made perhaps his most profound political statement, a personal commitment. At a rally sponsored by the National Joint Committee for Spanish Relief in aid of the Spanish Refugee Children at the Albert Hall in London on 24 June he said he was happy to join in the appeal for the 'greatest cause' that faced the world. Then finally he added: 'The artist must take sides.' In the fight for freedom and the elimination of all human slavery he had made his choice. Thus it was that the artist who in 1933 said that he did not understand politics, became overtly political.

Thereafter, Robeson's songs assumed a new meaning and significance. He was conscious of the fact that under fascism he would not be allowed to develop his voice because of his race, as he said in a radio broadcast from Madrid. He pointed out that although in the past black musicians, artists and entertainers played an ambassadorial role in Europe, the Blacks he saw in Spain were not entertainers but volunteer fighters. Robeson felt their fight for freedom in Spain was also a fight for freedom at home. Seeing them engendered, as he put it, a 'new warm feeling for my homeland . . . and I knew in my heart that I would surely return there some day'.

Robeson and his wife now travelled to Spain, and in January 1938 for the first time they experienced the horror of war in Barcelona. The soldiers, some of them black Americans, were glad to see Robeson at the front line. His songs boosted morale. In Barcelona Robeson met the Cuban writer Nicholas Guillen before travelling on to Madrid which was under heavy attack.

After taking his music to the people, and with the anguish of Spain a haunting memory, Robeson continued to pursue his art through a workers' theatre group of London trade unionists. His political thought, moulded by his experiences, his studies in Marxism and knowledge of life in the Soviet Union, led Robeson to take what then seemed like an unalterable position. Turning his back on a lucrative film career was a necessary first step.

He had been living in London for several years now, and had travelled considerable political mileage. In 1937 among his visitors were William Patterson and Max Yergan, whom Essie had met on her tour of Africa. Yergan had resigned as an official of the South African Coloured YMCA because he found the organization 'too conservative' and 'opposed the forces of peace and brotherhood'. After returning to New York, Yergan became a member of the National Negro Congress, which it was alleged included trained black communists towards the end of the 1930s, as well as a close friend of the Robesons. Later he became a co-founder (with Robeson) of the Council on African Affairs, which aimed at aiding the national liberation struggles in Africa. In the political frame of mind Robeson was in, it was most welcome for him to see Patterson again and to meet Yergan. Now his politics and art fused as never before.

After Spain, Robeson expanded his political activity and became more involved with the British labour movement. In the wake of the Spanish Civil War he sought creative efforts that would reflect his ideology. The theatre of the Left in Britain filled the bill. He became a member of the advisory council of Unity Theatre, a group that produced plays, often with a working-class message, not unlike the Provincetown Players. Many members of the theatre company were trade unionists, who could practise their art only after a day's work. Initially, in 1936, it was reported that the Trades Union Congress would subsidize a Left theatre to perform plays about labour and working-class interests. Among those in the advisory council were Tyrone Guthrie, Margaret Webster, Robeson, Ernest Toller, Victor Gollancz, Harold Laski, Maurice Browne and Sean O'Casey. With the aid of volunteer union labour, an old church was transformed into a modern theatre, which was dedicated to workers. Unity was a people's theatre, built to serve as a means of dramatizing their life and struggles, and as an aid in making them conscious of their strength and the need for united action. Equality was a fundamental principle. There was no star system. Robeson fully identified with its aims and objectives, and it presented him with a long overdue opportunity. He said that the play he wanted to act in would be done only in Unity Theatre and would deal with Negro and working-class life. He consigned most scripts sent to him to the waste-paper basket because they did not deal with the ideas of social progress. There was no doubt that he was now interested only in a play portraying struggle, and he stressed the need for working-class plays regardless of race.

He was also increasingly proclaiming his political outlook. The leadership qualities that Brown and others had seen in him earlier were now asserting themselves. His language was becoming qualitatively more Marxist. In late 1937 he told the *Daily Worker*: 'When I step on a stage . . . I go on as a representative of the working class. I work with the consciousness of that on my mind. I share the richness they can bring to art. I approach the stage from that angle.'

The following year Robeson explained that the Unity Theatre programme did not mention the actors' names, including his own. He was simply one of the cast, not a star. None the less, he was an international star and a powerful influence upon the left-wing amateurs and professionals. In June 1938 he appeared in Unity Theatre's production of *Plant in the Sun*, a play by the American writer Ben Bengal, directed by his friend Herbert Marshall. The play, which opened in June 1938, made a strong, dramatic appeal for trade unionism. Robeson was cast in the role of one of the five main characters involved in a sit-down strike. One of the few plays dealing with the triumph of a specific class, it was a success. The performances were all good. As one reviewer put it, Robeson 'never overshadows the others, he gives to them as only a great artist can'.

This encouraging and refreshing creation of a workers' theatre won the praise of London's press. Among the people who went to see the play were Jawaharlal Nehru and D.G. Tendulkar, whom Robeson had met earlier in Moscow. Robeson and Nehru had established cordial relations.

By about September 1938 Robeson wanted to return to films. He still thought that the film was a medium he could use to great advantage, although perhaps the concert stage was better suited to him. Through the intimacy of working close to the camera Robeson considered he could put across his personality more sympathetically than he could on the stage, and that film work was less of a strain. But his return to films was conditional: they must meet his standards. Until such a film came, he would stay outside the film business. In the play *Plant in the Sun* he considered he had integrated his job and his feelings about society. Given that part of his feelings about films were due to his 'integration of outlook', he saw the film industry as a clear expression of the workings of capitalism. He argued that workers in the studios (both in the United States and in England) had power which should be exercised. Thus, Robeson wanted nothing to do with the big film companies.

Early in 1939 what was left of the British battalion in Spain withdrew, and in January some 10,000 people assembled in the Empress Hall, Earls Court, to pay tribute to over 500 Britons who had died in Spain. Appearing before this massive audience were the British survivors. Then the spotlight shone on Robeson as he sang. One of the songs he introduced was 'Joe Hill', about a Swedish-American trade-union organizer who was framed on a murder change by the copper bosses in Utah and executed in 1919. The dead man symbolized the struggle for Robeson, who sang: 'Takes more than guns to kill a man,/Says Joe, I didn't die'; and says Joe, 'What they forgot to kill went on to organize.'

With the prospect of another world war looming larger each day, highbrow, conservative English people, because of Robeson's politics, kept away from his concerts. He did not lament this. As if to balance this reaction, he won new audiences among the people to whom he said he had always wanted to sing.

When *Plant in the Sun* closed, Robeson and Lawrence Brown went on a concert tour of the provinces, the most successful they ever had before their greatest fans, the people who formed the 'backbone of England'. Robeson and Brown next toured Scandinavia. When they left England in May 1939 they had no idea that it would prove to be an extraordinary experience. According to Brown the tour pleased Robeson. 'He was very surprised at the reception he received,' said Brown. 'The Norwegians, Swedes and Danes being the most Nordic people in Europe, Paul never expected to be greeted by them with so much warmth.'

Robeson's career was moving on, as a steadily growing audience, cutting across racial and national lines, came into contact with the man and his music.

After the Scandinavian tour Robeson was offered the lead in the play *John Henry*, to be produced in New York. As it turned out, this was one of Robeson's mistakes. 'I urged him to do a concert tour instead,' said Brown, 'but he wouldn't listen.' Robeson's stay in New York, where he had a discussion with Oscar Hammerstein concerning the play, was brief. Although he had repeatedly made public his overall dissatisfaction with films, nevertheless offers were made. He rejected them because he did not want to be part of the 'absurd, spear-brandishing act' any more. Only a worthwhile subject would be acceptable to him. The appropriate vehicle, as he saw it, for his return to films was in the role of David Goliath in the British production, *Proud Valley*. Robeson's friend Herbert Marshall and his wife put forward the idea of this film. Robeson, immediately recognizing its value, not only welcomed the shift away from stereotypes but liked the idea of working again with Marshall, who had of course directed *Plant in the Sun*. This was an opportunity not be missed.

Essentially *Proud Valley* concerned the struggle for survival of Welsh miners in the Rhondda Valley. The lives of the people centred upon the mine as the people worked, loved and sang. The cast was headed by Robeson who at last had found a role based on real life. And significantly, a 'typical Negro worker' was cast as the hero of the film. At once, it seemed all he had hoped for had come true. This unprecedented achievement increased the respect for Robeson among working people around the world who identified him with the cause of liberation. If he had been to them a 'hero', now he projected leadership.

During shooting on location in Mardy and at Caernarvon Castle Robeson and Marshall quickly established a warm, close and enduring relationship with the local Welsh people. Robeson felt a particularly strong bond with these villagers who respected him as a great singer and man of the people. The Welsh took Robeson to their hearts, and vice versa. The warmth and simplicity of this Welsh community reminded him of the black communities of Westfield and Somerville, New Jersey, where he had grown up. Welsh men and women were intimately involved in making the film. Auditions were held in Cardiff and, eventually, many local people appeared in the picture. An outstanding discovery was Rachel Thomas, a local housewife, whose acting received critical acclaim.

The onset of the Second World War, however, interrupted the shooting of *Proud Valley*. The schedule was rearranged and the film was completed quickly and had its première early in March 1940 at the Leicester Square Theatre. 'It was the one film I could be proud of having played in,' said Robeson. 'That, and the early part of *Song of Freedom*.'

His satisfaction was echoed by others. The film was used as war propaganda. And breaking from normal custom the BBC broadcasted the sound-track. If this was yet another plus for the film, there was at least one minus, not on artistic but on political grounds. Apparently Lord Beaverbrook was unhappy with Robeson's political leanings, and rumour had it that the Beaverbrook press was ordered to ignore *Proud Valley* because of remarks Robeson had made on international affairs that had some bearing on England's links to the war effort in the Caribbean. Eventually, although Beaverbrook decided not to criticize the film, he did not publicize it. While the trade papers gave favourable reviews of the film, the daily press and journals were less enthusiastic. Graham Greene expressed revulsion at Robeson's 'sentimental optimism'. But, perhaps the sharpest criticism of Robeson's performance came from the black American press, Robeson's most vigilant critic.

Robeson's departure from England marked the end of a significant stage in his ideas and political development. During his years in London he did not have many fixed ideas. He did, however, have a strong conviction that his conscience should be his guide and, as he put it, 'no one was going to lead me around by a golden chain or any other kind'. He reflected that, in the early days of his acting career, he more or less accepted the prevailing attitude of black performers that the content and form of a play or film scenario mattered little. The important thing was to grab the opportunities, particularly the rare offers of a starring role. Even so, Robeson was intuitively aware of the dangers. Years before, he had refused to sing and/or act before segregated audiences in America. Based in England he came to understand the British working class and from this location he shuttled back and forth to many countries, which helped to form his outlook on world affairs. This is the key to understanding why Robeson differed in certain attitudes from many people of his generation. He explained his decision to make his home in London at a time when opportunities for black artists in America were very limited. He felt that London was better than Chicago had been for Blacks from Mississippi. He was particularly mindful of the friendly welcome he received in English society. Treated as a 'gentleman and scholar' in London, he found a congenial and stimulating atmosphere.

During these 'happy days' he gradually moved away from the upper-class people who attended his concerts to the common people, among whom he felt at home. Although he insisted that the United States was home, occasionally he thought he was settled for life in London. Yet he realized London (where he had 'discovered' Africa) was the centre of the British Empire, about which much had been written by Marx and Lenin. This discovery was to have such a powerful impact on his political thought that it profoundly influenced the rest of his life. It was clear then that he would not live out his life as an adopted Englishman. Thus he arrived at the conclusion that 'I was an African'.

This meeting with his 'brothers' initially aroused in Robeson the artist an intense interest in African culture which, he argued, foreign rulers had made every effort to conceal and destroy. None the less, European artists and others were well aware of the value of African art; moreover, Robeson was able to immerse himself in the study of Africa at the London School of Oriental Languages. He came to see African culture as a treasure store of the world, and particularly to discover the richness of African languages. He studied Yoruba, Efik, Twi and Ga, among others. During his studies, always conscious of his people at home, he wrote about the culture of the Negro. He was especially critical of his fellow black Americans. He said he had met Blacks in the United States who believed that black Africans were incapable of communication by spoken language.

Long before Alex Haley had 'discovered' Africa for the American public, Robeson had come to discover the roots of his own people's culture and to learn of the kinship between African and Chinese culture. His pride in Africa had grown with the knowledge he had acquired through his studies. He championed African culture in argument and discussion with H.G. Wells, Harold Laski, Jawaharlal Nehru and with colonial students. Inevitably, at the centre of the British Empire, Robeson's understanding of this cultural struggle and exposition of it brought its detractors. British Intelligence cautioned him about the political meaning of his activities. 'If African culture was what I insisted it was,' Robeson responded, 'what happens then to the claim that it would take a thousand years for Africans to be capable of self-rule?' He recalled that it was an African who directed his interest in Africa. This individual had been on a visit to the Soviet Union and had seen the Yakuts, a people categorized as a 'backward race' by the tsars, and was struck by the similarity between the tribal life of the Yakuts and his people in East Africa. He was impressed by the strides the Yakuts and the Uzbeks had made, leaping ahead from tribalism to the heights of knowledge. They were culturally advanced, and their young men and women were mastering the sciences and arts, not in a thousand years but in less then twenty!

Through his interest in Africa, Robeson not only visited the Soviet Union but studied developments within the Soviet system. Indeed he found there a place where, it seemed, black people could walk 'secure and free as equals'. He was so impressed by the experience that he could not imagine any Negro not being pleased to witness it.

Thus Robeson's search for himself led him to find a voice for himself and his people. In other words, he had found his true identity and was now better able to relate to others. In retrospect, he had made a qualitative leap from being simply the interpretive artist of his time to political artist.

Although there were many in Britain who directly exploited colonial peoples, Robeson felt strong concern for the many millions who earned their living by honest labour. And even as he grew to feel more 'Negro' in spirit, or African as he put it then, he also came to feel a 'sense of oneness' with the white people whom he said he understood and loved. His belief in the 'oneness of mankind' had a parallel existence with his deep attachment to the cause of people of his own race. To Robeson there was no deep contradiction in this duality. In England he had learned there was a true kinship among the world's peoples, a prerequisite for mutual respect. Not surprisingly, this concept came through song, particularly those enduring songs that expressed the 'heart of humanity'. As a concert stage singer Robeson, in reaching new audiences, learned the songs of different peoples. In Britain he discovered the riches of English, Welsh and Gaelic folk-songs, melodies which he said expressed the same soulful quality that he knew in Negro music. About this kinship Robeson recalled what Frederick Douglass had written after visiting Ireland in 1847: 'Child as I was, these wild songs depressed my spirit. Nowhere outside of dear old Ireland, in the days of want and famine, have I heard sounds so mournful.' In Robeson's case, the beauty of these folk-songs drew him spiritually closer to the common people of Europe, particularly during the years that saw the rise of fascism. He had the notion that upper-class England was rather pleased by what the dictators were doing, and that the 'umbrella of appeasement' held out by Chamberlain did not blind the common people, who rallied everywhere for anti-fascist action, through the forces of labour – the trade unions, the co-operatives, the political parties of the Left – and others from the arts, sciences and professions. Thus he wrote, 'I, as an artist, was drawn into that movement and I came to see that the struggle against fascism must take first place over every other interest.'

4 · Home Again: Optimism and Disillusionment (1940–1946)

When *Proud Valley* was released in London Robeson had returned home to the United States. His long self-exile had ended on the eve of the Second World War. He returned to find that racial equality was the democratic ideal. Under the administration of President Franklin D. Roosevelt (in spite of the ravages of the Depression, which had severely affected Blacks) various government recovery programmes were initiated to employ the unemployed. Black scholars, writers and artists were assisted through grants in the furtherance of their work. Taken together, this unprecedented interest in black Americans was brought to the notice of white Americans. And although in the circumstances these measures were nowhere near enough to alleviate the poverty of Blacks, many of them sensed a wind of change in their favour.

Yet, almost immediately after his return, Robeson was subjected to racial insult. Unruffled, though concerned, he coped with the situation. At the time he was regarded as the most famous black man the world had ever known. He was indeed a great American, who was back where he belonged, among his people.

The Robesons now approached life in America dedicated to upholding the constitutional ideals of the country they loved, and with an evident degree of permanence. They settled in that city within a city, Harlem, at 555 Edgecombe Avenue, with their twelve-year-old son. Not far away were the residences of such notable Blacks as William Patterson, Walter White, Roy Wilkins and Thurgood Marshall. It seemed that the Pattersons' home was a place of welcome for many black artists, writers and professionals. Appropriately, Robeson's friend and partner Larry Brown had also settled in the city. Although Brown was a humanist, warm and helpful, avoiding involvement in political philosophy, Patterson regarded him as a great man. At this time, it seemed, Robeson allowed few people into his inner circle of friendship. The exceptions were Brown and Patterson, who symbolized a sense of continuity as the Robeson family was reunited on American soil. The ravages of the Depression, in spite of President Roosevelt's progressive policies, had already set in motion the forces of reaction.

When Robeson returned to the United States in September 1939 it was almost exactly ten years since the Wall Street Crash heralded the great Depression. This had initially brought hardship, unusually high unemployment, widespread hunger and poverty, especially to Blacks. Politically, economic stress brought a change from the 'rugged individualism' approach to a liberal influence introduced by the Roosevelt administration's New Deal policies. Against this background of optimism, many people in the United States were hopeful of a better tomorrow. But how did Robeson feel after many years of estrangement? In a powerful statement he said he felt more American than ever. The fear of prejudice had diminished. Some four years earlier he had been more interested in Africa and the sources of 'Negro art' than in returning to the United States. But what had prompted his return? He said he had learned that Negro people were not the only ones oppressed, that it was the same for Jews and Chinese (the question of colour was not considered), and that such prejudice had no place in a democracy; that racial barriers were false and therefore the oppressed would rebel against their oppressors. He had returned as an artist to sing his songs of freedom so that democracy in the United States would flourish.

For Robeson the year 1939 was full of activity. Early in June he appeared in a short run of a revival of *The Emperor Jones*, and in July gave his first song recital, following his return, at the AME Zion Church in Harlem where his brother Benjamin was pastor. He was engaged, too, in the production of *John Henry*. Standing by his principles, he refused to appear in the opening show in Washington, DC, because the theatre was segregated. Instead, he opened in New York. This decision which he was forced to take at home, never arose while he was abroad.

On 27 October Robeson signed a contract with Columbia Artists to sing *Ballad for Americans*, based on *The Ballad for Uncle Sam* by John La Touche, with music by Earl Robinson. The première of *Ballad for Americans* on CBS Radio was a memorable event. The *Ballad*, essentially a poem against intolerance and persecution, had an immediate appeal to Robeson. It contained such Marxist expressions as 'Man in white skin can never be free,/While his black brother is in slavery'. Robeson and Brown worked diligently over many hours to convey the message to the best effect. Robeson could not have been more fortunate. He had, reasonably quickly, found a means through which he could speak to millions of Americans about American democracy, both directly and through his art. No wonder Robeson impressed his personality upon the *Ballad*. 'Another singer might have interpreted it quite differently,' said Brown. 'He breathed life into it.'

At the inaugural performance on Sunday, 5 November 1939 the Master of Ceremonies, Burgess Meredith, announced, 'What we have to say seriously can be simply said. It's this: Democracy is a good thing. It works. It may creak a bit, but it works. And in its working, it still turns out good times, good news, good people. . . . Life, liberty and the pursuit of happiness – of these we sing!' Leading the American People's Chorus, Robeson then sang for about eleven minutes. The words could well have been his own, for they reflected his belief.

> Are you an American?
> I'm just an Irish, Negro, Jewish,
> Italian, French, and English,
> Spanish, Russian, Chinese,
> Polish, Scotch, Hungarian,
> Litvak, Swedish, Finnish,
> Canadian, Greek and Turk,
> And Czech and double-check American . . .
> For I have always believed it,
> And I believe it now,
> And you know who I am
> A-m-e-r-i-c-a.

No one had sung the *Ballad* as Robeson did. The audience, an estimated 600 in the CBS studio, broke into applause which lasted for about fifteen minutes. With this broadcast Robeson reached a vital cross-section of the American people in an unpredictable and dramatic way. He gained further access to the masses through a recording of the *Ballad*, which became the most popular song in the country. During the applause Marie Seton, who had seen Robeson for the first time in his homeland, observed a rare moment in American musical history, Robeson's triumph. She watched curiously as these Americans surged up to the platform and surrounded him. Marie Seton and Paul Robeson had been together in Moscow, Berlin and London. And what Robeson had said, after their unpleasant experience with Hitler's storm-troopers, that 'This is like Mississippi', had seemed far-fetched to her, although she had not been to Mississippi to witness the real problems of race there. 'Now it seemed as if his native land had changed under the guidance of Roosevelt,' she wrote. 'At last Paul Robeson appeared to be a free man in the land of his birth; one appreciated, loved, honoured.' The measure of his success on this occasion could be judged by the fact that his radio performance had aroused one of the greatest ever audience responses up to that date in the United States.

This was a major homecoming triumph for Robeson. Even so, did it really not matter that he was also a *black* artist? Marie Seton put this to the test soon after the CBS broadcast. She had invited the Robesons for lunch where she was staying at the Elysée Hotel, near the CBS studio. She told the hotel manager she was expecting the Robesons and wanted to be sure that they would not be asked to use the freight elevator. The manager said that would not be a problem. When the Robesons arrived, however, the manager telephoned Marie Seton. He said that if the Robesons were joining her for lunch in the restaurant, they would not be served because objections would be raised by other patrons. However, it would be all right for the Robesons to eat in her hotel room. Having been through the routine many times before, and in order to minimize Marie Seton's discomfiture, Robeson said they would do what had been suggested.

In spite of his busy artistic pursuits Robeson was greatly concerned about the Russian attack on Finland in November 1939. Did this act of aggression mean that the Russians were becoming fascist? Robeson could not believe it. When he turned down an invitation to take part in a benefit for Finland, sponsored by the Herbert Hoover Relief Fund, he was criticized by some newspapers. He was thoughtful of the events unfolding in Europe. By the end of the year, Great Britain and France had declared war on Germany. The Hitler-Stalin pact aroused bitterness and suspicion among Americans – something that would remain deeply embedded in the minds of certain sections of the society.

Yet the hostilities abroad did not affect Robeson's artistic career. As a personality and artist he was climbing the ladder of success in a dramatic way. The enormous success he enjoyed, and the consequent demands on his time and talents, necessitated the need for some private comfort, on those only too rare occasions when he could be alone with his family. Consequently, the Robesons bought the residence known as 'The Beeches' in Enfield, Connecticut. But even this hard-won acquisition was not without its problems. Making this place their home, a private retreat in their homeland, was largely dependent on the agreement of their neighbours.

The honours Robeson received did not deflect him from his awareness and concern about the stark realities of racial prejudice and discrimination in the United States. In fact, the contradictions within the society were abundantly clear in the way he was treated, personally, because he was black. There could be no more powerful impact than this, which served only to reinforce his commitment to progressive change. As if to remind him of what he knew so well, in July 1940 he was refused service in a fashionable San Francisco restaurant. With his legal background, and conscious of his rights, Robeson retaliated by suing the owner for discrimination on the grounds of race and colour.

His hectic schedule took Robeson in July 1940 to the Hollywood Bowl, Los Angeles, where he sang the *Ballad for Americans* to an estimated audience of 30,000 people. He also sang the *Ballad* for the San Quentin prison inmates, then to a mammoth crowd of 160,000 in Chicago's Grant Park, among other places. The gruelling schedule he had been on for years, now seemed to take its toll on him. Some reviewers detected signs of fatigue, deterioration in his voice.

In September Robeson appeared with the pianist Hazel Scott and novelist Richard Wright at a benefit for the Negro Playwrights' Company before 5,000 people at the Golden Gate Ballroom in Harlem. Throughout 1940 he was active on behalf of various organizations such as the Committee to Aid China, the Joint Anti-Fascist Refugee Committee to Aid Spanish Refugees and the Council on African Affairs, to name a few. And he devoted time, energy and money towards helping black theatre arts. Ever-encouraging to young people, he developed an interest in the emerging black singer Lena Horne, who later said that Robeson was 'deeply, deeply angry about what all our people suffer. But it was an understanding anger.

Never, never was he angry against white people as a group'.

As more of Europe fell to the Nazis, racial discrimination in the United States was linked to the war. Blacks saw the Ku Klux Klan's attacks as similar to the Nazi persecution of the Jews and the attacks on black soldiers who had been in Europe during the First World War. If democracy was what the Second World War was about, now as a resident Robeson was acutely conscious that the United States was woefully lacking in it, as far as Blacks were concerned. He considered that Blacks should not get involved in the war. More generally, he was emphatically against the United States being drawn into the conflict. The dangers inherent in these political statements must have been abundantly clear to Robeson. He could not ignore the fact that his artistic career was now being manifestly affected by his politics: sometimes his labour songs were sharply criticized, a radio engagement was cancelled and white youths campaigned against him in New Jersey. Was this the thin end of the wedge of American reaction? Robeson seemed unruffled. The sheer power of his mass appeal was behind him, and he knew it. He had unequivocally become the people's artist.

In the summer of 1940, as Blacks in America struggled for civil rights, Robeson was moved to action – providing leadership, long, long before Martin Luther King Jr. He lent his voice as narrator of the film *Native Land*, based on the La Follette report on civil liberties, a documentary film produced by Frontier Films, an independent company that produced films reflecting pro-New Deal ideas.

By the time his country-wide concert tour was under way, the positive spin-offs of the *Ballad for Americans* had preceded him. This tour was one of special merit. 'All our tours until 1947', said Brown, 'were a greater success than any of our earlier American tours.'

Occasionally Robeson ventured to the states south of the Mason-Dixon line, where 'Jim Crow' (total segregation) was the order of the day as decreed by the Ku Klux Klansmen. (Sixteen years before, the Klan had threatened the life of Eugene O'Neill's son, should Robeson appear with his white actress co-star in *All God's Chillun Got Wings*.) Robeson's only engagements in the South were at black universities and colleges where Whites were welcome. To Robeson's and Brown's surprise, something extraordinary happened at the schools where they performed. 'There was no Jim Crow,' said Brown, 'and quite a few white people came and sat where they pleased.'

At around this time Robeson sang a solo version of *Ballad for Americans*, often including Russian and Mexican folk-songs, the Hebrew Kaddish and arias from *Boris Godunov*. Of course Negro spirituals formed the core of his programmes. Songs from China were also included.

What was Robeson's technique as a singer? 'I have never been much interested in vocal virtuosity,' he said. 'I have never tried to sing A-flat while the audience held on the edge of its collective seats to see if I could make it.' This seemingly simple approach, unique to Robeson, was extraordinarily effective in its impact on his audiences generally, but particularly among working-class people, to whom he not only sang but also spoke. His message to them was becoming more politically direct. In December 1940 Robeson argued the case for Blacks joining the CIO (Congress of Industrial Organizations, the US trade-union body) during the campaign to organize workers in the Ford Motor Company. He was against separate unions for black workers. He was 'amazed' that the simple right to organize into a union was questioned in the United States. He stressed that the Negro problem could not be solved 'by a few of us getting to be doctors and lawyers'. The best way forward for his race to win justice, he argued, was 'by sticking together in progressive labor unions'. He warned that if Blacks failed to join the CIO, they could not participate in American democracy, of which the labour unions were an integral part. Those with the least rights would offer most, he emphasized. The relationship Robeson had forged with the British labour movement was a vital background to his involvement with the American trade unions, a relationship that grew with time.

On 19 May 1941 Robeson was again on hand to help workers. He spoke at the United Auto Workers rally in Detroit to aid the Ford organizing campaign. A few weeks later, as public demand continued to increase, an estimated 13,000 people heard him sing the *Ballad for Americans* at the Lewisohn Stadium in New York. There he proved once again that he was an uncommon artist whose fame was essentially a means through which he could focus the struggle of his people. And in an effort to improve wages, hours, conditions of work and to eliminate discrimination in employment and education, Robeson brought his influence to bear on the campaigns of mass organizations and labour unions.

The day before Robeson's Lewisohn triumph Hitler's armies invaded the Soviet Union. Now France and Britain had an ally in the

Soviet Union, which as a result was viewed more sympathetically by Americans. Thus Robeson's pro-Russian stance and knowledge of the country and her people seemed of a sudden eminently respectable. About this time US Government officials made serious efforts to prevent a 'march on Washington' planned by A. Philip Randolph. More than ever before, the goodwill and co-operation of Blacks were sought to bring about national unity. At least in the Northern states there were practical moves to effect better race relations.

In December 1941, with the Japanese attack on Pearl Harbor, the United States was drawn into the Second World War, which brought about even closer relations between the ideologically polarized Soviet Union and the United States of America, who were engaged in fighting a common enemy.

Earlier in the year pressure from black leaders had paid off. Roosevelt issued Order 8802 to prevent discrimination in factories and plants concerned with national defence. This order did not, however, result in a ban on discrimination in the US armed forces where, particularly in the Army, soldiers were completely segregated. Justifiably, this segregation in the fighting forces led some Blacks to believe that if the enemy did not get them, 'Whitey' would! Blacks questioned: Who then was the 'enemy'? Was the real enemy abroad or at home?

But war had its own dynamic, its pluses and minuses. In the United States black workers eager for employment after the ravages of poverty during the Depression years found that their labour supply was vitally necessary to the Government's demand, as they were integrated in order to increase arms production. In spite of the official line, the US Army, Navy and Air Force were almost entirely segregated, and the question of promotion was a major source of complaint among Blacks. Robeson was well acquainted with these issues, which were of central concern to his people.

If Robeson was disturbed by the Russian-Finnish problem, now because of his country's friendly approach to the Soviet Union he was heartened, and with seemingly renewed endeavours he launched himself into an all-out commitment to bring this 'war for democracy' to a successful conclusion. Although he was against American involvement in the war, now that they were in it, he felt he had to work for its end which he hoped would bring a lasting peace,

1   Phi Beta Kappa scholar, Rutgers University, 1919

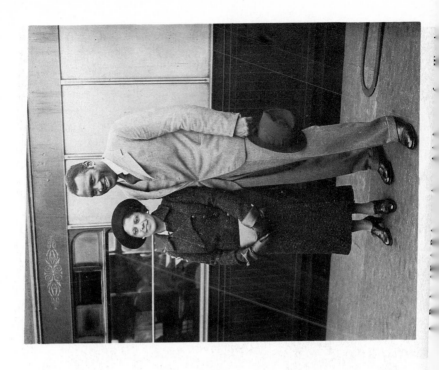

4 Robeson (*left*) in *Shuffle Along*, Harlem, 1922

5 Picketing the White House, Washington, August 1949

6 Paul Robeson with Nikita Khrushchev, 1959

7 Robeson as Othello with Mary Ure as Desdemona in the Shakespeare Memorial Theatre production at Stratford-upon-Avon, April 1959

equality and freedom. Towards this end, he joined organizations such as the Joint Anti-Fascist Refugee Committee, the Committee to Aid China and the Council on African Affairs. Through the last-named organization he worked for the liberation of Africa.

Often Robeson sought the refuge of his family, now settled in their Enfield home. This essentially socialist man was ill at ease with the capitalist trappings of private swimming-pool, tennis-court and billiard-room, symbols of affluence and success, yet the Robeson family became attached to the place. Based in these surroundings Essie pursued her anthropological studies, while Pauli attended Technical High School in Springfield, Massachusetts. In his new home Robeson had much to reflect upon. For one thing, his political position was in conflict with that of other black leaders (this had seemed inevitable for some time), such as A. Philip Randolph and Walter White. Many black spokesmen were attacked by pro-communists as being pro-war. Robeson, on the other hand, a friend of the communists and those on the Left generally, was anti-war and staunchly anti-fascist. Following Germany's attack on the Soviet Union, evidently Robeson became more open and increased his political activities. He was now in favour of military involvement and made a Herculean personal contribution towards boosting the American war effort, singing at ammunition plants and for various organizations wherever he was invited and whenever he could. And he spoke out on various issues: urging Blacks to fight back against the Klan, and calling for the mobilization of 'Negro and colonial people in the fight against fascism'. He sensed that the mood of the people would not remain optimistic and that the war should certainly not be prolonged. In May 1942 the film *Native Land* had appeared; and addressing 51,000 workers at the Yankee Stadium, Robeson called for a second front to shorten the war.

By August 1942 Robeson was again treading the boards. This time as the Moor in the long-awaited American production of *Othello*. Race prejudice in America was the main reason why the play with a black man in the lead had not been staged before. It was the persistence of Robeson's friend, the actress-director Margaret Webster, which led to the announcement in the spring 1942 that Robeson would play Othello at the Brattle Hall Theater in Cambridge, Massachusetts. In 1936 Lillian Bayliss (associated with the Old Vic Theatre in London) had tried unsuccessfully to involve Robeson in a new production of *Othello* directed by Tyrone Guthrie, with Laurence Olivier as Iago. Now that all of America knew of Robeson, such a production was timely. Although racism was an integral part of American society, it seemed that more people were prepared to tolerate intimate scenes between a black actor and white actress. While Robeson had triumphed in the part twelve years before at the Savoy Theatre in London, it was especially important for him to play the role in his homeland. Mrs Patrick Campbell's advice in 1922 that he should prepare for Othello was no idle comment. What had been an idea and a reality in England was about to be repeated in the United States. The theatre world waited expectantly.

Robeson was choosy about the people he wanted in the cast. His first choices were Basil Rathbone as Iago and Peggy Ashcroft as Desdemona. Ronald Colman and Greer Garson were also considered. Eventually José Ferrer and his wife, Uta Hagen, appeared as Iago and Desdemona, and Margaret Webster as Emilia. As he had done in 1930, Robeson prepared himself carefully for his role. But even so he was still an actor without a specific technique. Naturally, in his unpretentious way he compared himself with Ferrer. He did not regard himself as a great actor like Ferrer. 'All I do is feel the part,' he said, and make himself believe that he was Othello, acting as Othello would act. He was, in the opinion of many authorities, the ideal Othello. As Sam Wanamaker (the American actor who played Iago opposite Robeson's last portrayal of the Moor in 1959) has said, 'Robeson *was* Othello.' For one thing, both the director and Robeson agreed that Othello was black, 'not pale beige'. Establishing Othello's racial background was essential to Robeson.

The first preview performance was held in August 1942 at Brattle Hall Theater as scheduled. Robeson went into the record books as the first black actor to play Othello with a white cast in support. With so much going for the play, there was an air of anticipation and excitement as the 400-seat theatre filled. Although Robeson had lost some thirty pounds in weight, his bulk still loomed large on the small stage. For three hours the audience sat silently, trance-like, witnessing a rare moment in American theatrical history. When the curtain fell, their response was spontaneous and impressive. Robeson's dramatic artistry, though lacking in technique, was hailed by the pundits as being unequalled in that generation, if not in all previous generations.

After this 'extraordinary histrionic happening' there was unanimity on Robeson's artistry. He had used his voice and acting to such effect that, as one reviewer put it, 'For once, and with good reason, the playgoer can have sympathy for he who loved not wisely, but too well.' The theatre world could not ignore this event. Broadway's interest was aroused as telephone calls sought Margaret Webster. For Robeson another hurdle had been overcome. The sceptics and diehards of theatreland had been won over. *Time* magazine described his performance as 'vivid' and 'shattering'.

In the wake of this acclaim, the production moved on to Princeton, New Jersey, for another try-out. For Robeson, it was a triumphant return to his birthplace, at the height of his fame, to play the leading role in a Shakespearian tragedy. His reticence, which seemed undiminished, was perhaps the reason why little was left on record as to his feelings for his home town during his portrayal of Othello. A few years later, however, he reflected on the long, hard road that began in Princeton, where his brothers were not allowed to attend high school. They received their education ten miles away in Trenton. He also remembered his brother who died 'broken-hearted' because he found the humiliation of life in Princeton unbearable. His cousin Minnie who sat in the McArthur Theater where Robeson performed, for the first time in her life, later recalled how wonderful he was in *Othello*. In the audience, too, was the Shakespearian scholar, Arthur Colby Sprague, who was left at the end of the play wondering whether Robeson's performance 'had not approached the greatness attributed to actors in other times'.

Although the production was now good enough, it did not go immediately to New York. Theatregoers there had to wait until January 1943 for the announcement of a Theater Guild production of *Othello*.

If Shakespeare had intended that Othello should be a mature, well-built man, Robeson, now forty-four years old and of impressive physique, was ideally suited for the part. But he still felt a sense of limitation about his acting, that he had never been able to get the best out of the characters he played. Why? The answer seems to be that Robeson had never been convinced of the validity of any character he had played on the stage. He explained to Jerome Beatty of *The American* magazine that he saw the contrasting styles between himself and Ferrer as necessary. Thus, his calmness, during the early part, was effective against Ferrer's active Iago.

As his portrayal of Othello took shape, Robeson rejected the conventional view of this character as a jealous man, driven to murder his wife. He argued that the rage Othello felt 'is maddening, he is out of his head: and I know what that is like because I felt it once myself'. The one unforgettable occasion on which Robeson went off his head in rage was during a football game when his nails were ripped away because he wanted to become a Rutgers player.

In August 1942 Robeson made his last commercial film, appearing with Ethel Waters as a sharecropper in the final episode of *Tales of Manhattan*. He was unhappy about his role in this film, which reeked yet again of Hollywood's 'plantation' stereotype. He thought he could change the picture as the film was being made. 'But in the end,' he said, 'it turned out to be the same old thing – the Negro solving his problem by singing his way to glory. This is very offensive to my people.'

By October 1942 the outspoken Robeson was able to tell a mixed audience of Blacks and Whites, in New Orleans Booker T. Washington School Auditorium, that his evaluation of the courage and dignity of Blacks in the Deep South had been corrected by his visiting the area. There the bitterness and ugliness could be seen unadorned, and rising above it all were the Blacks.

While the majority of the American population at this time acknowledged that what Robeson had been saying was correct, there were those who had always been bigoted and racist, harbouring anti-liberal, anti-progressive, anti-communist views. It was an issue such as civil rights that led to Robeson's involvement in the film *Native Land*, which supported the ideas of President Roosevelt's New Deal. Although he was rated by many as one of the 'great Americans' of his time, he was acutely conscious of the double standards and ambivalence towards him among some elements in America. He was praised as an artist and discriminated against as a black man. The end of the war, Robeson hoped, would usher in an end to this system. Surely, he reasoned, black American soldiers fighting for a democratic Europe would not be denied their democratic rights at home! As he sang and spoke across the country he believed that racial equality would be achieved in a democratic America. At the time, anti-communism was not yet a strong movement, although there were deep undercurrents of suspicion and distrust.

In September 1942 a Texan Democrat Congressman, Martin Dies, head of the Un-American Activities Committee (and a man opposed to better black/white relations in the Southern states), submitted a list of names of people and organizations which he said were communist. Paul Robeson was among the names, and Frontier Films was one of the organizations. Dies was politically opposed to the Robert Marshall Foundation. Marshall was a government official who had left a large sum of money to advance the theory of production for use and not for profit. Subsequently the Foundation was formed. Dies, an upholder of white supremacy in the South, said that the Foundation had paid $6,000 to Frontier Films to make the 'communist' film *Native Land*. He alleged that the film was based on Richard Wright's book *Native Son* and that both Wright and Robeson were members of the Committee of the African Peace Mobilization, a front organization for the Communist Party. In fact, *Native Land* was not based on *Native Son*, as Dies maintained, but upon the findings of the Senate Report of Senator Robert La Follette, which revealed violations of the Bill of Rights.

Dies, as it turned out, was the first American official to label Robeson a communist. And so it was that at the height of his fame Robeson was looked upon, at least by Dies (and others like him), with deep suspicion. Although the American press was divided as to whether or not *Native Land* should have been released during the war, the *New York Tribune* felt it was a positive move in fighting for free speech, and that Robeson's involvement in the film was 'a stroke of genius'.

By the end of 1942 Robeson was probably the only man in the world who could transform a concert into a rally for civil rights. Increasingly the concert stage was becoming the pulpit for his 'propaganda' as he grew in stature. It was evident too that some of his reticence was giving way, of necessity, to more openness. His ability to hold an audience's attention was well known. Now, through his mission in song, interspersed with speeches, Robeson was able to get his message across directly to those who listened, and there were incalculable millions who heard his voice and intuitively knew and felt he was right in what he said. He had embarked on a path of no return in the struggle for peace and freedom in the United States, in Europe and in the world generally. Only a few years before, Europe was his artistic constituency. At home the internationalist Robeson was as much concerned, as he had been when it started, about the outcome of the war and its threat to democracy. Did he have doubts? And what were they? He smiled less now and with good reason.

There were reminders everywhere of the real divisions in American society. He had to face the stark question again and again: could his people become free at home? His answer had always been a positive yes, for struggle was endemic in his life. Although he was outwardly as warm and as gracious as ever, Robeson, according to his friends, was more lonely than before. The heavy responsibility as spokesman for his people had hardened his resolve. There had been a noticeable shift in the mood of Americans. Friends had always been valued, now they were at a high premium. The few people around him helped relieve his sense of loneliness as he found himself becoming more and more isolated. Yet there were always those who recognized his struggle. In January 1943 he received the Abraham Lincoln Medal for notable distinguished service in human relations in New York, a well-deserved honour. He seemed more concerned with what needed to be done, rather than directing his attention or energy to his detractors.

By the turn of the new year, 1943, perhaps Robeson's most honest critic and friend, Alexander Woollcott, died. Woollcott had seen greatness in the young Robeson and was witness to his developing talents and stature. Obviously touched by Woollcott's friendship, an an association that lasted for some twenty years, Robeson read with solemnity the 23rd Psalm at his friend's memorial service. His strong voice spoke the words:

Thou preparest a table before me in the presence of mine enemies: Thou anointest my head with oil; my cup runneth over
Surely goodness and mercy shall follow me all the days of my life . . .

Goodness was indeed shown to Robeson when he was honoured by the Schomberg Collection of the New York Public Library for promoting the folk art of many countries. This was followed by the Lincoln Medal by students of the Abraham Lincoln High School in Brooklyn. Robeson had a special attachment to young people, no matter which country he was in, and this award came as no surprise, since he appeared to them as a model for their own aspirations. They honoured him for his efforts of 'goodwill, tolerance and minority rights'. It is an award of special significance, because it was essentially an appreciation of Robeson by, above all else, American youth. In effect, a new generation was claiming him.

These honours reflected to some extent Robeson's prominence. He was asked to grace many occasions with his presence. On 17 April 1943 he was invited to attend the Teachers' Union Conference at the Tuskegee Institute, a Negro institution founded by Dr Carver. During the journey South Robeson experienced all the physical and psychological humiliation of Jim Crow. When he stepped off the train he was more determined than ever to destroy this disgraceful system in his own country. Although many in the conference audience were preoccupied with the more immediate concerns at home, Robeson, way ahead of his time, drew attention to the vital links of struggles elsewhere. His dedication to peace during this period of war had begun to emerge with absolute clarity; peace would release the rich possibilities for the peoples of Africa, China, India and the Pacific. He warned those who refused to accept 'any principle of equality of peoples at home or abroad'. The future must not be based on a new form of imperialism, but on the emancipation of the common man. To win the war against fascism would, in his opinion, mark the beginning of a new era for mankind. There was little to distinguish between Robeson the interpretive artist and Robeson the political artist. Now, more than ever, he seemed to have been at one with the mood of the American people, particularly his 'own people' who claimed him.

At the beginning of June Morehouse College in Atlanta bowed to Robeson's unparalleled, heroic efforts. The honorary degree of Doctor of Humane Letters was conferred on him. The college president, Dr Benjamin Mays, said to Robeson: 'We are happy to be the first Negro college in the world to place its stamp of approval upon the leadership of a man who embodies all the hopes and aspirations of the Negro race and who despite crippling restrictions breathes the pure air of freedom.'

Soon after this visit to the South Robeson received news of a race-riot in Detroit. Racial equality was still a far cry away. He was unhappy that the military hospitals in Washington were Jim Crow, and found it especially galling that he was due to sing at the Watergate concert in Washington, not far from the Lincoln Memorial.

The movement he had set in train had gathered momentum. His appeal to people as a whole was extraordinary. The 22,000 attending the open-air concert clapped rapturously, demanding encores of their favourite songs from their favourite singer. He sang

Ballad for Americans to the hushed audience of Blacks and Whites. This was an appropriate venue to sing such a song because of the Jim Crow conditions of Washington. Before him he beheld black/white unity as the audience stood up and applauded his rendition of the *Ballad*. This was of course more than just a gesture to an artist, and the *Ballad* was more than just a song. The mood of that gathering of thousands was, let us march for civil rights. The concert was followed by Robeson's attendance at an avalanche of meetings as he journeyed across the country once more. From the nation's capital he travelled to New York, Chicago and San Francisco in aid of the war effort. His call for freedom, early in June, had led to his addressing and singing at a black freedom rally in Madison Square Garden.

Wherever Robeson went, large crowds gathered to hear him speak and sing. In Chicago's White Sox Stadium 35,000 people heard him. The next day he met William Patterson, who was trying to organize the Abraham Lincoln School for adult education in Chicago. Emphasis was to be placed on black/white equality, the role of the labour unions and the arts. To this end, Robeson dug into his pockets, donating $2,000, his fee from the previous night's concert. This generosity was in keeping with his characteristic approach to the causes with which he had become associated.

The importance of Africa in the war was fundamental to his thinking at this time. He was so devoted to his work as Chairman of the Council on African Affairs that on one occasion he declined an offer of concerts that would have earned him $10,000 because they were scheduled on dates set for CAA meetings. Although Africans were involved in the war (fighting with the British and the French), Americans, both black and white, were still largely ignorant about Africa, in spite of Robeson's earlier efforts to impart the value of African culture to his countrymen. If India gained independence after the war, Robeson was convinced that the peoples of Africa would do the same.

Robeson continued to convey his message of peace, freedom, independence and racial equality, through song and speech, during this period. He addressed the CIO Minorities Committee's conference on 8 August, and at the Union-sponsored concert he sang foreign songs in both English and the original language. Appropriately he sang in Chinese at a symphony concert, perhaps the first Westerner to do so.

If Robeson's most loyal fans and supporters were those from the ranks of labour, there were other admirers who sought his services, also for worthy causes. An invitation from Mrs Winston Churchill was sent to Robeson asking him to give a concert in England to aid Russian War Relief. In spite of his desire to do so, Robeson was unable to accept the engagement. He later told Marie Seton that if he had gone to England then he might have stayed there.

Mrs Churchill's invitation was significant for another important reason. The *Pittsburgh Courier* carried the seemingly inconsequential report that 'Robeson had been denied a passport to travel to England to appear in a benefit concert sponsored by a British-Soviet Russian friendship group, under the honorary chairmanship of the wife of the Prime Minister Winston Churchill, was categorically denied by the State Department'. Was Robeson also aware at the time of being shadowed by the FBI?

On a visit to Chicago in September 1943 Robeson participated in an important meeting that underlined his political alignment. At the Win-the-Peace rally before 20,000 people he shared a platform with the Vice-President of the United States, Henry A. Wallace. This was no mean achievement for a black American at that time. Hitherto, Robeson may have stated his views clearly, but this association with Wallace was a political act that had an impact on the American public – a meeting between two major public figures, one white the other black, symbolizing future political possibilities. Adherents to white supremacy took note. Robeson was himself elated by the seemingly favourable turn of events as once more he prepared to tread the boards. In January that year the Theater Guild announced that Robeson would appear in the fall in *Othello* at the Schubert Theater, situated in New York. In due course, at the end of the first night at the Schubert Theater the cast took ten curtain calls, accompanied by twenty minutes of applause. Robeson, the American Othello, was a triumph. Many thought he was the embodiment of the Moor. Thirteen years after he had first played this demanding role Robeson had matured as an actor. The direction of Margaret Webster was an important factor in this new American production. According to Peggy Ashcroft, although Robeson's performance as Othello in 1930 was good, the production was a bad one.

Such rare occasions tend to produce their own unpredictable spin-offs. It was a strange change of fortunes that one of the Hearst newspapers, the *New York Journal-American*, which had been so vitriolic about Robeson's appearance on the stage with a white woman in the 1924 production of *All God's Chillun Got Wings*, now welcomed the black actor as Othello. 'I'd be surprised if thanks to the far-sightedness of the Theater Guild and the magnificent performance of Paul Robeson in the title role,' one newspaper critic wrote, 'we fortunate New York playgoers were not seeing the real "Othello", the Moor of Venice William Shakespeare actually had in mind.'

Whatever the pros and cons of his performance and the production itself, Robeson had undoubtedly reached 'the top of his game' both as an actor and singer. Yet he seemed genuinely astonished at his success, a reaction that continued to puzzle many who knew him. By December 1943 the new production of *Othello* had overtaken the record run of fifty-seven performances set by Walter Hampden in 1925. When the play finally closed in mid-1944 it had completed a record of 296 performances with 494,839 paid admissions.

The play had been on tour of America for over six months. Robeson's refusal to perform before segregated audiences in the South was endorsed by his supporting actors, José Ferrer and Uta Hagen. Given that this Shakespearian tragedy was about the problems of a black man, Robeson saw the play as a great challenge, one that could have special implications for young people. After his record-breaking performances, he had become so familiar with the role that he felt the part of Othello 'belongs to a Negro'. He argued that the naturalness was lost when a white actor plays the role 'under burnt cork'. For him there was no greater acting challenge. And he saw no reason why black actors should not play other Shakespearian parts.

While he was in Boston he was presented with the keys to the city hall by Mayor Tobin. Only a few weeks after receiving this public honour, there was evidence of anti-Semitism in the city. A Jewish synagogue and cemetery were vandalized. This was not Germany, where Nazism directed its venom against Jews, but the United States of America. For Robeson, who had linked the common oppression of the black and Jewish people, these incidents had serious implications. As the foremost spokesman for his people, it is not surprising that he spoke out. 'The struggle for freedom in which we are bloodily engaged means to me freedom of all individuals,' he said. 'To attack the Jews is to attack the coloured race and I trust that Negroes in Boston are as outraged as though the attacks had been on them.' A few days earlier he had been awarded honorary lifetime membership of the International Longshoremen's and Warehouse-men's Union, conferred by the president, Harry Bridges.

If Robeson was a hero to Blacks, it seemed Whites were at least willing to listen to him on a range of related subjects. At this stage he had gone beyond the part of merely accepting honours; he had committed himself to work as an official of the Council on African Affairs. On 16 November 1943 he addressed the first session of the New York Herald-Tribune Forum on Current Problems, not as a singer or actor, but as Chairman of the Council on African Affairs. To those who had been monitoring his speeches and statements the evidence was abundantly clear as he spoke. He sought (as he had done specifically with reference to Africa) to clarify the links on a broad level between the problems of American Blacks and those of minorities elsewhere in the world. He also spoke of China as the 'promise of the New World' and on the relations of Americans to Africa's place in the war and in the future post-war world, on which he pinned high hopes for a lasting peace and freedom. On this last question he concluded his opening remarks by saying: 'The winning of the war and the winning of the peace are interrelated things, not separate. Both depend upon the maintenance of the closest unity on the national and international levels.' And as formal spokesman on behalf of the Council Robeson wrote to President Roosevelt about post-war security plans affecting Africa. These African (and colonial) concerns, integrally linked with the problems of Blacks in America, constituted the broad outlines of Robeson's political thought. But, although his most immediate interest was always black freedom in the land of his birth, the colonial connection was fundamental. In this he was of course decades ahead of the Black Power advocates in the United States. Moreover, in December 1943, as part of a delegation, he presented a plea for the removal of a ban against Blacks in major baseball leagues before Commissioner Landis and League officials.

Towards the end of the year Roosevelt's New Deal liberalism and Robeson's self-declared democratic ideals were presented to the American public, as the war took a heavy toll in Europe. Above all else Robeson unstintingly hammered home his argument for freedom and a unified United States. Roosevelt was no doubt grateful that the most famous American, next to himself, was proclaiming his ideals in such a determined way. Inevitably Roosevelt's enemies, upholders of the status quo, now also felt threatened by the American Othello, who may have been expressing his love for his people and country perhaps not wisely but too well.

By the turn of 1944 Robeson's life was seen by many as an unprecedented success. Ed Sullivan, the columnist, ignoring the racism Robeson had suffered at Rutgers, eulogized his achievements there, and went on to advise Robeson that there was one more big role left for him to play 'as spokesman for his race'. Since Robeson had already been playing this role for some time, what did Sullivan mean? He warned Robeson to be wary of the Iagos whose innuendoes influenced the Negro and aroused white people. He felt that because Robeson was revered by his people and admired by Whites, he was poised to achieve the most important triumph. 'On both sides there are men of goodwill,' wrote Sullivan, 'on both sides, there are men who are fiercely intolerant. The kick-off will send these two teams crashing into each other. Robeson has figured in as many kick-offs, and has won; he must win this one for his country.'

Yes, Robeson clearly wanted his country to win convincingly against racial disadvantage and racial discrimination. But for so long as the status quo was fiercely defended by men such as Sullivan, Robeson would remain aligned to the progressive forces such as organized labour, which accepted him as their own. His alliance and commitment to the ranks of labour brought him further recognition as another year of war loomed ahead. In January 1944 he was made an honorary member of the State, County and Municipal Workers of America, and in addition to his lifetime membership, a few months later, the Union established a scholarship in his name at New York University.

The great Rutgers athlete also identified with sports in the United States, appearing on the special sports personalities broadcast with Babe Ruth and Jack Dempsey. In another broadcast of a different nature, the International Lincoln broadcast, sponsored by the American Office of War Information and the British Broadcasting Corporation, it was Robeson's honour to act as link-man between the American and British speakers, Vice-President Henry Wallace and the Archbishop of Canterbury. On that occasion, Robeson mentioned the names of Lincoln, Milton, Garibaldi, Lafayette, Sun Yat-sen and Lenin who, he said, would 'live forever in the minds and hearts of men for one reason mainly; they stand for liberty'.

The liberty-loving, revered black American was giving everything he could for the cause of peace and freedom. His voice reached everyone, for better or worse. Not everyone, however, agreed with Robeson's views, least of all the upholders of the status quo. In March 1944 Robeson was refused permission to sing at the Lyric Theater in Baltimore, Maryland, because of his insistence that the audience should be desegregated. This was yet another example of the contradictións in American society, reflected as a distinct pattern which emerged in Robeson's life: honours and awards followed by snubs and naked racism. The question he may have asked himself in March 1944 was: will this pattern continue or change after the war?

But if Robeson had enemies at that time, his true friends were always there. He was guest of honour at a dinner hosted by the National Federation for Constitutional Liberties, recognized for his outstanding efforts in helping to build international unity. Before the 800 guests, a big occasion for New York's liberals, Mrs J.B. Harriman (a former ambassador to Sweden) introduced Robeson and read a letter from President Roosevelt. A few days later, on 9 April 1944, at an extraordinary birthday party, more friends, admirers and well-wishers gathered, about 7,000 of them. This was a 'public party' for Robeson, and funds raised were donated to the Council on African Affairs. Reflecting Robeson's uniqueness, as man and artist, W.C. Handy (father of the blues), Duke Ellington, Joe Louis and Lillian Hellman were among the guests, and birthday greetings came from the people of China and trade unionists in Latin America, while Mrs Mary Bethune, a black educationist, described him as 'the tallest tree in our forest'. Robeson's trade-union friends, the Bakers' Union, Local 1, baked a six-tiered birthday cake topped with the message for a 'Better World'. For the thousands gathered, Robeson was indeed a friend. New York had seen few parties of this kind. This was an astonishing tribute, a measure of the stature and standing of the man. He was forty-six years old and recognized as truly a great American.

For many years now he had been giving of himself in what can only be described as superhuman effort. The physical demands of his engagements, over many years, especially since he had returned to the United States from Europe, were indeed great. Yet he never said no to an engagement that concurred with his belief. There was little time for a home life, although he regularly went to his home retreat for rest; moments which shielded him from the glare of publicity. The demands of *Othello* (he was still overweight) began to leave traces of physical wear and tear on him. On his birthday he looked a very tired man. Yet he sang with the same sense of conviction that had come to set his performances apart. And as if in reply to the Bakers' Union's 'Better World' slogan at the top of his cake, and because his tiredness must have been all too evident, he told his mammoth audience what his struggle meant. 'The mainspring of my life as an artist and as a person', he said, 'is a responsibility to the democratic forces for which I fight.'

Robeson, the man and artist, was indivisible. In May 1944 he received the coveted Medal for Good Diction on the Stage from the American Academy of Arts and Letters. Hitherto, since its inception in 1924, only nine people had received the award. At the awards ceremony Theodore Dreiser and Willa Cather also received awards from the Academy.

After a busy schedule the greying Robeson had earned himself a two-month rest before he began a cross-country tour (including the Canadian cities Toronto and Montreal) of *Othello* in September 1944. Of course the Southern Jim Crow states were omitted, except for black colleges and unsegregated audiences. This tour, covering some forty-five cities, gave him the opportunity to take the tragedy of the Moor to an even wider public. Above all the tour was instructive. The play had a unifying effect on educationalists. Schoolteachers – black and white – who had brought their classes to see the play, would crowd around Robeson's dressing-room with their pupils after the performance. In spite of the demands of the role, and a punishing schedule, Robeson always gave them the warmest welcome. For him, tiredness was no grounds for excusing himself, especially when children and students were involved. The next generation must know and understand the problems of the present, to ensure a more enlightened approach to the future. In effect, then, Robeson was not merely a symbol but a living example to American youth who looked to him.

He acted in a special benefit performance of *Othello* at the Abraham Lincoln School, spoke to the faculty and students at the University of Chicago, visited high schools and spoke in black and white churches and in synagogues. In Chicago, the last city of the tour, the play opened at the Erlanger Theater in April 1945. At Temple Sholem, perched on a truck at the entrance of a meat-packing plant, Robeson addressed 3,000 workers. 'The same cynical minds that approved of selling out Spain, Czechoslovakia and the rest of Europe would like to sabotage the San Francisco conference,' he warned, 'but the common people won't stand for it.' About this time 'Robeson's file' disappeared from the *Chicago Sun* library. Was this the beginning of the reactionary elements to 'bury him alive'? Evidently his participation in the political and economic drama of his time was being closely monitored in the United States, as it had been while he was in Britain.

Undeterred, the fearless fighter appeared at luncheons in between performances of *Othello*. On the last stage of this tour his experiences had tempered his optimism that reforms would indeed come. It was clear these would not happen without some major changes in American political life. And when President Roosevelt died, a few days after *Othello* opened in Chicago, Robeson was filled with foreboding. He considered the words of Carl Sandburg's tribute to Roosevelt: 'The art of the man is still now/Yet his shadow lingers alive and speaking. . . .' He thought of the war that had proceeded apace, engulfing the rest of the world. During the final performances of *Othello* in Chicago Robeson took the opportunity to renew friendships – as he had done in other cities. Just before a party held in May 1945, to which Robeson had been invited, was due to begin, the long-awaited peace was declared. The party become a celebration. According to one account, Robeson 'never seemed as happy as he was on this day. . . . His joy expanded into waves of well being. It was as if he wanted to embrace everyone who had come to this party'. The gathering of black and white, Jew and Gentile and the release of joy seemed to 'symbolize the America which could emerge with peace'. In spite of the war Robeson, through his portrayal of Othello, was among other things a 'revelation' to white people, a source of great pride to Blacks. 'He was one of us,' said a cab-driver. 'He was ours.'

More awards came with the euphoria of peace. In June 1945 Robeson received an honorary Doctor of Humane Letters degree from Howard University, Washington, and spoke at a Madison Square Garden rally for a Permanent Fair Employment Practises Committee against poll-tax, and for elimination of other obstacles towards equality for black people. But the artist, a true internationalist, always looked beyond.

For the first time since he left England in 1939, Robeson returned to Europe in August 1945. The fascist dictators, Hitler and Mussolini, were dead. Accompanied by Lawrence Brown, Robeson arrived in Europe to begin a tour which was to last several weeks to include France, Czechoslovakia and the American zone of occupation in Germany. During the war thoughts of the German war machine had preoccupied him as he worked unstintingly for peace from his American base. Now in the aftermath of great destruction he was back in Germany, the centre of war-torn Europe. He appeared in Hitler's opera-house in Nuremberg and in a stadium in Munich. He and Brown appeared in a theatre in Pilsen. 'In all we gave twenty-five concerts for the troops,' said Brown. Robeson sang for the troops and was upset by visits to Nazi concentration camps. He was particularly disturbed by the growing hostility towards the Soviet Union within the Allied High Command. Furthermore, he was worried by the attitude of Americans he had met in Europe. If this was the case abroad, what would it be like when they arrived back home?

On his return to the United States Robeson had little doubt that reaction would be maintained. The political hopes he had harboured under President Roosevelt now seemed threatened by the Truman administration. The prospects looked gloomy and demanded greater fortitude than Robeson believed possible after the war. In effect, the peace had brought its own intractable problems. But, characteristically, Robeson remained forthright in expressing his views. Of course he was now more conscious that the liberal views he had expressed, insistently calling for equality prior to and during the war (it seemed then largely a reflection of American opinion), were becoming no longer tenable. From now on, those who opposed Robeson's views (Southern Democrats and reactionary Republicans) would gain credibility as others joined them. Given this political trend, as Robeson saw it, there was no alternative but to face the growing reaction of his enemies head on. Thus, the artist who had taken sides during the Spanish Civil War was now faced with an ever-widening chasm dividing the haves and have-nots in American society. If previously his political adversaries had simply been making political statements, they were now ready to mount organized opposition. Indeed there was movement among Americans to return to 'normalcy'. Although the political tide had turned against all he had been fighting for, and had been recognized for in America, he remained fearlessly committed to his belief and struggle. To those who believed in the separation of art and politics the interpretive artist had become even more closely identified as the political artist. In effect, he had taken an irrevocable, uncompromising stand as he moved forward to face the mighty onslaught of American reaction.

Robeson's heroic stance received an opportune endorsement. The National Association for the Advancement of Colored Peoples awarded the coveted Spingarn Medal to him for his 'active concern for the rights of the common man of every race, colour, religion and nationality'. According to one of his close friends, this was the honour he most valued. It fortified him. A few weeks later, addressing the Central Conference of American Rabbis, he declared quite unexpectedly that the United States now 'stands for counter-revolution all over the world'. How prescient this remark has become in the 1980s! He urged the United States to share secrets of the atomic bomb with the Soviet Union, and predicted that it would be 'the greatest guarantee against another war'.

Although peace had come, one of the questions uppermost in Robeson's mind was: would freedom come to the colonized peoples who had loyally supported the Allied governments' commitment to the Atlantic Charter? His concern for Africans and Indians was matched by his immediate demands for full equality for Blacks in his homeland.

One important issue working against his pro-Russian views at this time was the fact that the Soviet Union had been involved in the establishment of people's republics in Eastern and Central Europe. They were now seen by the United States as a threat, not an ally. The Second World War had ended, but in its place there came into being a 'Cold War' or balance of terror between the two super-powers, a consequence of their very different ideologies and political systems. And as the 'Iron Curtain' divided Europe, the fear of communism in America was exacerbated. Thus social progress and change were seen as subversive, and racial discrimination in jobs and housing remained at an uncomfortably high level among Blacks.

It was with utter conviction, then, that Robeson had taken the message to the rabbis. He was not going to tell them what they wanted to hear. The time had come for plain speaking, something Robeson had never flinched from doing. He would not mislead. The speech had rattled the American establishment, which prided itself on democracy, especially in the post-war world. Or was 'democracy' simply an expedient war-time slogan? Anxiously Robeson watched with dismay and regret as his country drifted towards an anti-progressive position.

If as a personality Truman had little attraction for Robeson, as a politician he had even less. Both men seemed to be diametrically opposed on several fundamental issues. During the war Blacks had exerted themselves believing that the Roosevelt administration would indeed fulfil its promise of social and political advancement in a truly democratic society. Was this an illusion for the naïve? Robeson did not believe it was. In fact he had consistently warned that Blacks were tired of 'unfulfilled promises'. His worst fears were being realized under the Truman administration, as Blacks increasingly became the victims of violent acts by white racists. His popularity as a singer and actor had grown during the war years, his previous long absence from the United States apparently having increased his drawing power. During this period his repertoire included many Russian songs, which were well received, at least initially. He did particularly well singing Mussorgsky's songs and with political songs such as the 'Song of the Peat Bog Soldiers', 'Los Quatros Generales', as well as with melodies from Beethoven and Mendelssohn. Around this time Robeson was singing, as one reviewer put it, 'as a man who wanted something from the Lord very badly'. Of course the song that boosted American morale significantly was the *Ballad for Americans*. While the demand for the *Ballad* on the radio, in concerts and recordings increased, Robeson's album sales reached 30,000 within a year.

These years, according to Lawrence Brown, marked Robeson's 'greatest peak' as a singer, particularly the periods 1945-6, and later 1946-7. Yet during the moments of his greatest triumphs, Brown observed that 'he was more difficult to work with than during all the years before. He was in a terrible mood. He constantly felt he could not sing another concert'. Why? Evidently Brown did not understand that these were critical years for Robeson, who was disenchanted that little or nothing was being done to bring about the changes needed urgently in American society – matters of policy relating to such questions as fascism, colonialism and discrimination. The interpretive artist had done marvellously well in conveying the message, but the problem remained as to how to put it into practical effect for his people in the United States, not to mention the oppressed peoples in other countries. His strategy was to use his voice on the concert stage to alert and arouse his audience to real and disturbing developments.

Soon after his return to the United States he included labour songs in his programme, particularly 'Joe Hill'. His rendition of this song had an unfavourable response from one reviewer who regarded it as 'propaganda'.

Robeson's political views were now adversely affecting his career as an artist. Already a few people were labelling him 'communist'. Although his political activity was cause for concern by his concert manager, Robeson enjoyed continued popularity.

5 · From 'Great American' to 'Un-American' (1946–1949)

In January 1946 Robeson appeared with Marion Anderson at a rally for South African famine relief held under the auspices of the CAA at the Abyssinian Baptist Church in Harlem. At this time American public opinion was increasingly being influenced by international as well as national events. There was no question but that the United States had emerged from the war as the leading nation, commanding a powerful economic position over its rivals. The New Deal liberalism, it was hoped, would help to free the subjected colonial peoples after the war. This was not only a reasonable hope, but a realistic one; and Robeson was among those who had high expectations. But the advent of a new administration put paid to liberalism, as the American leadership steered the country towards more conservative and reactionary policies. Robeson's plea for friendly relations with other nations, particularly the Soviet Union, was being contradicted by anti-liberal, anti-socialist American foreign policy. Within the United States those who persisted in advocating progressive views became isolated, suspect. Although this shift to the right had not been clearly visible before 1946, it was a trend that had started many years earlier. President Truman was a Southerner, and naturally he selected Southerners – many of whom were pro-status quo – to become part of his administration.

Against this mood of apprehension, Robeson began an extensive concert tour. He was disturbed by what his people were saying about jobs and housing, as well as police brutality and lynchings in the South. The Ku Klux Klan and Klan-inspired terrorists were not the only culprits. Robeson pointed to the upholders of law and order; he remembered Isaac Woodward whose eyes were gouged out because a South Carolina sheriff did not like the idea of Blacks 'taking the war and its promises seriously'. In that case a white jury had found

131

the sheriff not guilty. Robeson was clearly unwilling to accept the situation. Ironically, while his concert tour proceeded and the violence against Blacks continued, he was at the peak of his success as a singer. It was as though the people's last hope of advancement was embodied in him, in his personal triumphs. He was a man of principle; he had spoken out on their behalf and would do so repeatedly. And so they flocked to his concerts. 'Certainly he never had such receptions in America as then, nor as many concerts,' said Brown. In 1945–6 they did 115 and in 1946–7 eighty-five.

On 6 June 1946 Robeson addressed a mass meeting for African freedom held in Madison Square Garden, under the sponsorship of the CAA. In July he crossed the Canadian border and joined striking automobile workers on the picket line in Windsor, Ontario. After singing a few songs he held a banner and marched with the strikers. This was a clear show of defiance and political commitment. Predictably, the American establishment took note and continued to monitor his movements.

In September, at the National Citizens' Political Action Committee and the Committee of the Arts, Sciences and Professions meeting held in Madison Square Garden, Henry A. Wallace (a member of President Truman's Cabinet) made a speech opposing the American 'get tough with Russia' policy, which resulted in his split with the Democratic Party. Wallace and Robeson had known each other before. According to one account, Wallace's position was 'an important factor in the Southern Democrats' opposition to Wallace's renomination for the Vice-Presidency in the 1944 election, and the substitution of Harry S. Truman'. Although Wallace's speech was controversial, Robeson received the greatest ovation for denouncing lynchings and attacking Governor Dewey of New York, who allegedly endorsed terrorism. Paradoxically, while Nazi war criminals were faced with trial for crimes against humanity in Germany, Blacks were subjected to lynchings in the democratic United States. In September 1946 Robeson was one of the sponsors and chief planners of a national conference on lynchings, representing a coalition of some fifty organizations from thirty-eight states. The conference mandated a delegation to meet President Truman to discuss anti-lynching legislation.

For both 'self-made' men this first meeting was significant. They were opposites to the extent that, as one writer put it, 'there was no common bond to engender even the most formal feelings of mutual respect'. In response to a statement read by Robeson demanding that the President issue a formal public statement to make clear his views on lynching, the President said such a statement could not be made and warned that Americans should not link national matters with the international scene. This was a clear indication of his feelings about Robeson's criticism of United States foreign policy. The President also tried to impress upon Robeson and his delegation that America and Great Britain were the only 'free' countries in the world. Of course Robeson disagreed, and urged the President to establish a definite legislative and educational programme to end the disgrace of mob violence.

By now Robeson's political activities were closely and widely publicized by the American press. The *New York Times* reported him as having said to the President that it 'seemed inept for the United States to take the lead in the Nuremberg trials and fall so far behind in respect to justice for Negroes in this country', and that the President told Robeson that America and Great Britain were the last refuges of freedom in the world. 'I disagree with this,' Robeson said. 'The British Empire is one of the greatest enslavers of human beings.' He declared that American and British policy were 'not supporting anti-fascism'. At that point in time Robeson's thinking was close to that of the vast majority of Blacks in America. As Walter White put it: 'World War II had given to the Negro a sense of kinsmanship with other colored – and also oppressed – peoples of the world.'

After his meeting with Truman, Robeson addressed mass meetings and spoke on radio against lynching. Perhaps the most important and brutal fact that Robeson had to face at this time was that the war-time American and Russian joint fight against fascism had virtually ended with the war.

In October Robeson was thrust further in the foreground of black struggle when he was elected Vice-President of the Civil Rights Congress, of which William Patterson was executive secretary. Soon after Robeson's meeting with Truman, a reporter asked Robeson if he was a communist. Robeson replied he was 'very violently anti-fascist'. In the climate of the cold war, the label of communist was designed to isolate and discredit Robeson in the public mind. Had he already gone too far with his statements on American national and international policies? Did he go too far in pressing the President?

Evidently he had become a major target for the new post-war

administration. It seemed that official endorsement of a process to 'bury him alive' had already begun. Pro-communism, far from being an acceptable ideology in the United States, was now the bogy. Robeson's outstanding achievements and extraordinary popularity had been enough to stifle his critics, who feared the kind of society he fought for, and hated him because he was a militant black spokesman. Until then, few black men (and for that matter few white men) had faced the President of the United States as fearlessly as had Robeson in the cause of his people. However, in spite of his stature as a great American, shameless officials in positions of power were planning his downfall. His political opponents, who had previously received little support, now felt the post-war pulse of conservatism, aided and abetted by Anglo-American big business, and sought to win public support for their cause.

Robeson, as co-Chairman of the National Committee to Win the Peace, was due to attend meetings in San Francisco in October. The process to malign him got under way officially that month when the California Legislative Committee on Un-American Activities (the Tenney Committee) subpoenaed him to attend a hearing. (At this time many others on the Left were also under attack.) Robeson was told that the purpose of his appearance before the Committee was to answer questions 'concerning the organization of certain groups' in which the Committee was particularly interested.

Robeson had never had to face this kind of interrogation before, but in spite of his suspicions, he co-operated. Inevitably the matter of his visits to the Soviet Union was raised. He told the Committee that he had last been in the Soviet Union between the end of 1937 and the beginning of 1938; that his son had been educated there and in London; and that both he and his son were citizens of the United States, where they were born. Turning to the black organizations, the National Negro Congress and the National Association for the Advancement of Colored People, the Committee counsel, Richard E. Combs, asked Robeson if he was affiliated to both organizations. 'Oh, I should say so,' said Robeson. He denied, however, that he was ever an officer of the Joint Anti-Nazi League Committee. He said he knew a lot about fascism and what it meant because he had seen it himself: 'I have helped to fight it . . . I know what it is. So I might have to participate a great deal more.'

Robeson's replies to searching questions from Chairman Tenney went as follows:

TENNEY: You don't mean to tell the Committee, I am sure . . . that merely because a man is a capitalist and has some money . . . that he becomes a lyncher or would condone those things?

ROBESON: No. I was giving a definition of fascism; that it is not necessarily the beast in man; it is the necessity of certain groups to protect their interests, like a former witness said, against social change, that is all. They want the status quo or even less than that. That was the essence of fascism. When people in Europe were pressing forward to social change the fascists said No and beat them back. I feel that is part of what is going on maybe in our own country today . . .

TENNEY: I may be going far afield here, Mr. Combs. But are you a member of the Communist Party? (Laughter) I ask it of everybody so don't feel embarrassed.

ROBESON: No. I am not embarrassed. I have heard it so much. Every reporter has asked me that. I will certainly answer it, Mr. Tenney. Only you might ask me if I am a member of the Republican or Democratic Party. As far as I know, the Communist Party is a very legal one in the United States. I sort of characterize myself as an anti-Fascist and independent. If I wanted to join any party I could just as conceivably join the Communist Party, more so today, than I could join the Republican or Democratic Party. But I am not a Communist.

TENNEY: You are not? I suppose from your statement, would I be proper and correct in concluding that you would be more sympathetic with the Communist Party than the Republican or Democratic Party?

ROBESON: I would put it this way: I said I could join either one of them just as well . . . I have no reason to be inferring communism is evil or that someone should run around the corner when they hear it, as I heard here this morning, because today Communists are in control or elected by people because of their sacrifice in much of the world. I feel that Americans have got to understand it unless they want to drop off the planet. They have got to get along with a lot of Communists.

In the years 1945–6, amidst the gathering forces of reaction, Robeson's involvement with the questions of labour and the problems of violence against black people was prominent. He spoke at the Sixth Biennial Convention of the International Longshoremen's and Warehousemen's Union and sang several songs. And he told *New Africa* (March 1945) that 'never again can colonialism be what it was'.

As the thirtieth recipient of the NAACP's Spingarn Medal for distinguished achievements in the theatre and on the concert stage, as well as his active concern for the rights of the common man of every race, colour, religion and nationality, Robeson had taken the opportunity to emphasize in his acceptance speech his preference for Soviet principles – economic, political and social. Impressed by what he had seen in Russia, notably the accomplishment in one generation by backward people, he shocked many in the large audience when he said: 'Full employment in Russia is a fact, and not a myth, and discrimination is non-existent. . . . The Soviet Union can't help it as a nation and a people if it is in the mainstream of change.' Ever vigilant against the rebuilding resurgence of fascism, optimistically he said, 'I feel America will choose on the basis of the democracy they represent.' Reflecting his socialist-humanitarian views – the oneness of mankind – Robeson urged the creation of a world where all peoples, regardless of colour, can live in harmony, and where resources can be used for the benefit of all towards the advancement of mankind.

Robeson posed questions on the domestic direction and policy of the United States towards the England of Winston Churchill or of British labour, towards France, Italy, Greece, Yugoslavia, China, the Near East, Spain, Latin America (especially the Argentine) and most importantly towards the Soviet Union. 'America's influence must be upon the side of progress, not reaction,' he emphasized. Preoccupied with his heritage, he pressed for food and freedom for Africa and called on anti-imperialists to defend the continent. It was not surprising to him that the imperialists were crying 'Stop Russia!' – a cry which, he argued, must be overwhelmed and made redundant by the voice of the American people demanding 'Big Three Unity for Colonial Freedom'.

In his unrelenting efforts as Chairman of the CAA Robeson wrote to the United States delegation to the General Assembly of the United Nations that the CAA was deeply concerned about the position that the US delegates had taken on the question of trusteeship relating to South Africa. Thus Robeson was not only engaged in a multiplicity of activities but argued forcefully for progressive change on a whole range of issues (on which he gave a reasonably clear indication of his position *vis-à-vis* communism and communists).

The fact that Robeson had been summoned before the Tenney Committee gave licence to his detractors to turn the heat on him. Reaction spread across the country. Yet that same month Robeson, undeterred, spoke (as co-Chairman of the National Committee to Win the Peace) at a strike meeting in San Francisco under the auspices of the Committee for Maritime Unity.

On balance, at the end of 1946, Robeson was still riding high. The vast majority of Americans believed he was entitled to the right freely to express his political views in the traditional democratic American way. Although this sentiment was strong, a few concerts were cancelled (a clear indication of the strength of feeling against him) as the great American artist began what was to be his 'last' professional concert tour in his country. It was clear to Robeson that politically the mood of the country had begun to move against his position. He observed, for instance, a split between 'liberals' and those who were pro-New Deal when it was popular. This cleavage was widening alarmingly.

Since the first German refugees arrived in London in 1933 Robeson had made great strides in his understanding of and involvement in political activity. Early in 1947 he was giving serious consideration to leaving both the theatre and the concert stage in order to undertake speaking engagements across the country against race hatred and prejudice. At that time the House Un-American Activities Committee had moved closer to its objective and the chief investigator, Robert E. Stripling, was looking for communists under suspicion. This lead was underlined by the Committee Chairman, J.P. Thomas: 'The Committee considers the Communist Party of the United States', he said, 'to be a subversive organization, and testimony or activities of any individual connected with the Communist Party of the United States is considered to be in the purview of the Committee's authority.'

In spite of this pronouncement, Robeson's artistic career was far from waning. His singing engagements were being supplemented by appearances at political and labour assemblies. Should the artist simply entertain and keep his politics to himself? How indeed would Americans react to him as a political artist? Before a largely white audience he expressed his disgust in January 1947 at a benefit concert in St Louis that black people were not allowed into the nearby American Theater, which was being picketed by the Civil Rights Congress. In this Jim Crow city Robeson again took the practical step of joining the picket line. Earlier in January his alignment with the labour movement was recognized by Local 600 of the United Automobile Workers in Detroit, who sponsored a testimonial dinner in his honour.

Robeson's picket-line action attracted the local newspaper reporters, who were keen to get details of his views. Anything he was likely to say could and would be used as evidence against him. And of course he knew this. In a determined voice he said: 'Some of us will have to speak up and appeal to the people to respect the common rights of others. It seems that I must raise my voice, but not by singing pretty songs.'

During this tour Robeson averaged three concerts a week, including in his repertoire English, French, German and Italian songs, selections from Mendelssohn's *Elijah*, arias from Mussorgsky and Negro spirituals. One of his popular recordings at this time was 'Songs of Free Men', including revolutionary songs which incensed his enemies. But his mission in song was inseparable from his political commitment. Thus composed and prepared, the forty-eight-year-old singer made his way to Salt Lake City, Utah, where he gave a concert in March 1947. Among the many songs he sang, 'Joe Hill' (a song of which he was particularly fond) was of major significance. Before him in the audience at the University of Utah was a cross-section of the community, who included low-paid mineworkers and the copper bosses. His close association with the miners and other groups of workers in Britain, his portrayal of a union organizer in *Stevedore* and his acting with trade unionists in *Plant in the Sun*, plus his own early unsatisfactory wage-earning experience, suitably qualified him to sing 'Joe Hill'.

> I dreamed I saw Joe Hill last night,
> Alive as you and me.
> Says I, but Joe you're ten years dead,
> I never died, says he,
> I never died, says he.
>
> The copper bosses killed you Joe,
> They shot you Joe, says I.
> Take more than guns to kill a man,

Says Joe, I didn't die,
Says Joe, I didn't die . . .

Says Joe, what they forgot to kill
Went on to organize,
Went on to organize . . .

Where working men defend their rights
It's there you'll find Joe Hill
It's there you'll find Joe Hill . . .
I never died, says he,
I never died, says he.

As the sound of the last note faded into a gap of silence applause rang out, though some sat in stunned silence. 'You've heard my final formal concert for at least two years, and perhaps for many more,' said Robeson. 'I'm retiring here and now from concert work. I shall sing now for my trade union and college friends. In other words, only at gatherings, where I can sing what I please.' The 2,000-strong audience stared in disbelief at the man on the stage who had taken a resolute, principled stand, ready to face the consequences.

Soon after Robeson left Salt Lake City Congressman Parnell Thomas (who was later in 1950 found guilty on a criminal charge of defrauding the US Government) had been engaged in trying to prove that Robeson was 'un-American'. By the end of this concert tour reaction against him was swift and effective. On 3 April 1947 he was prevented from appearing in Peoria, Illinois, when Shriners cancelled the contract for use of the Shriner Mosque and the mayor refused to allow the city hall to be used for the concert. In defence of the good citizens of his constituency, the mayor, with the support of the city council, took the necessary steps 'to prevent riots and other disturbances'. The city officials were determined to keep out propagandists for 'un-American ideologies'.

In Robeson's ensuing struggle for his civil rights, many friends and supporters in the CIO unions and other organizations came to his aid, demanding that they be allowed to use the city hall. Although the mayor relented and Robeson was to be allowed to use the hall, other forces were displeased. The American Legion protested against this violation of the city hall by Robeson (who, they said, advocated communism), and with their support the mayor withdrew his permission for the Robeson concert to go ahead.

When news of the decision in Peoria reached Robeson, who was in Decatur, he asked: 'Since when in America does a city dare to keep an artist out because of his political opinions?' This clear violation of civil rights, indeed of the right to assemble, strengthened Robeson in his resolve to sing in Peoria.

In effect Peoria, 'a microcosm of the nation', was a test case for Robeson. While the Methodist Association deplored denial of the use of a public building to Robeson (whose views the Association did not share), it felt certain that denial of the right of a citizen to express his views publicly was a 'disservice to democracy itself'. The *Peoria Star* criticized the 'misguided zeal' of the churchmen, one of its columnists making this pronouncement: 'The only organization that formally objected to allowing the City Hall to be used for a Robeson meeting was Peoria Post No. 2, American Legion. . . . We are hostile to Robeson's filthy communism, his sly methods of disseminating propaganda, and his apparent, stupid lies. What's more we are proud of our hostility.' It seems that Robeson's real opponents were the 'respectable' American Legion, anti-communists and upholders of freedom and democracy in America! The columnist's words acted as a signal to other newspaper writers and concert organizers to take up the cudgels against Robeson's progressive, pro-communist views.

Robeson was denied permission by the Board of Education of Albany, New York, for a concert at the end of the tour, due to be held on 9 May 1947, at the Philip Livingstone Junior High School. The Carver Cultural Society, sponsors of the concert, came to Robeson's defence. In the court-room drama that followed, Justice Brookstein ordered that the school be made available for the Robeson concert. Here in Albany, as in Peoria, the American Legion came out in open challenge. As it happened, the Legion's intimidation had little effect. The concert was held with over a thousand people in attendance. As a mark of respect for his audience Robeson, according to one report, avoided revolutionary songs and political remarks. If in his great moments of triumph he had seen the America he loved, now he was beginning to see and feel the dark forces at work in his native land, those that were contrary to all his post-war aspirations. To Robeson it was almost unimaginable that, given his public stature, he should be so vilified for the progressive views he held for a better America. What it seemed he failed to realize was the fact that free-enterprise American society was not structured for progressive change. At the end of his controversial concert, the artist, grey at the temples, said he would remember that performance 'with great warmth and affection'.

There was no doubt now that Robeson's artistic career had come into question. Of course he had read the signs and declared his position in Salt Lake City. And there had been many warning signs. For instance his manager, Fred Schang, had received complaints, one of which was that Robeson was using his concerts as a medium for communist propaganda. Those who complained felt there was no place in the United States for such propaganda, on the concert stage or elsewhere. Robeson was able to identify the sections of the public that held these reactionary views. There were others, however, with whom he felt comradeship.

At this time, he moved yet closer to the trade unions, playing an ambassadorial role. He left the United States for Panama to give four concerts, sponsored by the CIO United Public Workers of America, who were trying to unionize the predominantly black Panamanian work-force. Even here he found hostility. Because he cared about singing to his trade-union friends, at prices they could afford (a dollar each), he came under suspicion. What was the trick? The sterile attempts by his critics were swept aside by a crowd of 10,000 who came to hear him sing. Even the President of Panama had attended one of his concerts. Robeson treated the Panamanian people not only to songs but to selections from *Othello*. The applause was overwhelming. Brown was with Robeson on this visit and recalled that 'the vast majority of our audience were British West Indians who had been in Panama for a generation or so'. This trip underlined the fact that if Robeson were allowed to take his art to the people, the impact would be overwhelming. As an artist reflecting the struggles of the oppressed, he stood unrivalled both at home and abroad. He was indeed the people's artist. He would not disappoint them.

Later in June, he spoke at the National Maritime Union Convention. This was the last convention to which he was invited. Thereafter the union leadership under Joseph Curran turned anti-communist and supported the Cold War. This was a damaging blow to Robeson's hopes for labour unity. It was his hope and message that it was the united action of workers each day which would determine, to a large extent, when workers would be 'free from the shackles that forbid our full participation in a world where there is plenty for all'.

Faced with this disappointment in the United States, he drew some encouragement from his vast army of admirers and friends at home and abroad. In October 1947 he received an award from the Artists, Writers and Printing Workers' Congress of Bucharest, Romania. Such recognition, however, served only to deepen his political thought and involvement in the United States, which in turn led to closer monitoring of his movements by the House Un-American Activities Committee.

If Robeson the activist and artist could become so deeply pro-communist, how many other artists (particularly in Hollywood) were similarly committed? This was a logical question to pose, and Committee hearings to this effect were held on 20 October 1947. Nineteen people were called before the Committee, including Gary Cooper, Edward Dmytryk, Bertolt Brecht, Ring Lardner, Larry Parks, Ronald Reagan and Robert Taylor. Predictably, a wave of fear spread across the United States as the pro-New Deal (liberals and democrats of every profession) felt they could be implicated. Many, like Robeson, were ready to take a stand for their beliefs. Among the 'Red List' of subversive organizations was Robeson's Council on African Affairs. Publication of this 'List' had the desired effect: for example, it split the ranks of the CAA.

Perhaps the most vital target for HUAC was Robeson. In many ways he was unique, and successfully to pin charges on him would be a major step towards bringing the Left to heel. The Committee expected not only to justify its own existence but to make America free of the humbug and communist propaganda of the internationally famous black star. But perhaps even more relevant to the official attention Robeson had been receiving is the fact that the American public was, in modern times, unused to hearing a black man speak so intelligently and forcefully about the problems of his country. Was he an uppity 'nigger' who was unaware of the dangers in his own country? 'As a Negro in America', he said, 'I can speak here today, but I could go down to Georgia tomorrow and be dead.' Perhaps his cardinal crime was his refusal to say that the United States was good to him and that any black person could make it to the top if he behaved as he was told. If being black was unacceptable to the racists, this combined with his political views was even more galling to the white conservatives who were conducting the Cold War. Communist notions, and those who propagated them at home and abroad, were attacked through American foreign policy. Implementation of the Marshall Plan, which provided loans for the shattered post-war economies of Europe, whipped up further anti-communist fears. Thus the

Truman administration argued that 'so long as communism threatens the very existence of democracy, the United States must remain strong enough to support those countries of Europe which are threatened with Communist control and police-state rule'.

While the fear of communism at home was set against the campaign against communism in Europe, on 20 December 1947 Robeson announced his support of Henry A. Wallace as independent candidate for President of the United States in opposition to the Cold War policies of the Truman government. Later, Robeson attended a meeting to form the Wallace for President Committee, out of which emerged the Progressive Party. These last months of the year were of unusual significance in Robeson's life. In fact the year had seen the announcement of the 'Truman Doctrine', the proposed aid programme (the Marshall Plan) to Europe and growing Cold War tension between the United States and the Soviet Union and European countries.

The witch-hunt for communists and pro-communists in America threatened many individuals. Even the taint of such an ideology was enough for outright condemnation. Those on the Left were on their guard. Early in January 1948 James Hicks, editor of the *Amsterdam News*, tore up the negative of a photograph of Robeson shaking hands with the black American Ralph Bunche at a New Year's assembly in Harlem so that Bunche would not be politically tarnished if the photograph were published. (Later, in the 1960s, Hicks admitted that Robeson was saying what Blacks as a group would not begin saying for another five years, nor saying loudly for another ten years.) As it was, many black leaders were in a state of panic. Members of the Council on African Affairs, a prime target for the anti-communists, were deeply concerned. Even as far back as 1946 the *New York Times* identified that there were communists in the Council. Now, early in 1948, there was tension as the Council met. Among those present were Robeson, Max Yergan, Mary McLeod Bethune, Hope R. Stevens and W.E.B. DuBois. According to one account, Yergan argued for an alignment of the Council with American Cold War policies in order to evade the charge of subversion. Was this just a clever move by Yergan or a profound shift by him of his political position? Robeson confronted Yergan by standing firm on his and the Council's principles. This was the moment of truth for Yergan. Some members of the Council had much earlier suspected that his apparent commitment to the struggle for African freedom might not be genuine. Ideologically, the two co-founders of the CAA had drifted apart; Yergan was at loggerheads with Robeson, who viewed 'the freedom of Africa as affecting the freedom of Africans in America 100 per cent', Stevens recalled. 'He didn't care what the label was, and in those days the most vibrant direction to the black man's struggle in America came from men who were communist-trained.' At that important meeting Yergan, who had accused the Council of being communist dominated, was kicked out, and thus his friendship and long assocation with Robeson was ended.

Although communism had engendered growing distrust among capitalists abroad and at home, one of Robeson's main concerns was full citizenship for Blacks in America. So far he had been on the fringe of politics; the artist determined to publicize questions of civil rights for his people. Singing alone, he felt, was insufficient to get the support of white Americans for the cause of black Americans. This, some argued, was the job of politicians. But Robeson, the integrationist, saw a relationship between art and politics. (So it was that when a new and large, well-financed third political party became a strong possibility in America, he at once became a part of it.)

In January 1948 the time had come for Robeson to cross the footlights and become 'almost totally a political person'. Towards the end of the month he attended a meeting at the McAlpine Hotel in New York. The aim was to provide Americans with an alternative political programme, one that would follow the lines of Roosevelt's New Deal. A national 'Wallace for President' Committee was formed, to persuade the former Vice-President to run for President at the election in November. Wallace was opposed to the Truman administration's anti-Russian policy. An editor of the liberal magazine *New Republic*, he had the political clout to lead a third political party. Robeson was a member of this committee, which became the Progressive Party. By 1948 only two Blacks were in Congress. In fact, so uniquely placed was Robeson that hitherto (with the exception of the American Communist Party) no black American had been involved in formulating a political party's policies. Robeson now had an essentially political voice on behalf of his people. Domestically the Progressive Party stood for reforms, and in foreign affairs was against the Marshall Plan. And reflecting

Robeson's firm conviction, the Party believed in establishing friendly relations between the United States and the Soviet Union.

The American Labor Party, whose Chairman was Vito Marcantonio, supported the Progressive Party. On his resignation from the ALP, Marcantonio had suggested that Robeson ('labor's champion') should replace him. But Robeson made it abundantly clear he was not interested, and although he was totally committed to the Progressive Party, taking political office was not for him. Given his artistic constituency, was his involvement in the PP the extent to which he would go as an artist to indicate and effectively lead his followers in the appropriate political direction? There was, however, no denying his profound sense of social, cultural and political responsibility.

Robeson was a major asset for the progressives. Although he was one of their chief spokesman, the trend to discredit him continued as a book about him, *Paul Robeson, Citizen of the World*, was banned by the West Virginia Library Association. That same month the Transport Workers' Union for the first time in ten years withdrew its invitation to Robeson to attend its convention despite his honorary life membership. As if to counterbalance this drastic action, the International Longshoremen's and Warehousemen's Union invited Robeson to visit the Hawaiian Islands. Robeson toured these island communities with Lawrence Brown and Earl Robinson, doing some fifteen concerts, three of which were held in Honolulu. On this tour Robeson seemed to have been in high spirits. By all accounts it was an extraordinary trip. 'It showed what a lot of different people felt about Paul,' said Brown. 'As you know, Hawaii has many different race groups – Japanese, Hawaiians, Filipinos, Puerto Ricans, native Hawaiians. The thing that struck me was that each group welcomed Paul as if he were their own.' Moreover, Robeson had arrived not knowing one word of the Hawaiian language. Within twenty-four hours he learned a Hawaiian song so that the people could understand him. This was a remarkable tribute to the Hawaiian people from this unusually talented man. 'If anyone had told me this was possible I wouldn't have believed it,' said Robinson. 'But I saw Paul do it. You can imagine the effect upon the audience.'

On the tour Robeson commented on several issues. He told reporters at a press conference that he was much impressed by the islanders and felt there was a lesson in racial matters to be learned. 'It would be a tremendous impact on the United States if Hawaii is admitted as a state,' he said. 'Americans wouldn't believe the racial harmony that exists here. It could speed democracy in the United States.' Describing himself as an 'advanced New Dealer' (and now predictably uncritical of the communists), he expressed the belief that there would be no war with Russia. The whole talk about communism is absurd, he said. 'Either we get along with the communists, jump in the ocean, or blow up the whole world. Saying you can't get along with communists is like saying you can't get along with birds.' When he was shown a list of organizations in the United States branded as 'Un-American' he said he was a member of one, but also belonged to other organizations, including the staff of a Phi Beta Kappa publication and a number of Church organizations.

His concert selections during the tour were criticized. Talking quietly, he told reporters that he had sung the same selections for twelve years, ever since he had stopped making professional concert tours. It was therefore 'silly for a man to criticize the concert because of the material in it' – a somewhat subjective viewpoint. Finally he spoke about his plans to continue work on behalf of Wallace when he returned home, because Wallace was the man to continue the New Deal traditions of Roosevelt. To think of Wallace as a communist was preposterous. Robeson believed Wallace was a 'progressive capitalist'.

The Progressive Party gradually won national support from a wide cross-section of Americans, Blacks and Whites. By April, delegates representing trade unionists, student groups, ethnic organizations, businessmen and professionals met in Chicago to organize the Party officially. Wallace was introduced as leader of the Party by Robeson. After Wallace spoke, the delegates shouted, 'We want Wallace!' This call generated the kind of political excitement that had been absent from the American political scene for some time. Among those assembled at the Knickerbocker Hotel there was excitement and hope. The delegates then shouted, 'Robeson for Vice-President!' 'We want Robeson!' Suddenly all eyes were turned expectantly on Robeson. But it seemed he was not prepared for this call to political office. According to one account, 'he turned and walked off the platform. He had no intention of standing'. Although he had declined the obvious support offered, many Blacks were proud of that moment. 'I was politically naïve and didn't know anything of what was happening,' recalled a young soldier on leave, 'but I was absolutely enthralled at the sight of a giant black man on the stage, having an input. I have never forgotten that thrill.' One of the issues debated by the progressives at that historic meeting, and one which would preoccupy the American electorate and surround Robeson with controversy, was communism.

During the months that followed before the election in November Robeson campaigned enthusiastically on behalf of the Progressive Party. In May he addressed his friends at the International Fur and Leather Workers' Union Convention, of whom he was proud. Also present was the writer Howard Fast. Unaccompanied by Brown, who refused to travel by air, Robeson sang 'Water Boy' and 'Joe Hill'. He then told the convention that he had given up his professional career for over a year to visit many parts of his beloved America. He emphasized that in his travels from Pueblo through Colorado, to the cotton fields of the South and the fruit fields of California and the Midwest, he found people living 'at the edge of subsistence'. Inequality in the United States was far too great. 'I see too much poverty for us to boast,' said Robeson. He also felt that the US Government should not be allowed to support the British Empire, which supported the Smuts regime in South Africa, and pointed out to his union friends that the ranks of labour contained masses of people whose lives were controlled by a few capitalists, and that this imbalance should be redressed. He recognized this was the reality all over the world and fervently worked to change it. His father had believed that the major parties would solve all the problems, but much time had elapsed since his day. And perhaps he was ignorant of the fact that the plantation owners and industrialists had entrenched interests in these parties. He also recognized that his political involvement with the Progressive Party had brought him to a point of no return. He told his union audience that his manager was worried about bookings because he had been going around defending labour, and fighting for Wallace. In short, that his concert career was over. Then the political artist informed the convention how the concert business worked. He said that the concert society in most towns was composed of a few hundred people, thus excluding the thousands of ordinary people. In this sense 'American culture' was received by only a small minority of privileged people. In conclusion Robeson read 'The Freedom Train' to the convention.

About the same time he sought another appointment with President Truman to discuss anti-poll-tax, anti-lynching and fair employment legislation. His repeated requests, however, were turned down.

During the election campaign his uncompromising efforts won Robeson the admiration and praise of thousands of people who heard him speak up and down the country. The speeches he made received rousing approval as though he was *the* Progressive Party's presidential candidate. As a personality, Robeson had a wider mass appeal than Wallace. Evidently Robeson was good for the Party. But were his followers supporting him as an artist or for his politics? Put simply, it seemed he was the Party's major asset. But would this continue to be the case?

Already by the summer of 1948 it was clear that American democracy was on trial. Pro-Soviet Union policies and communism were seen increasingly as threatening issues. Behind Robeson's obvious popularity there were hidden forces at work that were gathering momentum with each day, to the extent that resort to the force of law was becoming necessary to forestall the Red menace.

In June Washington was abuzz with the Mundt-Nixon communist control legislative bill. The passage of such legislation would have serious and wide implications. For example, it would outlaw the Communist Party and nullify any effective government opposition. As a close friend of Robeson put it, a 'bad security risk' was anyone who read liberal literature or invited Blacks home. Government employees with liberal/progressive or communist views were seen as disloyal to the administration. Thus the Mundt-Nixon bill was expected to maintain the desired loyalty in Washington.

Against the threat of such grim prospects Robeson appeared before the United States Senate Committee which held hearings on the bill drafted by the House Un-American Activities Committee. The bill called for the registration of the Communist Party members and 'communist front' organizations. Robeson opposed this as violating the rights of American citizens.

While the HUAC deliberated over 'suspects', Howard Fast and ten Hollywood writers and directors were put to the test by being asked a number of political questions. Political beliefs were the object of the exercise. When Robeson faced his interrogators on the Senate Committee the *New York Times* reported that, asked several times whether he was a communist, Robeson's reply was that he would give an answer in due course. When Senator Ferguson again asked Robeson, 'Are you a Communist?', 'That question', Robeson replied, 'has become the very basis of the struggle for civil liberties.

Nineteen men are about to go to jail for refusing to answer it.'

After this confrontation Robeson joined a demonstration against the bill, demanding that it be replaced by a civil rights bill. 'If we can't get our liberties one way,' Robeson told demonstrators, 'we will build a new structure [through the Progressive Party] to get those liberties.' And at a Manhattan Center dinner sponsored by *Masses and Mainstream* magazine he urged all artists and writers to oppose the bill.

In July the Progressive Party held its convention in Philadelphia. Predictably, Wallace was nominated as presidential candidate, with Senator Glen H. Taylor as his running mate. Unpredictably, however, a black lawyer, Charles Howard, delivered the keynote address to the convention. For Blacks and white liberals, the appearance of Robeson and Howard on the PP's top level platforms was a sobering and welcome development. But, on this showing (for the supporters of the other parties), was it pushing social and political progress too far, too fast? Apparently, at the time, the answer from the estimated 37,000 people gathered at the convention rally to hear Wallace and Robeson was a resounding 'No'.

Robeson pledged to help the Party's ticket with all the power at his command. During his speech he attacked the cleavage between rich and poor America. He declared it was a mockery that in the world's wealthiest country the badly housed, homeless, jobless and hungry remained a major problem.

Meanwhile intense anti-communist feelings had been stirred to the extent that even President Truman was alarmed by developments. He said (at least with some recognition of the problem) that the 'menace of communism' lay essentially in those areas of American life 'where the promise of democracy remains unfulfilled'.

By the early summer it seemed Essie had moved closer to Robeson. She was engaged in a three-week campaign with Wallace, covering fifteen states. In her 'Double Talk' speech in Enfield, denying that she was a communist, she declared that as an American citizen she had no intention of leaving the country.

On his tour of the South, during the election campaign, Robeson was faced with the Ku Klux Klan. This was both a frightening experience and a reflection of the devotion that Blacks had for Robeson. In Memphis, Tennessee, for example, on the day of their meeting, the Klan mobilized in the hills. Yet the meeting was held. Some people came, but not many. The candidate and Robeson and a few others stood inside the church watching the handful trickle in. When the Klan came down in their cars towards the church hall, they were confronted by a hundred or more black men from the fields who stood in front of the church. The Klansman moved on. 'We had not called those men to defend us,' said Robeson proudly. They were not supporters of the Progressive Party, but men who opposed force and violence, because they were interested in what Robeson had to say.

Accompanied by Clark Foreman, a white Southerner and Progressive Party supporter, Robeson went to Raleigh, North Carolina. This was a significant visit for Foreman, whose ancestors were slave-owners, as well as for Robeson. 'Paul Robeson is a bigger man, a stronger man, a more talented artist and wealthier than I,' said Foreman. 'Yet by an artificial standard in our land, racism can wipe out all his accomplishments.' Robeson was touched by what Foreman said, acutely aware as he was of the history of the land in and around Raleigh, where his father and grandparents, Benjamin and Sabra, had toiled for 'Massa' Robeson. The tangible link with the past was meeting his 'own kith and kin, his cousins and their children'. His people were everywhere. Now, both men, black and white, believed progress would come in the South and elsewhere in the United States through the Progressive Party.

As the election campaign entered top gear, discontented democrats took heed of the PP's programme. Large crowds flocked to hear Wallace and Robeson. Truman, aware of the progressives' popular following, decided to adopt a more progressive domestic policy, 'almost a carbon copy of the domestic platform put forward by the Progressive Party'. After this bit of political opportunism, both the democrats and republicans launched an all-out attack on the Progressive Party. Truman even went so far as to promise the black voter a civil rights bill. This aggressive approach had the effect of confusing many voters. Inevitably 'red-baiting' against the Progressive Party began to mount alarmingly.

A few weeks before the election Wallace and Robeson appeared at a mass rally held at the Yankee Stadium in New York. After Robeson had sung 'Ol' Man River' and 'Let My People Go' the *New York Times* reported that his 'bitter tirade against oppression of the Negro brought the crowd to its feet with thunderous applause'.

During the closing stages of the election campaign the PP began to lose support as Truman gained a vital following. On election day the

American electorate favoured Truman instead of Wallace. (Consequently in 1950 Wallace severed his ties with the Progressive Party, and voiced regret for having criticized Truman on the Cold War!) But why should such a shift have taken place? The optimism of the spring was no longer there in December 1948. Earlier, during the rousing days of the campaign, Robeson told the Longshore, Shop Clerks, Walking Bosses and Gatemen and Watchmen's Caucus that he was proud to be a member of their union. Sadly many in the labour/trade-union movement had also changed their political affiliations. When, in early December 1948, the CIO Transport Workers' Union held its annual convention (which Robeson had attended regularly for several years) the new leadership, headed by Michael J. Quill, banned Robeson from attending. Robeson's faith in the workers was, and remained, fundamental. But now the foundation was being rocked; a portent of what was to come.

Perhaps it was for the best that Robeson had a concert engagement in the West Indies, a tour during which, the Caribbean sponsors had to be assured by Fred Schang, Robeson would concentrate on singing instead of politicizing. Robeson was impressed by his visit to Jamaica and Trinidad. His experience there encouraged him and, as the new year approached, he was ready to put greater effort into his relentless struggle.

In January he was in militant mood. He told a protest meeting called by the newly organized Negro Youth Builders' Institute Inc. that 'the suppression of the Negro in the United States varies only in degree in New York, New Jersey, Georgia and Alabama'; that the public must be 'aroused' to poor school conditions in Harlem and Brooklyn; and the inadequate housing, 'police brutality in the North, generally', which would include 'the railroading to the electric chair of six Negro youths in New Jersey' (the Trenton Six). And comparing what he termed 'children in cotton fields in the South, children in tobacco plantations and exploited children all over' with the 'neglected children of the North', said that conditions were 'of the same pattern – evidence of a coloured minority in a hostile white world'.

The pressure exerted on Robeson was evident for all to see, though least of all to Robeson himself. If he could not, or would not, perform professionally in his homeland, there were other places where he would do so. He decided to go to Europe, where he could continue his professional concerts. After a ten-year absence he arrived in

England in February 1949 for a concert tour. He told *Reynolds News* in an article, 'I, Too, Am American', that on his occasional trips to his home state, New Jersey, his former student friends would question what had happened to him: 'You used to be such a mild sort of chap and now you are so militant and political,' they would say. Robeson had no doubt of the value of his experiences in Britain to his political awakening and development. 'I think back and wonder how my attitude has changed since my student days,' he said. 'I realize then that I learned my militancy and politics from your Labour Movement here in Britain'.

When he had first arrived in Britain, he thought his sole job was to perform as an artist. This return visit to England put everything into international perspective. He realized that 'the fight of the Negro people in America and the fight of the oppressed everywhere was the *same* struggle'. Thus Robeson went out to sing for the Welsh miners, Glaswegian dockers and factory workers across the country.

On this return visit he felt at home in England. It was a relief to him to be able to leave his disappointments behind in the States. When he disembarked at Southampton he was greeted by dockers, who called out to him by his Christian name. 'Yes,' he said to them, 'I am part of this England.' He felt that one of his tasks while in Britain was to give the people the background to events in the United States. This had become an essential part of his ambassadorial role. In response to the accusation that he was 'un-American' and to the persecution of progressives for being more concerned with other countries than their own, Robeson argued that because no nation can live in isolation, he belonged to the America which sought peace with the Soviet Union and friendship with China. This, of course, did not preclude him from being American.

Given the changing fortunes of singers, Robeson was in the unique position of having left Britain as a star and returned as one of even greater repute. To reach the audience he wanted, he insisted on a £1 price ceiling for concert seats. The 10,000 tickets that went on sale in the morning at Belle Vue in Manchester were sold out by midday. At the Albert Hall 8,000 people turned up, and over 10,000 packed the Harringay Arena.

In the eyes of millions of people he was not the sinister communist he was made out to be in the States. Before his Manchester concert he visited a black people's club where, in a small room, he sang to a few people, and a crowd gathered outside to listen. In a speech on

'Racialism in South Africa', delivered at a protest meeting held in Friends House, London, on 25 March 1949, Robeson pointed out that while people were reminded of the 'Cold War', little attention was paid to the cold war of racial hatred and intolerance; a cold war which included the United States and the Union of South Africa among its participants. Although they differed in approach, they were in agreement on their policies of racial discrimination. Robeson defended the rights of the Indian minority in South Africa, and paid tribute to the Soviet Union which, he said, 'constantly champions the cause of the African and other oppressed peoples. Having itself abolished colonialism, which spells domination, abject poverty, degradation and death, the Soviet Union has by right assumed the leadership of the anti-imperialist forces to end the exploitation of man by man'.

The disruption of war had brought about new relationships and new perspectives. Robeson observed that the black British population had grown – a consequence of the arrival of black soldiers and voluntary workers who came to assist in defending Britain against fascism. Two groups, Africans and West Indians, were particularly strident in their demands for an end to racial discrimination in Britain and national independence in their colonial homelands. During Robeson's English tour issues such as the eleven Communist Party members who were being tried in the United States worried him. In this case, he felt that Marxism, a 'way of life' and a 'cultural philosophy' was 'on trial'.

Affairs in South Africa had always troubled Robeson. On 25 March he led a protest against the racist policies of the South African Government organized by the South African Committee of the India League (founded by Krishna Menon) in co-operation with the League of Coloured Peoples, the West African Students' Union and East African Students' Union, attended by 3,000 at Friends House, London. In addition to Menon (formerly a member of the St Pancras Council), Dr Dadoo (the South African Indian leader), the Revd Michael Scott and Julius Silverman were present. Robeson helped to raise funds for the cause of the oppressed in South Africa.

A few weeks later he travelled to Paris to attend the World Peace Congress organized by the Partisans of Peace. There he made an historic speech; one that would do irreparable damage to his popularity, political credibility and career in the United States. Among those present was W.E.B. DuBois. On 20 April, when

Robeson walked into the auditorium, the delegates rose to greet him with applause. After a brief silence he stood ready to address the Congress. In a short unprepared speech he said: 'It is unthinkable that American Negroes will go to war in behalf of those who have oppressed us for generations . . . against a country [the Soviet Union] which in one generation has raised our people to full human dignity of mankind.'

When these words reached the United States, it was as though the newspapers had been starved of headline news. The fact that they were Robeson's words made the message even more explosive and contentious. The attacks on him came quickly and ferociously. With few exceptions, his remarks were taken out of context and misinterpreted by the newspapers. The distorted headlines reflected the venom that Robeson's accurate analysis of his people's exploitation by the American establishment had generated. Although the *New York Times* quoted him correctly on this occasion, later editorials and articles showed it too had joined the chorus against Robeson. It seemed that he had committed so serious a breach with the American establishment that his words appeared as 'treason'. In Washington Robeson's words had the effect of drawing to the attention of politicians the fact that there were some 16 million Blacks in America. The *Washington Post* stated: '. . . when he [Robeson] said . . . that his views are shared by Negroes generally, he was actually betraying them in the interest of Communist tactics'. He was referred to as 'ungrateful and disloyal' by the *New York Journal-American*. Was Robeson aware of the implications of what he said in Paris? Years later he reflected that while speaking he had in mind the millions of Blacks in South America, the West Indies, the United States and Africa. The delegates were committed to the fight for peace, he said, and underlined the fact that he was definitely not speaking for the 15 million black Americans.

If the press was vitriolic, individuals also expressed their opinions with undisguised contempt. Yergan, no lover of progressive views of the Communist Party type, argued against the American Communist Party which, he said, Robeson idolized. American communists were the only Blacks ('miserable cowards', as he described them) who had achieved the 'full dignity of mankind'.

Walter White, the NAACP's executive secretary, had no doubt where he stood. 'In any conflict involving our nation,' he said, 'we will regard ourselves as Americans and meet the responsibilities imposed on all Americans.'

The comments of these two middle-class Blacks joined those of the growing number of Americans (white and black) attacking Robeson who, it was argued, did not represent the estimated 15 million Blacks in America. In fact letters and telegrams were received in the White House stating that Blacks would fight the Russians if necessary. Some Church leaders felt that Robeson's reported statement did not 'meet the approval of intelligent American Negroes'; and he was described by others as a 'Black Russian skunk' and a 'Russian-dominated, over-educated, black fool', who should be taken into 'protective custody' by the US Government.

As the controversy spread, few bothered to consider the essential point in Robeson's remarks – his unrelenting argument for *peace*, which he felt was threatened in the post-war world. He saw black Americans as still being 'colonized' in their country, a group of people who had helped to build the United States and should therefore receive their share of the nation's wealth. He denounced the US Government policy (which not for the first time he likened to Hitler's) and declared his readiness to fight for peace and liberty. This was consistent with other statements Robeson had made, but when related to the 'colonized' in the United States *vis-à-vis* the Soviet Union it was interpreted as treasonable. Robeson saw two main categories of Americans, Blacks and Whites, who were – except for the progressives and a hard core of workers – at loggerheads. The once unreservedly beloved American singer was now questioning the loyalty of Blacks to America and the platitudes of democracy and freedom, so often bandied about during the war.

As if to counteract, and/or temper the denouncement of Robeson, DuBois, who was present while Robeson was making his statement in Paris, wrote that while he was in absolute agreement with Robeson that Blacks should refrain from fighting in an 'unjust war', he did not share Robeson's view that all Blacks would not. He argued that a certain follow-the-leader attitude, the legacy of slavery, would persuade many Blacks to engage in any American enterprise 'provided the Whites will grant them equal right to do wrong'.

For Robeson, the fundamental tenet of the right of free speech on which the United States prided itself was denied. In exercising this right (and because he was an international figure) he was subjected to enormous pressures to make him feel he had done wrong. But would he seek forgiveness? If he could do this, life would be simpler.

While moves were made to keep him out of his house in Enfield, the 'nigger Robeson' had been in Stockholm to sing at a concert. On his arrival in Sweden, among the welcoming group were two Swedish communist reporters. This was hot news for the American reporters who emphasized this communist presence. Although Robeson's concert was successful, he was, according to one report, booed for singing songs about communism and revolution. Robeson said at a news conference in Oslo that he expected his political opinions and speeches would land him in gaol.

He maintained his principled stand in Copenhagen later in April and refused to sing when he learned his scheduled concerts on 27 and 29 April were sponsored by *Politiken*, a newspaper that supported the Atlantic Treaty. Ultimately another sponsor was found. Concerned that he should not be misunderstood, he explained to an interviewer in Copenhagen what his remarks about Blacks fighting against the Soviet Union really meant. His statement was directed not only towards Blacks in the United States but to millions of Africans and West Indians. He was bitterly disappointed with the reaction of the American press. He said he was authorized by the Co-ordinating Committee of Colonial Peoples in London to address the World Peace Conference in Paris, underlining the fact that his message was for peace, rather than on 'anybody going to war against anybody'.

On his return to London amidst the deepening controversy, Robeson would not be side-tracked. He was still concerned about the price of seats for his concerts. He expected working men to attend his concerts at charges of between one and two shillings. Predictably his agent – who was not in the business of charity – criticized this move. The 'workmen' concerts, which began at Gateshead, were also held in Liverpool, Manchester, Sheffield and in Clydebank town hall.

In May Robeson's tour took him to Czechoslovakia. Unfortunately, since their partnership began in 1925, Lawrence Brown, because of exhaustion, was unable to accompany Robeson. He was replaced by Bruno Raikin, a white South African (an admirer of Robeson) whom Robeson had met in London. Twenty years after his concert in Prague's Smetana Hall Robeson observed renewal work in progress following the ravages of the war. Now well attuned to the class content of his audiences, in addition to the Smetana Hall, Robeson informed the concert organizers that he would also like to sing to Prague's factory workers.

On the third of the four days he spent in Prague he was able to meet

Czech children, with whom he established an immediate rapport. This happened wherever he went. According to Lloyd L. Brown, Robeson had special feelings for the young. He never gave less than his full attention and, always a careful listener, he responded warmly to them. Brown, who had travelled around with Robeson, learned quickly that he could never interrupt a conversation Robeson was engaged in with either a teenager or child. A vast audience had assembled for his concert at the stadium. The performance on that sunny day was something more than a Robeson concert. It had an international flavour; included were colonial students then in Prague: Indians, Africans, Vietnamese, Chinese and Indonesians, among others.

On his last night in Prague Robeson gave voice to his innermost thoughts, as though he had reached another important juncture in his life. It was past 3 a.m. when he talked to Marie Seton. Convinced that peace was dependent upon Europeans, he said he had no illusions about the tough task he faced in the United States. In a rare admission, he confided that he did not know if he would live to see the struggle through. He had overcome his fear of death, but there was still much to live for. The next morning he was due to travel to Warsaw before going to Moscow, to join the people he loved. To live among the Russians for a while before he died was one of his great wishes. But even as he was expressing those heartfelt thoughts he was homesick. That night he yearned to be in the United States more than anywhere else on earth. He would go back, he said, and never leave 'as long as there is something I could do'.

Just before his concert in Prague, Robeson had a surprise: his friend Marie Seton had arrived. In Warsaw, the next stop on his tour, Robeson saw the devastation of war. He was deeply moved when he visited the Warsaw ghetto. He thought of the black peoples of the world. Here the Jews fought to the last man, woman and child for freedom, rather than live under oppression.

With the disturbing images fresh in his mind of the people's struggle in Warsaw, Robeson arrived in Moscow early in June 1949. In the twelve years since Robeson had last visited the country there had been many changes in the Soviet Union. The Muscovites, however, exuded the same warmth that Robeson had come to know so well. Robeson gave three concerts and took part in the 150th anniversary of Alexander Pushkin's birth at the Bolshoi Theatre. When he sang 'Ol' Man River' (by now it had become his theme song) at the Tchaikovsky Hall he changed the words to 'We must fight to the death for peace and freedom'. It seemed that Robeson, no longer able to ignore his growing unpopularity in the United States, was preoccupied with the furore following the Paris World Peace Congress. He sang 'Scandalize My Name', which he dedicated to the mainstream or bourgeois press.

The years of absence had not dimmed the Soviet people's memory; if anything, Robeson's Herculean struggles and artistic achievements had enhanced his reputation immeasurably. The Soviet press gave him unprecedented acclaim. A three-part series of articles on Robeson was published in the journal of communist youth in the USSR, *Komsomolskaia Pravda*. In 'First Joy' Robeson described impressions of his first visits to the Soviet Union in 1934 and 1936; in 'My Name Is Robeson' he related some episodes of his life; and in 'Ten Years of Struggle' he described the fight for peace, against war, and for a better life for the American people. 'Your country, dear readers,' he affirmed in the first article, 'is my second motherland.' Far away from his native land he was experiencing great joy and comradeship, as he had done before in Moscow. If the United States was a painful experience, surely there was a better way; one that was worth struggling for 'to the death'.

On 16 June Robeson flew into La Guardia Airport to face a cold blast from the American press and establishment, who waited ready to pounce. He was by now prepared for any eventuality; nothing would surprise him. But rather than being defensive, he was ready to take up the cudgels. Even so he was surprised to be met at the airport by uniformed policemen, a show of force that angered him. Also there to meet him was his son, Paul Jr, his fiancée, and a crowd of about sixty people (including Bessie Mitchell, sister of one of the six framed Blacks in death row at Trenton, New Jersey, as well as William Patterson and Dr Hunton).

The day 19 June was one that Robeson had looked forward to because his son, now twenty-one years old, would be married to Marilyn Paula Greenberg. This marriage between a black man and a white woman attracted undesirable attention from reporters and onlookers. At this essentially family affair, attended by Paul and Essie, reporters barged their way into the wedding, while cat-calls and boos came from members of the public. Robeson's patience and good nature were sorely tried by this ugly behaviour, and he was furious when cameramen violated the family's privacy. Unable to contain his utter disgust, Robeson underlined his earlier criticism of the press. 'I have the greatest contempt for the democratic press,' he said to the newsmen, 'and there is something within me which keeps me from breaking your cameras over your heads. . . . This marriage would not have caused any excitement in the Soviet Union.'

A few days later Robeson addressed a large audience at a protest rally in Madison Square Garden, held by the Civil Rights Congress. When he spoke in New Jersey fifty legionnaires (an ominous sign of the force to come) marched around carrying signs denouncing Robeson's appearance in the state where he was born. Such crude acts of intimidation only reinforced his resolve.

Those in authority now felt that only strong measures could make Robeson voiceless. The HUAC had again become active. In July 1949, monitoring the movements and membership of communists, black spokesmen testified before the Committee. One black witness said that Robeson dreamed of becoming a 'Black Stalin'. This was the thin end of the wedge in a concerted attack on Robeson. Jackie Robinson, the first black major league baseball player, told the Committee that Robeson's Paris statement sounded 'very silly'. Although he felt that American Blacks were stirred up long before the advent of the Communist Party and that 'they'll stay stirred up long after the party has disappeared – unless Jim Crow has disappeared by then', he told the Committee that he could not speak for 15 million people any more than any other individual could, 'but I know that I've got too much invested for my wife and child and myself in the future of this country, and I and many other Americans have too much invested in our country's welfare, for any of us to throw it away for a siren song in bass'.

In a long press conference held at the Theresa Hotel, New York, on 20 July, Robeson frustrated the persistent efforts of newsmen to get him to reply to Robinson's remarks before the HUAC. In other words, they wanted him to attack Robinson, but Robeson would have none of it. He stood for black unity, not division. He said, however, that the Committee's action by calling to Washington Robinson and other prominent Negroes 'to testify as to their loyalty is a campaign of terror and an insult to the entire Negro people'.

Amidst the steady decline of support for Robeson, there were principled Blacks who stood firm. The *Afro-American* said that Jackie Robinson had been invited to state his willingness to fight for the United States before the Committee, but that there were some

Blacks who would not fight for 'Uncle Sam'. The newspaper did not think that Robinson was a better American than Robeson. It took the view that Robinson could not 'begin to fill Paul Robeson's shoes', adding that while Robinson thought of himself, Robeson's thoughts were about millions of Blacks in the South who could not vote, who were terrorized by white racists and were denied decent education and jobs. Finally, the newspaper advised Robinson to concentrate on baseball and stay out of politics.

Unity among his people was one of Robeson's fundamental concerns. Years later, he commented on Manning Johnson's testimony before the HUAC which, among other things, alleged he was a member of the Communist Party on a 'highly confidential and secret assignment'. Robeson said that Johnson's was the only evidence that he was a Communist Party member in 1934 or 1935. However, Johnson could not substantiate his claim that he had been in a Party cell with Robeson, because Robeson was in England at the time. Such a liar had Johnson become, said Robeson, that even the witch-hunters disavowed him. The Communist Party was a legal party, he argued, and if he had wanted to join a political party he could well have picked the Communist Party. But he reiterated that he was not a member of the Communist Party.

With ample justification Robeson felt his fellow black Americans had misunderstood him. He was deeply concerned that they had failed to grasp his perspective, an international one, compared with their parochial views. Many Blacks wondered if Robeson had surrendered black American leadership to white integrationist international leadership. Although they all wanted progress for Blacks in America, sadly there was little or no communication. Politically, his was a Marxist world-view, though he was not a Marxist ideologue. At the time the Soviet Union, the only socialist country, offered the colonial liberation movements in the embryonic Third World countries the best alternative to the oppressive system under which they laboured.

If Robeson felt misunderstood, black American leaders in turn were unhappy that he had compounded their problems by adding the burden of 'red' to that of being black. They were at a loss to understand why his criticism of the United States had always to be linked to praise for the Soviet Union. Ideologically, then, Robeson's dogmatic position alienated him from these black leaders. Years later, however, Robeson's ideological stance would become the essential basis (whether or not they knew of it) for the advocates of civil rights and Black Power. Long before the horrors of Vietnam came to the foreground of the American mind, Robeson foresaw the dangers of civil war in Korea.

While the Committee's hearings continued, the NAACP announced its opposition. Literature was produced by a black undercover agent, linking Robeson with certain organizations that were later declared as 'subversive' by the Attorney-General. And although he had many Jewish friends, not all of them sympathized with his views. Rabbi Benjamin Schultz, national director of the American Jewish League versus Communism, denounced Robeson's Paris statements.

Against this background of controversy and hardening attitudes Robeson was preparing for a scheduled concert at Peekskill in August 1949. Earlier that month he had marched at the head of a picket line in front of the White House. Later, at a press conference, he challenged Truman to make good his civil rights promise and to enforce his FEPC (Federal Employment Practise Commission) order by protecting black workers from mass lay-offs and discrimination at the Bureau of Engraving and Printing. Accompanied by Charles P. Howard (keynote speaker at the Progressive Party convention) Robeson spent two afternoons in Washington, marching in a picket line that had been maintained for three weeks. He also maintained his international as well as national links by sending messages to the People's Drama Group, the Council on African Affairs and to the Youth Festival in Budapest.

Robeson was prevented from keeping his concert date at Peekskill by local agitation, culminating in a riot. In defiance of the demonstrations against him, Robeson, consistently concerned with civil rights, peace and freedom, announced that he was going to sing wherever the people wanted him to sing.

In the aftermath of Peekskill an assembly of 1,500 local residents formed the Westchester Committee for law and order. Undaunted, these Peekskill residents invited Robeson to sing, which was a brave decision. Their freedom and civil rights were at stake, they felt. Robeson agreed. The Committe had called upon 'People's Artists' to organize the concert and announced that the second concert would be held on 4 September at 2 p.m.

The venue was about half a mile from the scene of the violence.

This time several organizations (including the international Fur and Leather Workers' Union and the Bronx County American Labor Party) volunteered to defend Robeson. Solidarity was now the keyword. Just as in the play *Stevedore* when Blacks and white trade unionists fought together against a white racist mob, now in a real-life drama the stage was set for a show-down.

Predictably the concert announcement provoked counter-measures. The Verplanck Veterans planned a mass protest march outside the concert, and anti-Semitic and anti-black feelings were rampant. Encouraged by the last encounter, there were many potential protesters who were ready for blood. The county sheriff and the state police could no longer be mere onlookers. Instead, they faced the real possibility of a fight on their hands. Hundreds of law officers and state troopers were drafted in.

The Peekskill riot of 27 August had kindled enormous interest in Robeson's second concert. An estimated 20,000 people turned up to support and hear him. They also came to defend Robeson's and their own right to do so, several hundred men (Blacks and Whites) volunteering to form a Chinese wall around Robeson.

Finally, amidst jeers and screams from the anti-Robeson mob, the concert opened at 2 p.m. to the strains of music by Bach and Liszt, Verdi, Chopin and Mozart. Also appearing were Sylvia Kahn, who sang 'The Star-Spangled Banner', and a folk singer called Pete Seeger. Robeson sang 'Go Down Moses' and in 'Ol' Man River' in a voice deep, rich and proudly defiant he altered the lyrics yet again to match the mood, as he had done during the Spanish Civil War, to 'I must keep fightin''/Until I'm dyin''.

The concert was a resounding success. But for the protesters (who had prevented it a few days before) it was a failure. As the huge gathering made their way out of the concert area, they were attacked. Violence quickly escalated. Men, women and children, black and white, were hurt; and Robeson's effigy was burned far away in the Deep South. It was particularly distressing for Robeson to learn that Eugene Ballard, holder of the Croix de Guerre, the first black aviator of the First World War, was beaten by state troopers and local policemen; a good example of why Robeson was opposed to black Americans going to war in South-East Asia.

Although Mrs Roosevelt disliked everything Robeson had been saying, 'I still believe,' she said, 'that if he wants to give a concert, or speak his mind in public, no one should prevent him from doing so.'

No one who disagrees is obliged to stay or even go to hear him.'

The second Peekskill riot brought widespread protest. 'This is a tragic moment for America, as it was a tragic moment sixteen years ago for Germany and the world,' stated a letter in *The Nation* (signed by twenty-three leading Americans, including Oscar Hammerstein, Cheryl Crawford, Uta Hagen, Judy Holliday, Henry Fonda, Moss Hart and Fred Kirchway, editor of *The Nation*). But those in the press who were against Robeson, would have none of it.

6 · The Political Artist Disciplined (1949–1958)

Paris and Peekskill were behind Robeson, but the fall-out lay uppermost in the minds of the American establishment, who monitored his every move and utterance relentlessly. For Robeson a busy itinerary lay ahead. A few days after Peekskill he cancelled his visit to Mexico City to attend the Continental Congress for Peace. Essie spoke to the thousand delegates instead. By September 1949 even Robeson's 'friends' had second thoughts about him. The National Maritime Union Convention had been considering a motion recommending that his name be struck off the union's honorary membership. Support, however, came from the All-China Art and Literature Workers' Association and the All-China Association of Musicians of Liberated China, who protested against the attacks on Robeson at Peekskill.

Evidently Robeson's popularity had declined. Yet he maintained his stance, even though those in authority now felt they had licence to discipline him. They mounted a concerted attack to isolate him, in some cases by adopting a dismissive attitude. When he was called to testify as a defence witness at the trial of the eleven communist leaders, the Federal Judge Harold Medina allowed him to say only that he knew the defendants. 'May I . . .' Robeson began, but the judge interposed, 'No, Mr Robeson, I don't want to hear any statement from you. I can't find from anything in these questions that you have any knowledge of the facts that are relevant in this case.' According to Virginia Hamilton, Robeson, with his legal training, was convinced that his evidence indicating conspiracy certainly was relevant. Eight years later, in 1957, the Supreme Court would establish this fact in another case.

Robeson now started a singing and speaking tour sponsored by the Council on African Affairs; a tour that was not without considerable personal risk, since the American Legion and Veterans of Foreign Wars picketed his concerts and agitated the crowds.

While the American Legion in the Peekskill area continued to stir up anti-Semitism, free speech and assembly (constitutional guarantees) went by the board. To assert these constitutional rights Robeson decided to carry through a series of concerts and meetings stretching across the country from Pittsburgh to Los Angeles, sponsored by the CAA. The statement of the American Legion commander that Robeson was 'a personal disgrace to the nation' served to inflame the Legion in Pittsburgh, Cincinnati and Akron. The owners of halls rented for Robeson's meetings cancelled their engagements. Despite the opposition of the veterans' groups, the tour commenced in Chicago without violence, where a North Side Negro minister offered a prayer in which he said, 'Thank God for giving us Paul Robeson.'

The following day Robeson had a meeting on the South Side – the so-called Black Belt of Chicago. It took place at the Tabernacle Church. People poured in from all over the city, while thousands stood on the pavement outside. The old Negro minister, the Revd Rawls, had opened his church door to Robeson, whose name meant something to Blacks in this area of the city. Significant of how people felt about Robeson in Chicago was his reception at a baseball game in the White Sox Park where thousands greeted him and thrust out programmes for him to autograph. Newspaper reporters and photographers followed his every move in Chicago, but for the first time the Chicago press clamped down on reporting Robeson's activities.

Meanwhile every ruse was being employed in Los Angeles to intimidate the owners of Wrigley Field into cancelling Robeson's scheduled concert in September – a concert sponsored by the black newspaper *California Eagle*, which was celebrating its seventieth anniversary. The Motion Picture Alliance for the Preservation of American Ideals began a campaign by publishing advertisements 'red baiting' Robeson. Paid exhortations to stay away from the Robeson concert appeared in the movie trade papers *Variety* and *The Hollywood Reporter*. Threats were made against the life of Mrs Charlotta Bass, publisher of the *California Eagle*. The police chief called Mrs Bass and wanted to know if 150 police officers would be sufficient. She told the mayor that he need not worry about the event at Wrigley Field, because Robeson was coming to sing to his people who loved him.

Robeson won other allies – 4 million strong. When the campaign in Los Angeles was launched against him, the Negro Baptists were holding a convention in the city with 5,000 delegates who represented 4 million Blacks. The delegates registered unanimous protest over Peekskill.

Still the efforts to stop Robeson continued. The Los Angeles City Council passed a resolution to ban the concerts, but it was eventually held. According to Mrs Bass, the most enthusiastic members of the audience were the police officers. In Detroit and Cleveland, however, there was endless harassment. Robeson made one request in each city: that no Negro police should have punitive measures taken against them, no matter what happened. It was evident after he arrived in each place that the tension eased. The tour, it was argued, laid to rest the myth that Robeson's presence in a city was synonymous with a riot. None the less, the strain of Peekskill which continued in the series of meetings that followed, was great. Between June 1949 and January 1950 Robeson had visibly aged, but during these difficult months of personal trial, when after 'living at the top of the mountain' he had 'descended into the valley', his people responded magnificently wherever he went.

Every victory for free speech and assembly was met by a new attack against Robeson. On the very day of the Wrigley Field concert in Los Angeles the American Legion in Connecticut demanded that the state governor, Chester Bowles, ban Robeson from appearing publicly in the state of his legal residence. A year later his portrait as Othello was barred from exhibition in the Connecticut Senate Chamber.

Few people in the United States remained neutral towards him; they either stood for or against him. Among Negroes, certain businessmen and professionals turned against him. For them, as for their white counterparts, Robeson was a man to be marked down and hounded into submission by every known means, short of physical martyrdom, which appeared too dangerous, since nobody could gauge what percentage of the black American population would rise in wrath if Robeson were arrested or mauled: but everything short of this was to be tried in the next few years.

An economic boycott began. His records were withdrawn from all shops in the United States and thus a substantial source of his income was cut off. However, in England Robeson's voice was free, the BBC playing his records, particularly on request programmes.

In February 1950 Robeson was again in Chicago for the Progressive Party Convention. That same month saw the emergence of the communist witch-hunter, Senator Joseph McCarthy, who recognized his chance to make a name and took it, applying himself to the role with enthusiasm. He had friends and government officials aplenty to help him. McCarthy sought to purge the Government and the country of 'subversives' (communists and 'bad security risks'). His reign of terror lasted for about four years. Afraid of interrogation, many succumbed. Yet Robeson kept up his trenchant criticism of the US Government.

The media had in general treated Robeson badly. Now in March they were given the opportunity to make amends. Mrs Eleanor Roosevelt had chosen Adam Clayton Powell Jr, a New York democrat, Perry Howard, a black republican from Mississippi, and Robeson to discuss 'The Negro in American Political Life' on her National Broadcasting Television programme. Even Mrs Roosevelt – by then no supporter of Robeson – was criticized for selecting him. Protests came from other quarters, including the Vice-President of the National Broadcasting Corporation. All the while the FBI surveillance was maintained by agents who shadowed him, and his telephone was tapped.

On 25 June North Korean forces, assisted by the Chinese and backed by the Soviet Union, invaded South Korea. However, Robeson maintained his pro-communist stance. At a mass Civil Rights Congress rally in Madison Square Garden he spoke out against the United States' participation in the war, warning that unless American intervention in Korea and the rest of Asia was stopped, Africa would be next in line. He reiterated that the battleground in the Negro people's fight for freedom was in Georgia, Mississippi, Alabama, Texas, Chicago and New York.

Robeson's public criticism of his country's involvement in the war came at a time when he was preparing to begin a series of concerts in England, France, Italy, Czechoslovakia and Scandinavia. This tour, however, could not be undertaken. Robeson's remarks, either at home or abroad (especially during the Korean War) could no longer be tolerated by the American authorities. If he had once been a national asset, in their evaluation he had now become a national liability. Without further deliberation, the US Government acted. The State Department demanded that he hand over his passport. On the advice of his lawyer, he refused to do so. After all, he had not committed a crime. Should he attempt to leave the country, immigration and customs officials and the FBI were instructed to detain him. Soon after, Essie's and Paul Jr's passports were cancelled.

A statement was issued to Robeson's lawyers to the effect that Robeson's passport was cancelled in accordance with the 'discretionary powers' of the Secretary of State. Robeson demanded to see the Secretary of State, Dean Acheson. When eventually he visited the State Department he was told his passport would be reinstated on condition that he signed a statement that he would not make any speeches, but just sing, when he was abroad. Robeson refused to sign.

The cancellation of Robeson's passport was now public knowledge. It marked the beginning of a period of harassment that would last for almost a decade. It also saw a massive swing of public reaction against him, as McCarthyism instilled fear across the country. Robeson was treated as a non-person. Subsequent events were part of a process to expel Robeson from the American public consciousness. Records and books by and about him were removed from record shops and libraries. His home in Enfield was questioned by local residents (soon afterwards the house was put up for sale), and there were many at Rutgers University who called for his name to be deleted from the college records and demanded the return of his academic and honorary degrees. His name was left out of the *American Sports Annual*.

As the harassment intensified (rented halls, with few exceptions, remained closed to him), Robeson turned to journalism to communicate views he would otherwise have expressed in person. In November 1950 the first column of his 'Here's My Story' appeared in the monthly newspaper *Freedom*. The paper was published in Harlem, with Robeson's column appearing in most issues until August 1955. In December he brought a lawsuit in an attempt to regain his passport, the denial of which he considered was a blatant denial of his rights and privileges. Early the following year the suit was dismissed. Early in 1951 Walter White attacked Robeson in an article entitled 'The Strange Case of Paul Robeson'. While White appreciated Robeson's sacrifice in terms of time, money and popularity, to unveil the racial and economic evils in the United States, he was puzzled by Robeson's inability to see through the opportunism of the Soviet Union's domestic and foreign policy. It was an indication to white democrats in the United States and Europe of the extent to which Blacks could be driven in frustration and despair. Fortunately for white Americans, there were few Robesons. Finally, White pointed out that, unlike the vast majority of Blacks who saw the Soviet Union's and the United States' faults and decided to fight for freedom in an imperfect democracy, Robeson chose to adhere strictly to a totalitarian philosophy.

In April the United States District Court for the District of Columbia ruled against Robeson by insisting it had no power to act in his case, but also denied a government motion that he be compelled to turn in his cancelled passport. (In the summer Robeson's son's application for a passport to attend the 1951 Youth Festival in Berlin was turned down.)

Journalism was one way for Robeson to alleviate the physical constraints placed upon him. Between January and April, in his *Freedom* column, he wrote on several themes, including emancipation, Negro history, a tribute to DuBois and the power of the American people. Sustained by his family and friends, he maintained a punishing schedule of meetings. Between the end of June and the beginning of July, speaking at the American People's Congress for Peace before 7,000 people in Chicago, he again criticized the United States' action in Korea. By mid-August he continued the fight to regain his passport by appealing against the April dismissal of his passport suit. In November he made two major addresses: first he opened a session of the Conference for Equal Rights for Negroes in the Arts, Sciences and Professions, held in New York, and ten days later, with the Soviet ambassador, Alexander S. Panyushkin, and Corliss Lamont, he addressed the World Peace Rally sponsored by the National Council of American-Soviet Friendship in New York City.

By about mid-December Robeson headed a New York delegation which presented a petition to the United Nations by the Civil Rights Congress charging genocide against Negroes of the United States on the grounds that '15 million black Americans are mostly subjected to conditions making for premature death, poverty and disease'. Robeson also urged unity for peace, pleading for a cease-fire in Korea.

Even though the Robeson family were now virtual prisoners in the United States, there were many requests for Robeson to sing abroad. Invitations came from England, Israel, Canada and Holland. Early in 1952, when Robeson attempted to cross the United States border to Canada, where he was invited to speak at a meeting of the Mine, Mill and Smelter Workers' Union in Vancouver, BC, he was advised by a State Department representative that, if he left the United States, he would be liable to five years' imprisonment and a $10,000 fine. Instead, Robeson established communication with his intended audience by speaking and singing to them by telephone. Some 2,000 Vancouver citizens heard Robeson sing and speak to an open session of the Mine-Mill national conference in the Denman Auditorium, and such was Robeson's magnetism that although he was not there in person, at the end of his speech the entire assembly rose and gave him a thunderous ovation. After singing 'Joe Hill' Robeson pointed out that refusal to allow him across the border was an act of the American administration, not an act of the American people. He spoke about labour's struggles, the struggles of colonial peoples for freedom and the struggles for world peace. In conclusion, he reiterated the lesson he had learned as a little boy from his father: 'Stand firm, son, stand firm to your principles!' He was ready to adhere to his father's words 'as long as there's breath in my body'.

At this time, during the early fifties, Americans were permitted to enter Canada without passports. Ironically, when the US Government had finally removed the ban on his going to Canada, Robeson was refused admittance by the Canadian authorities. But despite his inability to travel, Robeson remained active during the year. Between April and June he undertook a birthday tour to raise $50,000 to aid the National Negro Labor Council, the Council on African Affairs and *Freedom*. In May he received the support of Senior Bishop William J. Walls of the AME Zion Church at the 34th quadrennial conference for the return of his passport; and sang to an estimated 40,000 people at Peace Arch Park on the US-Canadian border. Later he became Vice-Chairman of the newly created Peace Liaison Committee for Asian and Pacific Peace chaired by Madam Sun Yat-sen. And in November civic and 'patriotic' groups protested in Hartford, Connecticut, against his concerts scheduled as part of the People's Party presentation at a public school.

Robeson battled on courageously as his government and others took note. In December he was awarded the Stalin Peace Prize, being hailed as 'the standard-bearer of the oppressed Negro people'. Unable to obtain a passport from the State Department, he could not go to Moscow to accept the prize. Instead, at a gathering of 300 persons in New York a $25,000 cash award which goes with the prize was presented to Robeson by Howard Fast who, at that time, described the prize as the highest that 'the human race can bestow on any one of its members'. The initial claim of the US Government that the prize should be taxed for 'services rendered' to the Soviet Union was that Robeson would not have to pay income tax. The Internal Revenue Service had claimed $9,655 of the award, but Robeson successfully argued that no tax was due, since he had performed no services for the Soviet Union and had made no effort to win the prize. Thus the Soviet award fell in the same tax-exempt category as the Nobel and Pulitzer Prizes.

With recording companies refusing to issue his records or record new ones, and all the concert halls, theatres and so forth closed to him, Robeson, who had been listed among the top ten highest paid concert artists of 1941, saw his income dwindle from over $100,000 in 1947 to about $6,000 in 1952. Moreover, the prospects looked gloomier when in December a concert scheduled in Chicago was called off because mortgagers of the Church where it was to be held threatened that, if Robeson sang, they would demand immediate payment or foreclose. Some Blacks holding federal jobs were even threatened with dismissal if they attended the concert.

Under the constant gaze of the FBI Robeson adapted to a more itinerant way of life, staying intermittently with Essie, his brother Ben and various friends as well as in his own apartment. Against this background of claustrophobic suspicion and harassment in the land of the free, a few young black artists, Sidney Poitier, Harry Belafonte, Ossie Davis, Julian Mayfield and Leon Bibb, voluntarily accompanied their path-breaking hero whom they loved and admired, because he was so hated by Whites in America. Robeson did not shun the protection they offered. 'It was a question of choosing sides,' said Mayfield, 'and we chose Robeson.' Poitier recalled that although Robeson sometimes laughed heartily, much of the time there was an air of sadness about him. 'He was angry because I think he did not understand how he could be the golden boy all these years and then they turned on him,' said the black superstar. Evidently the years of exile had already begun to take their toll. There was clearly more sadness in Robeson now than happiness. His extraordinary and seemingly invincible creative energy was now under-used and faced the real risk of dereliction. It was, as Louise Patterson put it, 'a terrible period'. His brother Ben provided good company when Robeson was at the parish house. Often the solitary singer would sit in a small room playing his records. He knew he would sing again, but was allowed to do so only in the parks, schools, colleges and, of course, in the churches where his people welcomed him and where he first heard the spirituals and learned to sing.

Early in 1953 the for and against Robeson pattern of events continued. In his recent book *First Book of Negroes: A Child's History of the Negro* Langston Hughes had not mentioned either Robeson or DuBois. This was counterbalanced later on by an award for 'selfless service to Africa' from the National Church of Nigeria, which named Robeson a 'Champion of Freedom'. Commenting on the Stalin Peace Prize, Robeson made it clear why the Soviet Union was important to him and his people. The Negro people today, he stated, were interested in Africa and Asia and closely followed the liberation struggles in these lands.

Robeson realized his freedom was relative. In February he joined six others in an appeal to the parole board for the freedom of Ben Davis, the black communist imprisoned under the Smith Act, and he sang and spoke to 6,000 people in Detroit at the Sacred Cross Baptist Church under the sponsorship of Freedom Associates. He could not forget – and indeed he informed those who did not know and reminded those who did – that his discovery of Africa in London profoundly influenced his life. Robeson also issued a statement urging protest against the imprisonment of black leaders in Kenya, and again urged support for the gaoled leaders in the United States and Africa and freedom struggles in Kenya and South Africa.

Robeson saw no cause for criticism of either Stalin or the Soviet Union. The following month Robeson sang where he was welcomed, at a religious concert at the Calvary Baptist Church in Detroit, sponsored by Mrs Vera Smith, Chairman of the Church's Evangelistic Commission; and began a second nation-wide concert tour with an appearance at the Greater St Peter's Baptist Church in Detroit. The tour, sponsored by Freedom Associates, spanned five months and took Robeson to the West and Deep South. Thereafter he sang in Washington Park before a crowd of 25,000.

During the latter part of 1953 Robeson's concern over the policy and practice of racial discrimination and oppression in South Africa was spotlighted. In August, referring to the US Government's reluctance to let him travel abroad, in a speech at the Peace Bridge Arch, he referred again to the deep feelings he had for the community of his youth.

Although Robeson's legal costs had risen and his earnings had declined alarmingly, he again applied for his passport so that he could fulfil engagements in several European countries. His request was rejected. The pressure on him was mounting steadily. Towards the end of 1953, after several months of close government surveillance, the Robesons sold their house in Enfield, Connecticut. Not only were they unhappy living in that state but Robeson's income was insufficient to meet his expenses.

The fact that Robeson was forbidden from travelling outside the States was receiving increasing attention abroad. In June 1954 the All-India Peace Council circulated a plea for the return of his passport, and another application he made later in the year to regain it so that he could attend the Soviet Congress of Writers Conference in Moscow was turned down. He challenged the State Department's right to deny him his passport on the grounds that he was thus deprived of his constitutional rights of freedom of speech, thought and assembly, and freedom to earn a living guaranteed by the First and Fifth Amendments of the United States Constitution. In his struggle Robeson also received the support of Charlie Chaplin. On the day when Chaplin's acceptance of the communist 'peace' prize was announced, a cablegram from Chaplin was read to a mammoth audience in New York to honour Robeson. The purpose of the affair, as the Communist Party explained, was 'to launch the campaign for his right as an artist to travel abroad'. Such pro-communist support for Robeson hardened anti-communist feelings in America.

During 1954 Robeson did much writing and speaking on the issues that troubled him, such as possible American involvement in South-East Asia. And time and again he urged his friends in the labour movement to fight on for an expansion of American democracy.

In 1954 the Korean War and McCarthyism raged on. That year, however, was marked by the official end of the US Communist Party and the Supreme Court decision on *Brown vs Board of Education* which, according to Dorothy Butler Gilliam, 'changed the political alignment of many Negro leftists. The victory catapulted the NAACP to new heights and pushed the Supreme Court into a new social revolutionary role'. Consequently many Blacks left the party (or what was left of it) and the last issue of *Freedom* published was for the July-August period. With the demise of the CP black intellectuals came forward to criticize those with communist views. Harold Cruse, for instance, could not accept Robeson's 'middle-class left-wing ethos' which idealized 'Negro workers' and considered that Robeson had failed to get his *Freedom* message across to the masses in Harlem. Robeson's black nationalist middle-class critics had begun to emerge with some credibility during these years of persecution.

Nevertheless, Robeson as always took great pride in his work for the Council on African Affairs. Although, as Dorothy Gilliam argued, it was 'barely known' beyond the East Coast and was 'never a mass-based group' during the 1930s and 1940s, the Council was 'a pioneer in bringing the question of Africa, and the fight against colonialism to the consciousness of people in America'. As if to add insult to injury in mid-1955, the Council's Executive Board was forced because of 'government harassment' to discontinue its work. Thus Robeson's sadness was compounded as the channels through which he could express himself dwindled. His sense of isolation deepened, but he was resolute in his attempt to travel again and fulfil his mission in song. This was a sad year for Robeson, yet he remained a shining example of fortitude. His son Paul Jr, now in his late twenties, wrote of his father that the most wonderful thing he had learned about him was that he belonged to millions of people throughout the world. He was proud that his father never wavered from his principles.

With the news that a main street in a new state farm settlement in the Soviet Union had been named after him, Robeson prepared to sing and speak again. Earlier, in March 1955, he gave two sell-out concerts in the auditorium of the First Unitarian Church in Los Angeles. He also sang and spoke at Swarthmore College, Pennsylvania, under the sponsorship of the Forum of Free Speech. This was one of the few occasions since he had been blacklisted that he performed to a mixed audience. He sang sixteen songs, ranging from a chorale to Bach's 'Christ lag in Todesbanden' to a Warsaw ghetto freedom song. Accompanied on the piano by Alan Booth he sang in English, German, Russian, Yiddish, Chinese, Persian and an African language. The high point of the evening, according to one reporter, was the reading of the closing speech from *Othello*. Song was mixed with serious comment; his concert performances were no longer just entertainment.

In May Robeson was offered the role of Othello by Sergei Yutkevich, director of the Mosfilm Studio of the Soviet Union, in either English or Russian. Robeson accepted the offer and applied once again for a passport from the State Department.

By July 1955 the State Department had rescinded the special order restricting Robeson's right to travel outside the continental limits of the United States. The order, in effect since 1952, had prevented him from travelling to Canada, Mexico, the West Indies, Hawaii, Jamaica, Trinidad and British Guiana, places where in general no passport was required. This was not an indication of a change of heart within the State Department. Rather, the Department decided to resist the attempt by Robeson to regain a passport, arguing that he had not exhausted the administrative means of doing so. More bluntly, the Federal Judge Burmita S. Matthews refused to order the State Department to grant a passport to Robeson. After listening to arguments by Robeson's lawyer, Leonard B. Boudin, and the US Attorney, Leo A. Rover, the Department ruled that before his application could be considered, Robeson would have to file a non-communist affidavit. Of course Robeson refused.

Meanwhile, he received growing support, particularly from abroad, and his friends renewed their pledge of support for him. In addition to that of such newspapers as the *Los Angeles Herald-Dispatch*, *San Diego Lighthouse* and *Pittsburgh Courier*, British support was much in evidence. Delegates at the TUC meeting at Southport appealed to President Eisenhower to allow Robeson a passport to visit Britain. And Cedric Belfrage wrote: 'The British workers and people are anxious again to hear this great son of America.' These words concluded a cable from Stockport, England, to the White House in September. The cable was a plea to Eisenhower for the release of Robeson from behind the 'Cadillac Curtain' in the spirit of the President's post-Geneva suggestion that 'all curtains should begin to come down'. Belfrage warned that this was a sample of the windy weather in Britain which threatened to reach gale force if Robeson's passport was not returned soon. The cable was signed by almost 300 people at the annual TUC meeting, 249 of whom were delegates. Five of the signatories were MPs, including the secretaries of the Weavers and Chemical Workers' Union, Ernest Thornton and

Robert Edmunds. Five were TUC General Council members.

Among these British workers the fight to liberate Robeson took on a new emphasis, as the central symbolic expression of their concern over American 'thought-control'. Within a few weeks, three union bodies – the Belfast Trades and Labour Council and the Scottish and South Wales branches of the Miners – renewed invitations to Robeson to come and sing for them. They all considered him not merely a 'great son of America' but a towering man whom workers everywhere were proud to call comrade. Scottish Labour MPs and trade unionists, according to *The Times*, were among those sponsoring a petition to be presented to the US Government through its Glasgow consulate for the restoration of Robeson's passport. The petition was addressed to President Eisenhower.

Earlier, in February 1955, three alleged communist front organizations were charged with deception and for the collection and spending of $3\frac{1}{2}$ million in the previous twelve years. These organizations were the American Committee for the Protection of the Foreign Born, the Joint Anti-Fascist Refugee Committee and the Civil Rights Congress. According to the *New York Times*, Robeson was national director of the Civil Rights Congress and testified on its behalf. He stated that he had no idea of how much money the Congress had raised and told the Court: 'I sing for Hadassah, and the Sons of Israel and any number of worthwhile causes and no one asks me how much money they raised.'

Within Robeson's beloved America the tide was slowly turning in his favour. There was evidence of growing public sympathy for his constitutional right to travel. According to Ellen Keeler in the *Daily Worker*, Robeson held concerts in Oakland, San Francisco, San Diego and Berkeley, California. He spoke and sang to trade unions, churches, fraternal organizations, women's groups and youth groups. He told the different groups that he spoke for peace, equality for Blacks and an end to colonialism, the same things that were called for by leaders of the 'dark races' who had met at the Asian-African Conference in Bandung. He identified these reasons as the basis for the warmth and friendliness with which his people greeted him.

In January 1956 the British-based Committee to Restore Paul Robeson's Passport issued a brochure, *Let Paul Robeson Sing Again*. Robeson wrote to Mr Loesser, representing the Committee, stating how pleased and grateful he was to receive their support and to hear of their plans for a mass meeting in Manchester in support of his right to travel to practise his profession. He also expressed 'Heartfelt greetings' to his 'dear friends' in Manchester in a recorded message to a 'Let Paul Robeson Sing' meeting at the Lesser Free Trade Hall, Manchester. He commented on the richness of the folk culture of Lancashire which had given England and the world the artistry of Gracie Fields and many others.

The American authorities were still determined to get Robeson to admit his membership of the Communist Party, so that the tags of 'treason', 'traitor' and 'un-American' could stick. Such an attempt was repeated on 12 June when Robeson was again brought before the House Un-American Activities Committee. The hearing, presided over by Francis E. Walter as Chairman, was also attended by Gordon H. Scherer (Ohio), Richard Arens and Bernard W. Kearney, among others. Robeson's counsel was Milton H. Friedman. It was due to begin at 10 a.m. in Washington, DC, on the 'vital issue of the use of American passports as travel documents in furtherance of the objectives of the Communist conspiracy'. Robeson arrived early, an indication of the seriousness with which he approached the matter. Early in the proceedings there were signs of deep tension. The dialogue which followed, reflected the intense feelings that had accumulated over many years. When Arens asked Robeson – the first witness to be called – if he was appearing in response to a subpoena that was served upon him by the HUAC, Robeson responded: 'Just a minute. Do I have the privilege of asking whom I am addressing and who is addressing me?' This exchange between Robeson and Arens and the Chairman followed:

ARENS: Are you a member of the Communist Party?

ROBESON: Would you like to come to the ballot-box when I vote and take out the ballot and see?

ARENS: Mr. Chairman, I respectfully suggest that the witness be ordered and directed to answer that question.

CHAIRMAN: You are directed to answer the question.

ROBESON: I stand on the Fifth Amendment . . .

ARENS: Do you mean you invoke the Fifth Amendment?

ROBESON: I invoke the Fifth Amendment.

ARENS: Do you honestly apprehend that if you told this committee truthfully whether or not you are presently . . .

ROBESON: I have no desire to consider anything. I invoke the Fifth Amendment and it is none of your business what I would like to do . . .

CHAIRMAN: You are directed to answer that question.

ROBESON: I invoke the Fifth Amendment and so I am not answering. I am answering it, am I not?

ARENS: I respectfully suggest the witness be ordered and directed to answer the question as to whether or not he honestly apprehends that if he gives us a truthful answer to this last principal question, he would be supplying information which might be used against him in a criminal proceeding.

CHAIRMAN: You are directed to answer that question, Mr. Robeson.

ROBESON: Gentlemen, in the first place, wherever I have been in the world and I have been in many places, Scandinavia, England and many places, the first to die in the struggle against fascism were the Communists and I laid many wreaths upon graves of Communists. It is not criminal and the Fifth Amendment has nothing to do with criminality. The Chief Justice of the Supreme Court, Warren, has been very clear on that in many speeches that the Fifth Amendment does not have anything to do with the inference of criminality. I invoke the Fifth Amendment.

ARENS: I respectfully suggest, Mr. Chairman, that the witness be ordered and directed to answer this last outstanding question.

CHAIRMAN: He has been directed to answer and he has invoked the Fifth Amendment and refused to answer . . .

ROBESON: I invoke the Fifth Amendment. . . .

Robeson was then asked if he had ever been known under the name of 'John Thomas' or if he had known Nathan Gregory Silvermaster. In response to the former question he invoked the Fifth Amendment, and to the latter he replied 'No', again invoking the Fifth Amendment. The hearing continued with Robeson's being subjected to questions, *inter alia*, about Max Yergan, communism, the Council on African Affairs, his Paris statements, trips to the Soviet Union, the schooling of his son, Stalin and finally on his friend Ben Davis. Before being questioned on Davis, Robeson unexpectedly told Arens: '. . . I sent a message to the Bandung Conference and so forth. That is why I am here. This is the basis and I am not being tried for whether I am a Communist, I am being tried for the rights of my people who are still second-class citizens in the United States of America.' The following dialogue brought the hearing to an unexpected end:

ARENS: . . . Now I would invite your attention, if you please, to the *Daily Worker* of June 29, 1949, with reference to a get-together with you and Ben Davis. Do you know Ben Davis?

ROBESON: One of my dearest friends, one of the finest Americans you can imagine, born of a fine family, who went to Amherst and was a great man.

CHAIRMAN: The answer is 'Yes'?

ROBESON: And a very great friend and nothing could make me prouder than to know him.

CHAIRMAN: That answers the question.

ARENS: Did I understand you to laud his patriotism?

ROBESON: I say that he is as patriotic an American as there can be, and you gentlemen belong with the Alien and Sedition Acts, and you are the non-patriots, and you are the un-Americans and you ought to be ashamed of yourselves.

CHAIRMAN: Just a minute, the hearing is now adjourned.

ROBESON: I should think it would be.

CHAIRMAN: I have endured all of this that I can.

ROBESON: Can I read my statement?

CHAIRMAN: No, you cannot read it. The meeting is adjourned.

ROBESON: I think it should be and you should adjourn this forever, that is what I would say.

CHAIRMAN: We will convene at two o'clock this afternoon.

FRIEDMAN: Will the statement be accepted for the record without being read?

CHAIRMAN: No, it will not.

Thus the hearing was adjourned at 11 a.m. and a recess was taken until 2 p.m. that same day. In part, Robeson's statement, which he was not allowed to read or submit as a record, was as follows:

It is a sad and bitter commentary on the state of civil liberties in America that the very forces of reaction, typified by Representative Francis Walter and his Senate counterparts, who have denied me access to the lecture podium, the concert hall, the opera house, and the dramatic stage, now hale me before a committee of inquisition in order to hear what I have to say. It is obvious that those who are trying to gag me here and abroad will scarcely grant me the freedom to express myself fully in a hearing controlled by them. . . . My fight for a passport is a struggle for freedom –

freedom to travel, freedom to earn a livelihood, freedom to speak, freedom to express myself artistically and culturally. . . . My travels abroad to sing and act and speak cannot possibly harm the American people. . . . By continuing the struggle at home and abroad for peace and friendship with all the world's people, for an end to colonialism, for full citizenship for Negro Americans, for a world in which art and culture may abound, I intend to continue to win friends for the best in American life.

Moreover, Robeson told the press what he thought of the hearing:

I am not in any conspiracy. It should be plain to everybody and especially to Negroes that, if the Government had evidence to back up that charge, they would have tried to put me *under* their jail. . . . They have no such evidence. . . . I have made it a matter of principle to refuse to comply with any demand that infringes upon the constitutional rights of all Americans.

Repeated requests for his passport and repeated rejections from the US Government did not discourage Robeson. In fact these setbacks spurred him on to even greater efforts. In September 1956 he requested the intervention of the Supreme Court in his passport case. Although his appeal was rejected, his appearance before the HUAC was widely reported, varying in tone and emphasis. The *Washington Daily News* reported that the Committee 'voted unanimously to cite Robeson for contempt of Congress'; the *New York Times* saw the contempt of Congress action as 'the upshot of a shouting, table-thumping and gavel-banging hearing at the Capitol'. Robeson received support from the black newspapers *California Voice*, the *Pittsburgh Courier* and the *San Francisco Sun-Reporter*, which commented on his stand before HUAC. The *Sun-Reporter* declared that in the eyes of most Blacks Robeson held a special position in the United States and in the world. As the conscience of the United States in the field of 'color relations' he was feared and hated by Whites. Black workers and black intellectuals, however, idolized him because he addressed the issue of black/white relations in a manner that attracted international interest.

More support for Robeson's passport campaign came from Britain's musicians. Distinguished composers and musicians wrote to President Eisenhower asking him to make valid Robeson's passport.

They said in a letter that they were admirers of Robeson's vocal artistry and that no artificial barrier should be placed in such a way that it might adversely affect the cultural exchange between peoples of different nations. As participants of British culture, they were confident that the majority of British people were eager to hear Robeson sing again. In the United States even those who disagreed with Robeson's views were none the less anxious that he should be able to exercise his American right to state them.

Earlier in the year (1956), according to the *New York Times*, Robeson was ready to sing after recovering from surgery. He had undergone an abdominal operation the previous October. During this relatively inactive period he announced that he was returning to 'public activity'. Of course, once the matter of his passport was resolved, he hoped to resume his artistic career. As it was, many offers for concert, stage and film engagements could not be undertaken by him. At this stage his passport case was before the United States Court of Appeals.

At last, in mid-February, a packed audience in the Massey Hall, Toronto, heard once again the golden voice of Robeson, in person. Permission to travel to Canada was an important step forward for Robeson. In Toronto he received rapturous ovations. His concert included songs of love and struggle; of peace and of freedom; of life and death and the spirituals of his people. While in Toronto Robeson also gave a fifteen-minute broadcast and appeared on CBC television.

But this breathing-space was soon cut off. A few weeks later, in April, Robeson was banned from entering Canada. Another act of maliciousness against Robeson came in November when his name was omitted from the 1956 edition of the College Football and All-American list of players on the 1918 Walter Camp All-American team. It was a year not only of hope and disappointment but of irony. *Sanders of the River*, one of Robeson's most regrettable films, reported to have had only indifferent success in the United States, was awarded the annual gold medal presented by the Institute of Amateur Cinematographers for the most significant picture of 1935. Korda had at last received recognition from the British, whom he admired, by receiving the most coveted British trophy for producers.

While the Soviet Union called on the US Government to let Robeson out of the country, it was Robeson's British friends who were at the forefront of the campaign to regain his passport. At the annual general meeting of the British Actors' Equity Association a resolution was carried congratulating the Council on its decision to support the Robeson campaign in Britain, and urging 'representations in whatever quarters may have influence in allowing him to perform in this country'. In a letter to *The Times* the actress Flora Robson wrote to say that while she had no sympathy for Robeson's politics, she would consider it a tragedy if he were not able to appear in London again as Othello. A few days later Professor J. Dover Wilson wrote to *The Times* urging Washington 'in the name of Shakespeare' to let 'that great African gentleman with the golden voice' come to Britain to sing and 'above all interpret for us once again the heroic Negro who is Shakespeare's noblest tragic figure'. Professor Gilbert Murray, Basil Spence, Father Trevor Huddleston, Sir Compton Mackenzie, Augustus John, Sir Arthur Bryant and Benjamin Britten, Sir Herbert Read, Kingsley Amis, Lord Baldwin and dozens of other prominent Britons expressed warm support for the campaign to 'Let Robeson Sing'. None of these people inquired into the political beliefs of Robeson, even though for many years it had been taken for granted by most people around the world that Robeson was a communist or, as the State Department put it, 'under the direction, domination and control' of the communist movement.

Referring to his testimony in 1946 before the Tenney Committee in California, where he had declared under oath that he was not a communist, Robeson said that because he had spoken the truth, he was not tried for perjury nor was he gaoled. Johnson's unsubstantial evidence was all they had. He explained that he had refused to answer the question of the HUAC in 1947 as to whether or not he was a communist because by then several Hollywood writers were incarcerated and the onrush of anti-communist hysteria was so fierce that answering the question would have added fuel to the fire. Thus Robeson, as a matter of principle, invoked his constitutional rights, stating that his political beliefs were his personal concern and nothing to do with anybody else. He left no doubt where he stood. He reiterated his position as a left-winger with a belief in socialism. This did not mean he favoured a Russian take-over of the United States. Revolution was not the only means through which socialism could be achieved. And to the charge that the Russians 'brainwashed' him and filled him with ideas other than his own, he laughingly reasserted what he had said on many earlier occasions to his friends – that he formed his viewpoint between 1928 and 1940, not in Russia but in

London. When he first arrived in the Soviet Union it was as an artist, not as a politician. The fact that British labour struggles had shaped his political philosophy explains why he identified with the black working class in the United States.

At this stage in his passport campaign the music of Robeson was again reaching large numbers of people who had gradually come to his aid. This time, however, there was tacit acceptance of him both as artist and the man whose political views, not his music, had brought him imprisonment worse than gaol. By August 1957 Robeson had attracted an estimated audience of 10,000 people on the West Coast of the United States. He appeared five times in California, singing in Los Angeles and San Francisco.

But for many among the black intelligentsia the question posed at the time was: Has Robeson betrayed the Negro? Part of his problem *vis-à-vis* the American public and Blacks in particular was his hesitancy to criticize the Soviet Union even when such criticism was valid, which irritated and angered black Americans. It had become painfully clear to many that Robeson's principled views were inflexible, deeply rooted, provoking other Blacks to assess him, to put him in perspective.

At about this time Robeson was in collaboration with Lloyd L. Brown on Robeson's autobiographical book, *Here I Stand*. Its publication in the United States in 1958 was something of a non-event, so far as the white press was concerned. However, it received critical acclaim from the black press and several foreign newspapers. The *Baltimore Afro-American* serialized parts of it, while the NAACP's *Crisis* found it 'disorderly and confusing'. Although this magazine did not regard Robeson as a Negro leader, it agreed that he should be free to travel abroad.

Already by the fall of 1957 there was a change of mood in the United States. Although Robeson's views and militancy had not changed, times had; the American people were growing up. The sacrifices Robeson had made thus far to highlight the evident injustice existing in his country and elsewhere were undisputed. Now, more than ever, his music reflected the wails and woes of an oppressed people. Almost as though to mark another year in the relentless campaign, the Welsh miners invited Robeson to be their honoured guest at the 1957 Eisteddfod. He could not of course attend the gathering but he made his presence felt via transatlantic telephone between New York and Porthcawl in Wales.

For twenty years Robeson had been waging a fight for peace, equality and freedom. Now there had emerged in the United States other Blacks who were also passionately committed to act upon their beliefs. In 1955 and 1956 in Montgomery, Alabama, an important new leader of black people, Dr Martin Luther King Jr, forged a civil rights movement, to deal specifically with the American problem. He believed in non-violence as a tactic and a philosophy of life. King became the most articulate black leader when the pro-segregationists were convinced that racial equality was a communist idea and that those who asked for it were subversive.

Meanwhile more black Americans began to question the validity of the Government's denial of Robeson's passport. Their support for Robeson was met with an almost equal resolve by the State Department to maintain the ban on his right to travel. Ellsworth Bunker, the US ambassador in New Delhi, informed the State Department that the Prime Minister's (Nehru's) daughter, Indira, was organizing a national committee to sponsor a 'Paul Robeson Day' in the Indian capital. The State Department made a frantic effort to halt plans to celebrate Robeson's sixtieth birthday in India. According to the *New York Times*, Nehru and his daughter were giving warm support to a nation-wide campaign to honour the American singer. In a letter to the All-India Committee organizing the celebration, the Prime Minister wrote: 'This is an occasion which deserves celebration not only because he has represented and suffered for a cause which should be clear to all of us – the cause of human dignity. Celebration of his birthday is something more than a tribute to a great individual. It is also a tribute to that cause for which he has stood and suffered.'

Interest in and support for Robeson's cause were now being reflected in the sales of his book. It was reported that the first edition of 10,000 copies of *Here I Stand* was sold out six weeks after publication and that a new edition of 25,000 copies would soon be issued. Although this new edition was to be sold at less than the price of the first, in many cities (Cleveland, Ohio; Washington, Miami and Atlanta) bookstores blacklisted the book.

In the build-up to Robeson's sixtieth birthday an estimated twenty-seven countries were planning to celebrate it. In Mexico City twenty top figures in music, art, dance, movie, trade-union and farm organizations were sponsoring a concert; in Aleppo, Syria, a committee of lawyers and teachers was headed by an Economic Ministry official; in Peking, a joint group of literary, art, peace, music and cultural relations committees met. Throughout Hungary and Bulgaria concerts were planned. And in London distinguished sponsors of the Robeson Committee were throwing a big birthday party to launch the campaign on what it hoped would be the 'final lap'. Did Robeson's supporters at last sense victory? The British publisher Dennis Dobson announced the forthcoming appearance of a new Robeson biography by Marie Seton, with an introduction by the eminent historian, Sir Arthur Bryant. Robeson sent a message to the Chinese people saying, 'one day I hope to greet you on Chinese soil'. In fact, he never visited China. He thanked the Chinese people for celebrating his sixtieth birthday, and expressed thanks to their brave leaders and to all the Chinese people for their socialist contribution and their defence of peace. In his 'Letter' from Peking, the journalist Sidney Shapiro wrote in *The Worker* that Robeson's birthday was celebrated in China as an event of major international significance. For two days preceding his birthday and on the day itself the national radio network played recordings of his songs.

In May, although Robeson had been triumphant in his coast-to-coast appearances, his scheduled appearance on the ABC-TV Chicago Station WBKB was cancelled. The vice-president of the station was quoted as saying, 'Robeson is a free citizen. Let him hire a hall if he wants to make a speech. But I'll have no part of it.' Yet another concert hall was closed to him. The superintendent of the Soldiers' and Sailors' Memorial Hall said that Robeson's concert (scheduled for April) was cancelled because it would not \be consistent 'with the memorial character of the building'. The closure of this hall to Robeson led to the opening of two black churches (the Central Baptist Church, Wesley Center AME Zion and St Matthew's AME Zion Church), which offered Robeson facilities for his concert.

In addition to the help and encouragement of individuals, Paul Robeson committees were organized in Australia, Bulgaria, Ceylon, China, Ecuador, England, France, Germany, Hungary, India, Japan, Mexico, Norway, Poland, Sweden, Switzerland and the USSR as well as in the United States.

By now the earlier hysteria of anti-Robeson feeling was giving way to arguments in support of the political artist. Carnegie Hall, the scene of earlier concert successes, now opened its doors to Robeson. When he appeared there in May 1958 (his first city recital in eleven years) he sang in several languages – English, German, Russian, Hebrew, Yiddish and Chinese. There was unanimous agreement that this come-back concert was a triumph. It was, however, noticeable that Robeson was weakest in his spirituals and at his best in the folk-songs.

In March the American Actors' Equity Association had followed the British Actors' Equity Association's example by passing a resolution to consider helping Robeson to regain his passport. In April the State Department had relaxed its restrictions and Robeson was at last free to travel, but only in the Western Hemisphere where no passport was required. Europe was therefore still out of bounds to him. Thus Robeson's punishment and frustration persisted. Finally, in June, when the United States Supreme Court ruled that passports could not be withheld because of a citizen's 'beliefs or associations', Robeson, instead of mounting a bitter attack on those who had imprisoned him in his own land, showed his deep respect for justice by saying: 'I wish to thank Mr [Leonard] Boudin, and of course the Supreme Court, for what has happened, and also the thousands and thousands of people of all races and creeds who have been my passport.' At last he was free to honour his many commitments abroad.

7 · The Last Journey Abroad (1958–1963)

Before Robeson left for London he told a *New York Times* reporter, who asked if he planned to stay abroad, that this was his land. His grandfather and father had been born in the States, too, and he did not plan to leave the country. And long before he actually made the journey to Britain there were moves to welcome his return. No American – indeed few men of any nationality – had won such widespread and warm support from the British public. British television, according to one report, was ready to give the British public what it wanted in a 'big way'. In July Robeson signed for a series of televised concerts. After his television appearance *The Times* described Robeson as 'a fine and thoughtful artist' who sang his songs with 'huge delight'. During what was to be his final tour of Britain it became abundantly clear that age had not brought either a loss of vitality in his music or a mellowing of his political voice. In fact, in spite of the intense pressures he had endured to bring him to his knees, to beg forgiveness for his 'crime', he remained the essential political artist.

As expected, Robeson went to Wales where he appeared at the autumn Eisteddfod – the music festival at Ebbw Vale. Will Paynter of the South Wales Miners' Union told a large audience that they were honouring a great man and a great artist. Dr D.D. Evans, the area general secretary, then presented Robeson with a miniature miner's lamp. The miners and their families gave Robeson a great ovation. They had never forgotten the role he played in the film *Proud Valley*. When he finally appeared on the stage at this important event, surrounded by the choir of Welsh children, the vast audience joined the children in singing 'We'll Keep a Welcome in the Valley for Him'. During this visit to Wales, Robeson also shared a platform with Aneurin Bevan, the Labour leader, at a curtain-raiser to the

Eisteddfod.

Robeson then returned to London to perform again, after an absence of almost eight years, at the Albert Hall, scene of memorable concerts and meetings during the Spanish Civil War. A capacity crowd cheered and shouted for their special favourites as Robeson was welcomed back to London.

The exposure he received on this long-awaited visit was, in a word, extraordinary. He was not only spotlighted on television, and his activities widely reported in the press; his concert appearances were compared to those of another, lesser known black American singer, Harry Belafonte, then thirty-one years old. Both singers were performing simultaneously in London. The British press made a great ado about which performer was the 'greatest'. The London *Chronicle* had made up its mind: 'For 20 years Paul Robeson has symbolized the art of his race. But it would seem now that 31 year old Harry Belafonte, the slim six-footer from Harlem has displaced him. . . .' Was Robeson now too old to continue to hold centre stage? Or had his politics devalued his artistic credibility in the eyes of perhaps a biased reviewer? According to Shirley Graham, both Robeson and Belafonte received good reviews by the British press. Although Belafonte created somewhat of a sensation on his first appearance in Britain, obviously commercial attempts to play the young Belafonte against his 'hero' Robeson fell very flat.

After his London concerts, Robeson travelled by air to Moscow where he received an enthusiastic welcome. He sang on television, and in the Sports Palace to an audience of 12,000. On this two-week visit Robeson's every movement in the Soviet Union was monitored. The *New York Times* published a large photograph of Robeson and the Soviet Premier, Nikita Khrushchev at a Black Sea resort near Yalta, where the Soviet leader was vacationing. Later, in September, Robeson was made Honorary Professor of the Moscow State Conservatory of Music, and he began a tour of the German Democratic Republic. After years of relative inactivity this was a rigorous, if not punishing schedule. But Robeson was doing what he did best: speaking and acting on behalf of disadvantaged communities in the United States and elsewhere.

In August Robeson's autobiographical book *Here I Stand* was published in London, New York, Bucharest, Berlin and Moscow. Still no leading American publisher would publish it.

One of the truly exciting moments of his tour of England was the announcement that Robeson would sing at the evening service in St Paul's Cathedral on 12 October. He was to sing for half an hour, following which a collection would be taken for the defence and aid fund established by Christian Action for the 'treason trials' in South Africa. This was to be an historic occasion, for Robeson was the first black man to stand at the lectern in St Paul's.

After the Supreme Court decision made it possible for Robeson to travel abroad, Glen Byam Shaw, the new director of the Shakespeare Memorial Theatre, Stratford-upon-Avon, sent Robeson a telegram congratulating him on regaining his passport. Shaw also invited Robeson to play Othello, to which Robeson agreed. It was announced that Robeson would play Othello at Stratford Memorial Theatre in the 1959 season.

On 1 January 1959 Robeson was welcomed by Nikita Khrushchev at the Kremlin's New Year Ball. Robeson and his wife were in Moscow for a month's visit. However, before the end of January it was evident that Robeson was in poor health. During the years of waiting for his passport to be cleared he had put on a lot of weight. His recent concert tour of Europe had suddenly changed the rhythm of his life and left him exhausted. He was confined to a Moscow hospital – the first of successive hospital visits over the next four years. He was suffering from a deteriorating disease of the circulatory system. Doctors forbade him from making any stage appearances, for the time being.

Partly through his determination and will, and partly as a result of his enforced convalescence near the Black Sea, Robeson recovered. His doctors thought he could play Othello on condition that he used his voice more, minimized his physical activity and reduced the number of performances each week. Yet soon after Robeson arrived in England he was put through a demanding rehearsal by the director Tony Richardson. Often they worked on the play until midnight. As it happened, Robeson had the assistance of Sam Wanamaker, who played Iago. This was a fortuitous reunion of the two Americans who had first met in the early 1940s. Wanamaker, a progressive artist, had been subpoenaed to appear before the HUAC but he remained in Britain.

The long-awaited production opened the hundredth season of the Shakespeare Memorial Theatre, a few days before Robeson's sixty-first birthday. He led a relatively unknown cast, among whom were Mary Ure as Desdemona and Albert Finney as Cassio. At the end of this performance Robeson and the cast took fifteen curtain-calls. The mature Robeson had triumphed as Othello yet again. But how did his performance compare with his earlier ones? W.A. Darlington, who had reviewed Robeson's performance as Othello in 1930 for the *Daily Telegraph* and *Morning Post*, recalled that his praise then for Robeson was not whole-hearted though he had 'many fine moments, but there were times when he lacked that air of confident authority'. But now in the 'vale of his years' Darlington felt Robeson had that authority. 'He is completely in control. . . . Only Iago can shake him.' Robeson now had all the qualities that go to make the ideal Othello, in spite of lacking the 'ability to deliver Shakespeare's verse so that it touches the heart'. Other critics, however, saw Robeson's Othello as 'strong and stately . . . a superman of a general'. 'Nobly spoken,' said another; and 'superb' added a third. The critic in *The Times* argued that when Robeson last played Othello in England he was handicapped by a freakish production and grotesquely maimed text. Now he had greater assurance than he had in 1930, but alas, no greater command of Shakespearian verse, and again he was sadly lacking, handicapped by an 'over-clever' production. This critic concluded that the 'miscasting' of both Sam Wanamaker and Mary Ure robbed Robeson of his 'best chance of making something memorable of the part'. Ironically, it was Wanamaker's co-operation and help that were instrumental in helping Robeson achieve the high point of his dramatic career. Kenneth Tynan considered that Robeson had very little Shakespearian experience. In more appropriate company, he said, he was sure that Robeson would rise to greater heights than he had in this performance. As it was, he seemed to be murdering a butterfly on the advice of a gossip columnist. His voice, he affirmed, was incomparable, though perhaps it was too resonant, too musically articulated for the very finest acting. Tynan added that the greatest players – Kean and Irving, for example – had seldom been singers as well. On the contrary, their voices had been humanly imperfect, 'whereas the noise made by Mr Robeson is so nearly perfect as to be nearly inhuman'.

Thereafter Robeson played to full houses, until the final curtain brought to an end his long, tempestuous, historic and often controversial stage career. Wanamaker thought that this was Robeson's finest performance as an actor. But what were Robeson's own feelings about his demanding performances at Stratford? 'Playing at Stratford', he said, 'did fulfil one of my ambitions and I can now relax, feel that my artistic life has been fulfilled and hope to continue at a good level without any startling plans.' He agreed with Wanamaker that this was indeed his finest dramatic performances and thanked him for the improvisation they had worked through together.

In June Robeson sang at the base of Nelson's Column in Trafalgar Square during a large rally in support of nuclear disarmament organized by the British Peace Committee. Earlier he had participated in a May Day parade in Birmingham.

Several weeks later Robeson had, according to the *New York Times*, attended a meeting of the world youth festival in Vienna and declared that the American people could not 'talk of giving full freedom in the United States'. Apparently Robeson had alleged that United States foreign policy was being infiltrated by fascism and he suggested that Mr Nixon's trip to the Soviet Union and Poland would demonstrate to the Vice-President that the people who live in those countries really want peace. According to the newspaper, when delegates to the festival (attended by an estimated 17,000 from 82 countries) tried to question or criticize Robeson's statements, they were shouted down or ruled out of order by the communists, who controlled the programme.

It was rumoured that Robeson would ignore US passport restrictions and visit communist China and Hungary to give concerts. Travelling through Budapest on his way to Romania, he told the Hungarian newspaper *Nepszabadsag*: 'For ten years I have been a prisoner in my own country. I was not allowed to go abroad and I was prevented from meeting the European soldiers of the world peace movement.'

Robeson's presence in England gave him the opportunity to put his message across as clearly as possible. His aim was to get the British and US people together. In a lengthy interview he told George Matthews of the *Daily Worker* of his part in this process. 'Since Mr Dulles and Mr Macmillan can get together,' he said, 'the American people ought to get together with those in other countries. There is another America besides that of Mr Dulles – progressive America. I am very proud to be part of that America and the people of Britain.'

It had become well known that London was his cultural centre and that much of his political and artistic development had taken place against a background of life in Britain. Age had brought no change in his political commitment. He said again that it was in Britain that he became aware of the struggles of the Indian people and others who were under colonial rule. His nine-year absence prompted him to make various working plans during his stay. He had always found it to his advantage working from London and travelling to and from the United States. He was pleased to have given several concerts and anticipated appearing before millions of fans on television; an opportunity not to be missed, particularly because television appearances for progressive artists like Robeson were rare in the United States. He then returned to the unhappy years of 'imprisonment' which were linked to his profound sense of responsibility to the Negro people in the United States and their struggle to become first-class citizens. Predictably he was concerned with the events in Little Rock and Montgomery. Similarly, as he had done before he left in 1959, he expressed readiness to help. From Britain he viewed the working-class movement in the United States. He saw the unity of this class as vital to its struggles, and was prepared to return to the United States at short notice. And again he emphasized the relationship between his art and politics by saying that his work as an artist and his political work were inseparable. This was his uncompromising approach in the struggle for a better world.

Desegregation in the South had become a burning issue on which Robeson had been utterly uncompromising. On the question of race relations, and specifically Little Rock, on which the US Supreme Court had made its judgement, Robeson spoke out boldly against Faubus, whose actions must be strongly opposed. But, of course, he was unsure whether American citizens would be prepared to defend those whose rights were violated in the South.

The situation in America was one thing, but Britain was shaken by its own racial practices when race riots had exploded in Nottingham and Notting Hill in 1958. What did Robeson think about this? According to Matthews, Robeson said he was glad that the majority of British people and especially the labour movement recognized the need for unity of all peoples. This idealism had blinded Robeson to the fact that a colour bar had existed for many years and race riots in Britain had been recurring since the first decades of the twentieth century (e.g. in 1911 in Cardiff, and in 1919 again in Cardiff and in Liverpool). In any event, the labour movement was itself essentially racist. None the less, Robeson had an abiding faith in workers and was sure that the British labour movement would not allow continued attacks on West Indians and Africans, on the grounds that these were against the interests of white citizens also.

Since his arrival in Britain, after regaining his passport, Robeson had yet again to face the thorny question of confirming or denying that he was a communist, especially to the press. 'This question of refusing to say if one is a communist is an important part of the battle for civil rights,' he told an interviewer, for the benefit of his beloved British public. 'If you start demanding the right to know whether a person is a communist or a Republican or a Democrat, then you are taking away one of his most fundamental rights.' For Robeson the Communist Party in the United States was a legal political party and therefore it should have the right to propagate its ideas, and accordingly its members, who were not conspiring to overthrow the state by 'force and violence', should not be victimized. 'I have travelled in many countries,' he said, 'and wherever I have gone I have always laid a wreath on the tombs of those who laid down their lives in the battles against fascism. And every time I found that communists were among the first to do so.' He expressed satisfaction that among the people of Harlem 6,000 signatures were collected to support the candidature of his friend the communist leader Ben Davis, for the New York State Senate. He passionately believed in the Soviet Union and the accomplishment of socialism there. Each visit to the Soviet Union confirmed his belief that the 'backward races' could make progress under socialism.

In contrast with the way he was regarded by many in his American homeland, Robeson was a hero in the Soviet Union. Since he had first visited that country the USSR and the world had indeed changed, especially after 1945. The Soviet Union had, for example, become a great power and behaved as great powers do; through military occupation it had established communist governments in several Central and Eastern European countries. The Utopian view of socialism, however, had been challenged in these 'people's republics' by dissidents and opposing factions. For many socialists, especially in the West, it was unacceptable that those who opposed these 'republics' or regimes were not allowed to do so. And to ensure that the ruling Party line was followed, the new Communist International was established in 1947, Cominform (the Communist Information

Bureau) acting as the co-ordinating agency for Soviet-imposed policies, especially during the Cold War. Under the iron hand of Stalin, by the 1950s the Soviet Union had made a dramatic recovery from the Second World War. After Stalin's death in 1953, the Soviet Union, under the leadership of Nikita Khrushchev, adopted a more flexible attitude in its dealings with the West. Yet the fifties were years when Robeson moved in the shadows (while being shadowed by secret agents). Americans remained deeply distrustful of the Soviets and communism which Robeson believed was the only way through which the workers of the world would be free from exploitation. But it seemed communism had gone dreadfully wrong. Pro-communists and Party members were shocked by the behaviour of communists. Eric Bentley put the disaster in perspective by stating that, given Stalin's concentration camps which exceeded those of Hitler's, the Russian disaster was far worse than the German one because it brought 'desolating disappointment', crushing high expectations and the desperate hopes of the oppressed.

Publicly at least Robeson declined to comment on the Stalin regime. He went no further than saying that any discussion of Stalin was a matter best left to the Russian people. 'It is their problem,' he told the House Un-American Activities Committee. Robeson's affection for the Russian people was so deep that any public criticism would have been counter-productive to his position as a socialist and to his promotion of the Russian system. This inflexibility on his part, his dogged loyalties, was both a strength and a weakness. The critics could have their say but Robeson, who had experienced freedom for the first time in the Soviet Union, remained unmoved and unrepentant.

By the turn of 1960 Robeson was back again in Moscow, singing and speaking to plant workers. He also attended a theatre production with Khrushchev, marking the 100th Anniversary of Chekhov's birth in Moscow.

At this stage in Robeson's life, there were few parts of the world his voice had not reached. More people had heard of him than perhaps any other human being of his day. In November 1960 he made his last concert tour, which took him for the first time to Australia and New Zealand. Here, he took the opportunity to link music with race. He told reporters in Adelaide: 'I sing folk music because it covers the whole world. I am interested in all peoples. I am deeply concerned with the problems of people who were here before you – the indigenous people of Australia. I don't call them the aborigines. I call them indigenous peoples.'

Being in New Zealand was quite an experience for Robeson, and he felt very close to his audiences. Many people, some of them elderly, had hoped for a long time that they would one day hear him sing in person. He was particularly interested in the Maoris. In Auckland he visited the Maori Centre. 'I want to learn Maori songs and as much as I can of the Maori language,' he said.

Over the years, by highlighting the black Americans' plight, Robeson had made many enemies. His journey and comments down under, however, did not escape the American journalist George Sokolsky who, in a critical assessment of Robeson's views, vented his feelings towards Robeson in the *Washington Post*. He said that unlike other singers, black or white, Robeson chose to preach hate against the United States. Robeson's unrivalled rendition of 'Ol' Man River', Sokolsky felt, should not exempt him from making statements that were close to 'treason' abroad. To counteract Robeson's seeming lack of national pride Sokolsky went around calling him a liar.

Among the few who had consistently defended Robeson feelings ran high. Robeson's reputation had taken a qualitative leap; already he belonged, it seemed, to history, to the history of the black people, one to be eulogized. His friend William Patterson felt that Robeson was 'made in America'. The composition of the society, he argued, left Robeson no choice as a man but to fight back. His life was therefore an example worthy of emulation, so far as the struggle for human freedom was concerned, by American youth, black and white.

During the regular trips he made at this time to East Germany Robeson spent much time with an artist called Oliver Harrington. His years of incarceration in the United States, Harrington felt, had made Robeson suspicious of those Americans – white liberals and Blacks – who posed as friends but had deserted him. In contrast, the Soviet Union (and other socialist countries) and his friends there gave him unflagging support. This man of strong feelings naturally formed strong attachments, and for all his warmth and charm he could not forgive or forget those who had so shamelessly disciplined him. All his life certain Americans had done this to him, in one form or another. Not surprisingly, therefore, he could not trust them in the way that he could trust the Russians, to whom he now turned for treatment during this awkward time of ongoing illness.

Robeson's illness was terminal. In the months that followed he spent much time in hospitals and nursing homes. When news reached him that he was being considered by President Kwame Nkrumah for the post of lecturer at the University of Ghana's Institute of African Studies (in spite of an attempt by the United States State Department to block his appointment), unfortunately he had become too ill to accept. This would have been a fitting home-coming to the continent he loved so dearly.

Illness incapacitated him grievously. Instead of appearing at the Africa Freedom Day concert at the Festival Hall in London, he was admitted to hospital in Moscow, suffering from exhaustion and a circulatory disease. All his engagements for several months were cancelled. Away from his 'own' people, he was alone and very depressed. He was delighted to see his friends Dr and Mrs Alphaeus Hunton, who visited him at this time. Dorothy Hunton recalled that Robeson got up, embraced Alphaeus, and then both of them strolled out to the garden for about half an hour. After this, she was struck by the marked change in Robeson: he had become cheerful, which made him feel a lot better. According to one account, Essie thought that more rest for her husband was absolutely necessary after the more than thirty-five years of insistent work, controversy and tension which he had absorbed. But by now she too, the devoted wife and companion who had weathered years of private and public turbulence in their relationship, was also ill, suffering from cancer. In spite of this, as the more 'aggressive' partner, she valiantly protected Robeson from the ever-intrusive press. Her unwavering commitment to her husband was never really in doubt. She did everything humanly possible to get him started as an actor, a singer and a political activist; she was his earliest champion and critic. Thus far, theirs was a relationship fraught with difficulties but one which had stood the test of time.

It was as though, by the end of 1962, people intuitively felt Robeson's illness marked the waning of a Titan. Appropriately, the Soviet people had been the first to recognize him: they now named a mountain peak after him, attributing to him the qualities of a great internationalist. His activities on behalf of peace, the extent to which he had fought against war and its causes between the great powers was the yardstick by which the Soviet people measured his role and work. He was the most honoured living American among socialists, who continued to lionize him.

It was now that rumours were rife about Robeson's disillusionment with socialist countries. His close friend Harry Francis said it was sheer nonsense to suggest that Robeson was disillusioned in this way. Published reports on the matter and assertions that he was being held in East Berlin against his will were described by his son as 'lies out of the cloth'. Paul Robeson Jr, according to the *New York Times*, declared that his father's recent flight to East Berlin had 'no political overtones'. He said his father had been suffering from exhaustion for several years and was planning to take a long rest. But this explanation was not enough for those who were interested in Robeson, particularly his detractors.

In August 1963 Robeson was interviewed at London Airport, *en route* for the United States, in connection with a mass march on Washington. 'The turning-point has come for the American people,' he declared. Later, from his sick-bed, he sent greetings and best wishes to his fellow-Americans involved in the march. Sadly he could not be there himself, and his old friend DuBois had died in Ghana just before the march.

In December 1963 tragedy struck the Robeson family. Benjamin Robeson, pastor of the Mother African Methodist Episcopal Zion Church in Harlem for twenty-seven years, died at the age of seventy. Soon afterwards the American public learned from the *New York Times* that Robeson was returning to the United States to retire. Retirement was at the request of his doctors, who advised him against performing professionally again because of his poor health. His agent, Harold Davison, said in London that Robeson was returning to the United States because it was his home and that the singer's politics were behind him.

Later that year Robeson eventually went back to the United States after an absence of almost five and a half years. Robert G. Spivak in the *New York Herald-Tribune* stated that *Figaro* in Paris had run a story in which it was claimed that Robeson was totally disillusioned with Russia and communism. The *Figaro* report allegedly said that Robeson had long believed that minorities in the Soviet Union had 'complete freedom' and could live 'without the least restrictions'. But he acknowledged that experience had taught him this was untrue.

According to Spivak, Robeson declared that Soviet customs were imposed, and one was told of the superiority of Soviet culture, Soviet writers, art and music. Moreover, Robeson allegedly said he was disillusioned because the so-called liberation was a façade – in the Soviet Union oppression went under a different guise. Spivak referred to Robeson as 'Moscow's fortunate Negro' and that one of Robeson's friends, Edric Connor, a West Indian actor, seemed to accept the *Figaro* story. Spivak quoted Connor as saying that Robeson was proud of the Stalin Peace Prize, but by the time Khrushchev assumed power Robeson was a changed man. With more than a hint of satisfaction, Spivak concluded that Robeson's magnificent voice was, perhaps, now silent for ever.

So for the last time the Robesons, both in bad health, returned to their homeland. They had travelled widely and experienced more than most Americans. They had been celebrities abroad for more than four decades. Yet while for the mass of Americans they were simply well-known Blacks, having fallen from grace, for many in the black population they were (particularly Robeson) heroic figures. Physically, Robeson was a mere shadow of his former self. Thin, old and bespectacled, he was met on arrival at the airport by his son, daughter-in-law and two grandchildren. He smiled but barely responded to the press.

Back in Harlem, the scene of much of their early courtship and life, the Robesons now lived quietly at 16 Jumel Terrace. Uncharacteristically, Robeson saw few people, which was extremely difficult for a man whose life had always been public and not guardedly private or personal. From this retreat he observed and encouraged a new generation of Blacks involved in the American struggle and, as ever, he monitored events abroad. His brother Ben and his old and trusted friend DuBois were no longer around to engage in conversation which would have comforted him. He was left alone to speculate and brood; but he was not forgotten, although his voice was broken. The American authorities had done much damage, but they had not destroyed everything. Robeson's records (not all were destroyed) evoked a life always striving to rise above the oppression and sorrow of his people. In the past he did not need to be told there was work to be done; he just got on with it. Now in his utter helplessness, in the words of one of his songs, deep inside, he could 'Hear de Lam's A'cryin''.

8 · The Last Years (1964–1976)

Robeson's health continued to deteriorate. As they had done in the Soviet Union, the Huntons visited Robeson in Harlem. For Dorothy Hunton it was a sad thing to see Robeson in his present physical condition. Another blow was struck when Robeson's dear friend Ben Davis, whom he had known for some thirty-five years, died. At the funeral Robeson spoke of the 'glowing inspiration' that Davis had always been, a dedicated fighter for freedom and peace. In his sorrow, Robeson said goodbye in the words of a song Davis had often heard:

> Farewell, beloved comrade,
> We make this solemn vow:
> The fight will go on,
> Until we win, until we, the people win.

Robeson was against Barry Goldwater running for the presidency; after all, Goldwater was a candidate who not only refused to support the Civil Rights Bill (and who was also against labour union organization and the whole social welfare programme) but was against it in principle. Robeson argued that at a time when the peoples of the world were working for peace in order to avoid nuclear war Goldwater talked irresponsibly of using nuclear bombs 'to defoliate the forests'. 'Survival of the world', Robeson added, 'demands that the leaders and the peoples of all nations understand the dreadful implications of nuclear warfare, and completely reject it.'

Robeson's resonant and consistent voice did not fall on deaf ears. In his physical decline people no longer took him for granted. Elizabeth Gurly Flynn observed that his 'crimes' endeared him to instead of isolating him from thousands of people. The behind-the-scenes moves to bring Robeson back to the foreground, to recognize his magnificent, selfless contribution, became a reality in April 1965 when *Freedomways* (quarterly review of the 'Negro freedom movement') sponsored a 'Salute to Paul Robeson' at the Hotel Americana, chaired by the actor/playwright Ossie Davis and the actress Ruby Dee. Among the packed audience of admirers was James Baldwin, who noted that 'in the days when it seemed that there was no possibility in raising the individual voice and no possibility of applying the regions of conscience, Paul Robeson spoke in a great voice which creates a man'.

Robeson's voice rang out. He said he was thankful to *Freedomways* for giving him a reception unlike anything he could remember. He recognized the fact that the journal had come into being along with the thrust of the Negro freedom movement 'to express, record and to contribute in this history-making activity in our country'. He saw *Freedomways* as playing a splendid role in interpreting black struggle in America and abroad. It was one of the poignant moments of the evening when he said: 'I would like for a moment to call your attention to an artist who has been closely associated with me in my career. I hope Larry is still here, my friend and colleague, Mr Lawrence Brown, an authority on Negro and classical music who has been my partner in concerts for forty years.' Robeson recalled his own work in music and the theatre in the Village in the twenties and thirties, and was encouraged by the strides black playwrights and artists were making in almost every aspect of cultural life in America. It was an historic moment, he said, to see the participation of black and white artists in the freedom struggle and to note their brilliant contributions to the understanding so necessary for all sections of the American community.

He then told his audience of the respect people abroad had for 'our music especially for the songs expressing a deep desire for friendship, equality and peace'. He also mentioned the great rallies for peace he had attended abroad, in Paris, Moscow and London. But while he was abroad Robeson never lost touch with the remarkable progress of the freedom struggle at home. Freedom now was the struggle in the South and elsewhere in the United States, he said; a struggle reflecting unity as in the Great March from Selma to Montgomery when Blacks and Whites marched together. He was optimistic that the struggle would continue, even during the dark days of the Progressive Party campaign. He noted that in claiming their rights, black Americans were as determined as never before. But he pointed out it was most important to recognize that these demands in no way lessened the democratic rights of white American citizens. On the contrary, it would enormously strengthen the alliance between the Negro people and the white citizens at every level of American society. A living connection, deeper and stronger, between black and white Americans was vital in the struggle for democracy. Only in this way could the Negro question be solved.

These defiant words stirred the audience. Robeson then turned to the theme of music and struggle. In the black Americans' struggles, from slavery through reconstruction – on the marches, in the demonstrations and at mass meetings or in the churches – the part played by music was of central importance, for songs inspired, encouraged, sustained and united thousands of people. As well as the song 'Go Down Moses' (one that had come from the struggles of the people), which he had sung in many languages and in many countries over many years, Robeson said there was another from such a tradition:

> Never say that you have reached the very end,
> When leaden skies a bitter future may portend:
> For sure the hour for which we yearn will yet arrive
> And our marching steps will thunder 'We Survive'.

The audience was enthralled by this man whom they loved. Now he was preparing to leave them. It was the last time in his long, distinguished, controversial career that he would address a public audience in person. 'I certainly go home knowing and feeling more and more deeply "We shall overcome, deep in my heart I do believe, we shall overcome some day",' he said.

After this renewal by Robeson of his lifelong commitment to his people, at home and abroad, more Americans were coming to recognize the true value and selfless dedication of his long struggle for human betterment. Hope R. Stevens, a friend of his, saw Robeson as democracy's 'most powerful voice'; a man who championed the cause of freedom and fought for peace and justice all over the world.

The life of a recluse was so alien to Robeson that, in spite of his condition, he found it necessary at times to go out. Occasionally he would slip out of the house, when few people would recognize him. While out one night in October 1965 he was found lying injured and semi-conscious on waste ground near High Bridge Park in the Washington Heights section of New York City. He was taken to hospital and released after treatment for cuts on his face and other injuries. According to one account, Essie reported her husband missing and stated that he sometimes suffered from loss of balance and dizzy spells. After treatment at the Vanderbilt Clinic, Robeson told the police he did not know how he was injured or how he came to be in the 'lot'.

During these long, inactive days of retirement, Robeson reflected on the few Americans who had provided Blacks with leadership. DuBois's contribution was of special interest. In the winter of 1965 Robeson's 'Legacy of W.E.B. DuBois' was published in *Freedomways*. He cited DuBois's brilliant and practical mind, his intellectual courage and integrity, his awareness of the world and the place of Blacks in it, which helped to arouse black consciousness. 'I remember too his deep kindness,' wrote Robeson. 'DuBois was, and is in the truest sense an American leader, a Negro leader, a world leader.' This was Robeson's tribute to one of the few black Americans who had been consistently on his side before, during and after his Paris statement.

There was now a marked upturn of interest in Robeson world-wide. Following the establishment of the Paul Robeson Choir in East Berlin in 1963, the Academy of Arts set up the Paul Robeson Archive to collect and preserve the many documents, records, tape recordings, photographs, newspaper cuttings and so forth connected with his life and work. This announcement was made by the Paul Robeson Committee of the German Democratic Republic, composed of leading personalities, many of whom had been associated with Robeson, such as Professor Ernest Herman Meyer, Professor Albert Norden, Professor George Knepler and Dr Franz Loeser. The Committee stated that Robeson's work belonged to the whole of progressive humanity and with this in mind the Committee invited support from all parts of the world. Further east, in the Soviet Union, the Russians announced plans for a Paul Robeson movie. And at home, for this 'prophet in his own time', it must have been sweet music to his ears to hear John Lewis speak of him as an inspirer of youth at the *Freedomways* salute: 'We salute more than a man, we salute a cause. We salute the dreams and aspirations and the hopes of an oppressed people whether they be in Selma, Alabama, in Jackson, Mississippi or in Vietnam. . . . We of the SNCC [Student Non-Violent Coordinating Committee] are Paul Robeson's spiritual children because they, too, have rejected gradualism and moderation.'

Amidst the acclaim, however, Robeson suffered a severe personal loss. In December 1965 Essie died aged sixty-eight. Only months after he had been found unconscious, this was a cruel blow to Robeson. He had been reluctant, at least publicly, to say much about his wife before. But according to the editor of *New World Review*, on a number of occasions Robeson spoke of his deep gratitude to his wife for her influence in determining his course as a singer; and for her many contributions to his development as an artist and as a human being. He also spoke of his wife's lifelong work for full equality for the Negro people, for human advancement and peace.

After Essie's death Robeson lived alone at Jumel Terrace. He saw only Paul Jr, Marilyn and their children, and perhaps a few others. Previously he had often spent time with his sister Marion, and now he needed to be cared for constantly, Marion (a retired teacher) took him in at her house in Philadelphia. His son bore the full responsibility of attending to his affairs. At this time Robeson was loved and comforted by his family and saw very few friends. His association with the Church and Church matters never wavered. One of his visitors was the Revd Hoggard, pastor of the AME Zion Church. Occasionally he went to the theatre, but much of the time he spent reading.

Robeson's sixty-ninth birthday was marked by a special ceremony in East Berlin's Museum of German History. The audience included leading personalities from the arts, sciences and other fields. A brief, illustrated account of Robeson's life and work was distributed to everyone present. Several of his records (including 'The Other America') were released in the GDR, and a number of books about Robeson were published. In the Soviet Union and elsewhere many tributes followed. For black Americans, especially those who had been close to him over the years, such occasions were worthy reminders of a remarkable man who was still in their midst.

A year later, interest in Robeson had become widespread among the students and staff at Rutgers. By the time of his seventy-first birthday, Rutgers University had succumbed to the cry for justice by dedicating a music and arts lounge in honour of its famous student. While the awards and tributes came in quick succession, as if in recompense for past neglect, Robeson's life was gradually slipping away. Yet it must have gratified him that at last his old university had recognized him, thus taking a step against anti-racism, that black artists and students honoured him and were investigating his contribution, and that his friend C.L.R. James had written a tribute to him in *Black World*. James pointed out that if Robeson had wanted to he could have built a movement to succeed the Garvey movement. But Robeson did not want to start a movement that would evolve around him; he felt himself committed to the doctrines and the policies of the Communist Party. This strict adherence by Robeson to ideology, however, brought him sharp criticism. As Edwin Hoyt put it, Robeson lost prestige in the United States through his strong allegiance to the Soviet Union, a loss that had to be weighed against what had become known about certain Soviet leaders. The destabilization of the Soviet Union, for example, was a sudden blow, which brought about some questioning of his uncompromising stance. Apart from this, there was the Soviet Union's anti-Semitism policy, which drove American communists such as Howard Fast out of the Party. If all this was cause for concern, outwardly at least Robeson remained unshaken.

If in fact the 'perfect nation had turned out to be less than perfect', Robeson's answer to any disillusionment with the Soviet Union was clearly set out in his book *Here I Stand*. On other issues, however, Paul Robeson Jr, now spokesman for his retired, incapacitated father, attempted to set the record straight. In a speech delivered at Rutgers University, at an affair sponsored by the Eastern Region of Alpha Phi Alpha Fraternity and the Rutgers Student Center, he said that in the Rutgers library there was a letter from a white student which called for Robeson's execution because of his Paris statement in 1949. Amidst this racist atmosphere, he said, a campaign to silence his father began and steadily gained momentum, with the result that Robeson's passport was cancelled. Such detractors, determined to devalue Robeson's stature, tried to project an alternative image of a 'tragic, misled figure, victimized by the times'. Robeson was a trailblazer, who understood well the price exacted for the path he took and paid it with dignity.

Between 1970 and 1976 Robeson was the recipient of several awards. Paul Jr received the coveted Ira Aldridge Award on his father's behalf, and further underlined his father's unhappy experience. He said that in spite of attempts by leaders of the United States and the Establishment to hide the truth about his father and his achievements, Robeson displayed uncommon courage by allowing his people's struggle to take precedence over personal success. And because his father appeared as a threat to the Establishment, a 'curtain of silence' was drawn around him. The award, he said, would help to move that curtain aside.

By the turn of 1973 it seemed that many more sections of American society were making amends for their neglect of Robeson. In April a 'Salute to Paul Robeson' on his seventy-fifth birthday was held in a packed Carnegie Hall. Robeson was too ill to attend but sent a taped message. He expressed his warmest thanks to his friends assembled there and to those around the world who had sent him greetings. Despite his inactivity he wanted everyone to know that he was the 'same Paul', and that his dedication to the cause of freedom, brotherhood and peace remained undiminished. He was particularly concerned with his own people in the United States who were struggling for complete liberation from racist domination. In short, equal rights with an equal share in the fruits of their labours was the goal he envisaged for all minority groups. He concluded:

In the same spirit, I salute the colonial liberation movements of Africa, Latin America and Asia, which have gained new inspiration and understanding from the heroic example of the Vietnamese people, who have once again turned back an imperialist aggressor. Together with the partisans of peace – the peoples of the socialist countries and the progressive elements of all other countries – I rejoice that the movement for peaceful coexistence has made important gains, and that the advocates of 'Cold War' and 'Containment' have had to retreat. On this occasion, too, I want to say a warm hello to the many friends who have sent me encouraging messages during my long illness. . . . Though ill-health has compelled my retirement, you can be sure that in my heart I go on singing:

> But I keeps on laughin'
> Instead of cryin'
> I must keep fightin'
> Until I'm dyin'
> And Ol' Man River
> He just keeps rollin' along!

Among those involved in the Carnegie Hall tribute were Harry Belafonte, Sidney Poitier, Dizzie Gillespie and Angela Davis.

Gillespie saw Robeson as his 'personal champion', Poitier said that 'before, no black man or woman had been portrayed in American movies as anything but a stereotype', and Angela Davis spoke of Robeson as 'a partisan of the socialist world', and 'above all, a revolutionary'. In a tribute to his father Paul Robeson Jr, pointing out that the most unique and important thing about his father was his personality, the man himself, said that his father was one of those rare people who exuded light and warmth, rather than casting a shadow on those he met. (Many people have independently claimed this to be true.) Robeson's personal qualities were vital, he said. To appreciate him fully one had to *see* and *hear* him, an experience that was almost always unforgettable. And from the Soviet Union, Konstantin Kudrov, the Russian journalist, wrote that the Soviet people were proud of and honoured and valued their unbreakable friendship with Robeson. Kudrov's work as a journalist enabled him to appreciate the life and work of Robeson as a 'splendid example for the world of the indivisible unity of a man of art and a class-conscious fighter'. Finally, the Russian wished Robeson good health on his seventy-fifth birthday. Kudrov's heartfelt message was one of impending loss.

Later that year the black American Bertrand Phillips was asked by the Soviet Government to paint a portrait of Robeson for the rededication ceremony of Mount Paul Robeson. And Rutgers University, which had kept Robeson in its 'alumni closet', finally honoured him *in absentia* by conferring an honorary doctorate on him as part of a programme marking his accomplishments in the arts, scholarship and on the sports field. The citation read, in part: 'By songs, deed and word you have touched men's minds, no less than their hearts. You have given the common man of all races and all lands a new vision of himself.' Moreover the *New York Times Book Review* published a review of *Here I Stand*, fifteen years after it had first appeared.

By the end of 1973 the Cold War seemed to have thawed, and China was becoming part of the wider world. The Soviet leader Leonid Brezhnev, on a visit to the United States, said that the Cold War did not serve the interests of the countries involved. Moreover, the tragedy of the United States military involvement in Vietnam was followed by internal political corruption, which came to be known as the Watergate scandal. In a sense, these kinds of events had long pre-occupied Robeson, who did all he could to bring attention to them.

In spite of or because of the accolades that had been heaped on Robeson, he was still viewed as a highly dangerous man, even at the age of seventy-six, as was evidenced when a letter from the United States Supreme Court Justice William O. Douglas to Simeon Booker, the *Jet* Washington bureau chief, was opened and delivered six months after it was written. Booker wrote to Douglas that the latter's mention in his letter of the name Robeson, perhaps the most hated Black this century, had maybe engulfed the two of them in a 'communist threat'!

Even such acts could not stop the momentum of pro-Robeson feelings. In his seventy-sixth year, among those who honoured Robeson was Actors' Equity. Unable to attend the presentation of this annual award, Robeson sent a message stating that he was moved by Actors' Equity making him the first recipient of its award. He reflected on the kinship he felt with fellow actors since O'Neill had expounded on the 'oneness of mankind'. In retirement, he was encouraged that a new generation, black and white, were passionately concerned with human betterment. And he urged 'old-timers' who were still involved in the struggle, 'Right on!' Subconsciously he was urging himself on.

Late in December 1975 Robeson suffered a mild stroke and was admitted to the Presbyterian University Hospital in Philadelphia. Diagnosis showed he was a victim of cerebral vascular disorders. In the days that followed, his life slowly ebbed away. On 23 January 1976 he died, and the voice which many had taken for granted was at last silent. As Pablo Neruda wrote:

> Once he did not exist
> But his voice was there, waiting.
> Light painted from darkness,
> day from night.
> And the voice of Paul Robeson
> was divided by the silence.

At Robeson's funeral on 27 January thousands gathered to pay their last respects, although it was supposed to be a family affair. Bishop Clinton J. Hoggard, who delivered the eulogy, said that Robeson had lived a long, active life until harassment took its toll on his physical frame. Yet he was comforted by words of long ago from his famous performance of Othello:

> Good name in man or woman, dear my lord,
> Is the immediate jewel of their souls:
> Who steals my purse steals trash; 'tis something, nothing; . . .

Paul Robeson Jr also spoke about his father, who had never regretted the stand he took almost forty years before when he made a crucial decision. He had said then: 'The artist must elect to fight for freedom or for slavery. I have made my choice. I had no alternative.' He said his father felt a deep sense of responsibility to the people who loved him and to all to whom he was a symbol. When he could no longer fulfil their expectations, he had retired completely. And when his voice and music – his mission in song – no longer produced the desired effect on his audiences, he decided to become silent. By now it was crystal clear to many that Robeson viewed life, work and art as 'all of one piece'.

The cohesion of these elements in Robeson was a microcosm of what he understood and sought to convey in his belief in the 'oneness of mankind'. From this perspective he never lost sight of the value of human freedom, especially the freedom of the people from whom he sprang. 'Nobody can say that I betrayed the Negro,' Robeson had consistently said. 'Everything I did, I did for the Negro, for the cause of his dignity and self-respect.' Bidding his father farewell in the AME Zion Church, Paul Robeson Jr concluded with the words of a poem: 'I may keep memories of him, but not his essence . . . for that will pour forth tomorrow. . . .'

In thought and deed Robeson was a man for all peoples, a political messenger, an activist, an artist not content with interpreting the world but in changing it. This was his total commitment in life and he fought to the end, unbowed and undefeated. Ever-conscious of his humble beginnings, he had for decades acted according to his firmly held principles and beliefs (he was not a politician, nor did he pretend to be Moses) – as a Negro leader, an American leader, a world leader. He was above all a product of American institutions. The words of Frederick Douglass, which Robeson quoted in his book, serves as a fitting epitaph for himself: 'A man is worked on by what he works on. He may carve out his circumstances, but his circumstances will carve him out as well.'

Bibliography

BOOKS AND EXCERPTS FROM BOOKS

Bradley, A.C., *Shakespearean Tragedy*, London: Macmillan, 1904.

Browne, M., *Too Late to Lament*, London: Gollancz, 1960.

Cousins, E.G., *What I Want from Life*, London: Allen & Unwin, 1934.

Cruse, Harold, *The Crisis of the Negro Intellectual*, New York: William Morrow, 1967.

Davis, Lenwood G., *A Paul Robeson Research Guide: A Selected Annotated Bibliography*, Westport, Conn.: Greenwood Press, 1982.

Embree, Edwin R., 'Paul Robeson, Voice of Freedom' in *13 Against the Odds*, New York: Viking, 1944.

Fast, Howard M., *Peekskill, U.S.A. – A Personal Experience*, New York: Civil Rights Congress, 1951.

Foner, Philip S. (ed.), *Paul Robeson Speaks*, London: Quartet, 1978.

Gelb, Arthur and Barbara, *O'Neill*, New York: Harper, 1960.

Gilliam, Dorothy Butler, *Paul Robeson: All American*, Washington, DC: New Republic Book Company, 1976.

Graham, Shirley, *Paul Robeson, Citizen of the World*, New York: Julian Messner, 1946.

Hamilton, Virginia, *Paul Robeson: The Life and Times of a Free Black Man*, New York: Harper & Row, 1974.

Himber, Charlotte, 'Let My People Go, Robeson' in *Famous in Their Twenties*, New York: Association Press, 1942.

Hoyt, Edwin P., *Paul Robeson*, London: Cassell, 1968.

Hughes, Langston, *The First Book of Negroes: A Child's History of the Negroes*, New York: Franklin Watts, 1952.

Lamparski, Richard, *Whatever Became of . . . ?*, 2nd series, New York: Crown, 1968.

Miers, Earl Shenk, *Big Ben*, Philadelphia, Pa: Westminster Press, 1942.

Moritz, Charles (ed.), *Current Biography*, New York: H.W. Wilson, 1976.

Nazel, Joseph, *Paul Robeson*, Los Angeles, Calif.: Holloway House, 1980.

Noble, Peter, *The Negro in Films*, London: Skelton Robinson, 1949.

Ovington, Mary White, *Portraits in Color*, New York: Viking, 1927.

Paul Robeson: The Great Forerunner, compiled by *Freedomways*, New York: Dodd, Mead, 1978.

Redding, J. Saunders, *The Lonesome Road*, New York: Doubleday, 1958.

Robeson, Eslanda (Goode), *Paul Robeson, Negro*, New York: Harper, 1930.

——, *African Journey*, New York: J. Day, 1945.

Robeson, Paul, *Here I Stand*, London: Dennis Dobson, 1958. (For more on Robeson's writings *see* Davis, L.G., and Foner, P.S.)

Robeson, Susan, *The Whole World in His Hands: A Pictorial Biography of Paul Robeson*, New York: Citadel Press, 1981.

Rogers, J.A., 'Paul Robeson, Intellectual, Musical and Histrionic Prodigy' in *World's Great Men of Color*, 2, New York (published by the author), 1947.

Rosenberg, Marvin, *The Masks of Othello*, Berkeley, Calif.: University of California Press, 1961.

Sergeant, Elizabeth, *Fire under the Andes*, New York: Knopf, 1927.

Seton, Marie, *Paul Robeson*, London: Dennis Dobson, 1958.

Webster, Margaret, *Shakespeare without Tears*, New York and London: McGraw-Hill, 1942.

——, *Shakespeare Today*, London: Dent, 1957.

Woollcott, Alexander, 'Colossal Bronze' in *Portable Woollcott*, New York: Viking, 1946.

Wright, Charles H., *Robeson: Labor's Forgotten Champion*, Detroit, Mich.: Balamp, 1975.

ARTICLES, PAMPHLETS AND THESES

Beatty, Jerome, 'America's No. 1 Negro', *American Magazine*, CXXXVII, May 1944.

Brown, Lloyd L., *Paul Robeson Rediscovered*, Occasional Papers no. 9, American Institute for Marxist Studies, 1976.

Buxton, L.C., 'The Development of the Political Thought of Paul Robeson', unpublished Master's thesis, University of Delaware, 1979.

Cripps, Thomas, 'Paul Robeson and Black Identity in American Movies', *Massachusetts Review*, XI, summer 1970.

DuBois, W.E.B., 'Paul Robeson, Right' and White, Walter, 'Wrong', *Negro Digest*, March 1950.

Ellison, W. James, 'Paul Robeson and the State Department', *Crisis*, LXXXIV, May 1977.

Fishman, George, 'Paul Robeson's Student Days and the Fight against Racism at Rutgers', *Freedomways*, IX, summer 1969.

Garvey, Marcus, 'Paul Robeson and His Mission', *The Black Man*, II, January 1937.

Gilmore, Mildred, 'Profile: King of Harlem', *New Yorker*, September 1928.

Hentoff, Nat, 'Paul Robeson Makes a New Album', *Reporter*, 12 April 1958.

Hitchens, John L., 'Paul Robeson', *Theatre Arts*, October 1944.

James, C.L.R., 'Paul Robeson: Black Star', *Black World*, XX, November 1970.

Kolodin, Irving, 'Paul Robeson in Carnegie Hall', *Saturday Review*, August 1958.

Lewis, John, 'Paul Robeson Inspirer of Youth', *Freedomways*, V, summer 1965.

Miers, Earl Shenk, 'Paul Robeson – Made in America', *The Nation*, CLXX, May 1950.

Mitchell, Loften, 'Time to Break the Silence Surrounding Paul Robeson', *New York Times*, August 1972.

Moos, Elizabeth, 'Free Paul Robeson', *Masses & Mainstream*, October 1951.

Patterson, William, 'In Honour of Paul Robeson', *Political Affairs*, XLVII, May 1968.

Pittman, John, 'Mount Paul', *New World Review*, February 1962.

Robeson, Paul, Jr, 'My Dad', *New Challenge*, February 1955. (See also Davis, L.G., and *Paul Robeson: The Great Forerunner*.)

Rowan, Carl T., 'Has Paul Robeson Betrayed the Negro?', *Ebony*, October 1957.

Schlosser, Anatol I., 'Paul Robeson: His Career in the Theatre, in Motion Pictures and on the Concert Stage', unpublished doctoral dissertation, New York University, 1970.

Smith, Anna Bustill, 'The Bustill Family', *Journal of Negro History*, 10, October 1925.

Stevens, Hope R., 'Paul Robeson – Democracy's Most Powerful Voice', *Freedomways*, V, summer 1965.

Stuckey, Sterling, 'Paul Robeson Revisited', *New York Times Book Review*, October 1973.

——, '"I Want to Be African": Paul Robeson and the Ends of Nationalist Theory and Practice, 1914–1945', *Massachusetts Review*, XVII, spring 1976.

Weaver, Harold D., 'Paul Robeson at Rutgers', *Black Voice*, April 1973.

——, 'Paul Robeson: Beleaguered Leader', *Black Scholar*, V, 4, December 1973–January 1974.

——, 'Paul Robeson and Film: Racism and Anti-Racism in Communications', *Negro History Bulletin*, 37, January 1974.

White, Walter, *see* DuBois above.

Yeakey, Lamont, 'The Early Years of Paul Robeson: Prelude to the Making of a Revolutionary, 1898–1930', unpublished Master's thesis, Columbia University, 1971.

OTHER NEWSPAPERS AND JOURNALS

Afro-American, American Dialog, Baltimore Afro-American, Burton Evening Gazette, The Bystander, California Voice, Chicago Crusader, Chicago Defender, The Cinema, Cleo, Daily Express, Daily Film Renter, Daily Gleaner (Jamaica)*, Daily Herald, Daily Mail, Daily Mirror, Daily News, Daily Record, Daily Sketch, Daily Telegraph, Daily Worker, Daily World, The Era, Evening Post* (Wellington, New Zealand)*, Evening Standard* (London)*, Everyman, Figaro, Film Pictorial, Film Weekly, Freedom, G.K.'s Weekly, Illustrated London News, Jet, Jewish Chronicle* (London)*, Jewish Life, Leicester Evening Mail, Los Angeles Times, Manchester Guardian, Melody Maker, Middlesex County Times* (Ealing)*, The Millgate, Musical America, Nash's Pall Mall, Negro Worker, New Africa, New Statesman and Nation, New Theatre, New World Review, New York Amsterdam News, New York Herald Tribune, New York Journal-American, New York World Telegram, News Chronicle, The Observer, Oxford Mail, Pearson's Weekly, Peekskill Evening Star, Peoria Star, Philadelphia Tribune, Pittsburgh Courier, Pravda, The Referee, Reynolds News, San Francisco-Sun-Reporter, Screenland, Spectator, The Sphere, The Star* (London)*, The Sun* (New York)*, Sunday Dispatch, Sunday Express, The Sunday Times, Sunday Worker, Swarthmore Phoenix, Swindon Advertiser, Tass, The Times* (London)*, Variety, Wall Street Journal, Weekend Review, West African, West African Review, Yorkshire Post.*

Index

213